CHORA: Intervals in the Philosophy of Architecture
Managing Editor: Alberto Pérez-Gómez

Volume 1 (1994)
Edited by Alberto Pérez-Gómez and Stephen Parcell
Volume 2 (1996)
Edited by Alberto Pérez-Gómez and Stephen Parcell
Volume 3 (1999)
Edited by Alberto Pérez-Gómez and Stephen Parcell

Chora 3: Intervals in the Philosophy of Architecture

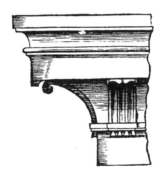

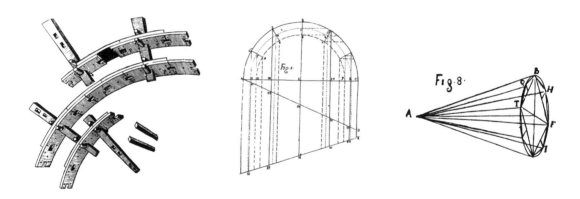

Intervals in the Philosophy of Architecture

C H O R A

V O L U M E   T H R E E

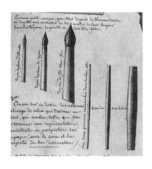

Edited by Alberto Pérez-Gómez and Stephen Parcell

McGill-Queen's University Press

Montreal & Kingston · London · Ithaca

CHORA is a publication of the History and Theory of Architecture graduate program at McGill University, Montreal, Canada.

MANAGING EDITOR

Alberto Pérez-Gómez

EDITORS

Alberto Pérez-Gómez, *McGill University*
Stephen Parcell, *Dalhousie University*

ADVISORY BOARD

Ricardo L. Castro, *McGill University*
Marco Frascari, *Virginia Polytechnic Institute and State University*
Donald Kunze, *Pennsylvania State University*
Phyllis Lambert, *Canadian Centre for Architecture*
David Michael Levin, *Northwestern University*
Katsuhiko Muramoto, *Pennsylvania State University*
Juhani Pallasmaa, *University of Helsinki*
Stephen Parcell, *Dalhousie University*
Louise Pelletier, *McGill University*

SECRETARIAL ASSISTANCE

Susie Spurdens

Canada Cataloguing in Publication Data

Chora: intervals in the philosophy of architecture
Vol. 1 (1994) –
ISSN 1198-449X
ISBN 0-7735-1711-1 (issue 3, bound)
ISBN 0-7735-1712-X (issue 3, pbk.)
1. Architecture – Philosophy – Periodicals. 1. McGill University.
History and Theory of Architecture Graduate Program
NA1.C46   720'.1   C94-900762-5

Typeset in Sabon 10/13 by Caractéra inc., Quebec City.

Contents

Preface

THE ESSAYS in this third volume of the CHORA series continue to explore diverse historical and critical issues in architecture. They are driven by a genuine desire to seek architectural alternatives to simplistic models based on concepts of aesthetics, technology, or sociology. In their refreshing, interdisciplinary readings of our architectural tradition, these essays explore the expanded field of architecture and meditate on its potential for human life. In the absence of a living architectural tradition, these "stories for the future" reveal possibilities in places often ignored by conventional historiography and positivistic epistemology. While avoiding the dangerous delusions of absolute, transparent truth and logocentric power represented by History, they recognize the need for *histories* in normative architectural discourse.

In a world increasingly reduced to electronic impulses, architecture finds itself in a precarious situation. To redefine its role in the perpetuation of human culture, effective architectural discourse is needed. This can no longer be the traditional discourse of metaphysics or theology, nor of the specialized theories of science. While the architect's work is unquestionably a work of the personal imagination, an appropriate mode of discourse is needed to prevent this work becoming merely a simplistic formal play or an irresponsible will to power. Appropriate words are imperative for the practising architect, whose activity demands an ethical stance and is always language-bound. Beyond their specific interests, the essays in this volume contribute to the formulation of an appropriate language for articulating political practices related to architecture. CHORA thus continues to pursue a possible reconciliatory architecture that respects cultural differences, acknowledges the globalization of technological culture, and points to a referent *other* than itself. In a world where new paradigms of communication continue to approach the ephemeral nature of embodied perception and the primary orality of language, architecture may indeed be able to carry intersubjective values and embody a cultural order beyond tyranny or anarchy.

As in previous volumes of CHORA, most of the thirteen essays explore concrete historical topics within a critical framework that opens horizons for the present. Indeed, the past is never truly past, nor is the future truly in the future. This third volume also includes speculative theoretical texts and "projects" in which conventional boundaries between history and fiction are intentionally blurred. It includes Ricardo Castro's original reading of the Koguis culture in Colombia. As inheritors of a pre-Columbian tradition, the Koguis today still dwell "along the path," challenging our assumption that architecture is defined by permanent, place-bound objects. Two other essays are concerned with origins in the Western tradition. Maria Karvouni explores philological and architectonic connections between the Greek *demas* (the political individual) and *domus* (the house). Mark Rozahegy speculates on relationships between architecture and memory – a "constructive" memory that may be potentially repressive or liberating. In commenting on Vitruvius's account of the origins of architecture, he draws from Nietzsche's notion that memory "burnt into the body" is the locus of culture.

The essays that investigate particular historical topics focus on the period between the late sixteenth century and the present. Myriam Blais discusses technical inventions by the sixteenth-century French architect Philibert de l'Orme, whose work is situated at the origins of our modern understanding of architecture. The late-sixteenth-century reconstruction of the Temple of Jerusalem by Juan Bautista Villalpando is examined by Alberto Pérez-Gómez, who ponders the significance of this incarnation of the divine archetype and the ethical dilemmas that result from the modern mentality of its Jesuit author. Janine Debanné's study of Guarino Guarini's Chapel of the Holy Shroud in Turin challenges the prevalent belief that a scientific mentality underlies this remarkable building. She investigates the theological and philosophical framework of Guarini's architectural theory and suggests why this building continues to touch us so deeply in the late twentieth century. Katja Grillner's study of the early-seventeenth-century writings of Salomon de Caus and his built work in Heidelberg describes a curious Rosicrucian-Protestant world that is situated between the traditional cosmos of the Renaissance and the mechanistic universe of Baroque science.

Two architectural writers of the late eighteenth century are studied by David Winterton and Franca Trubiano. Winterton reflects on Charles-François Viel's "Letters," an important text that is practically unknown in the English-speaking world. Viel questioned the hegemony of classical (Vitruvian) architecture and sought an alternative architectural practice that was grounded in a "Nature" invested with spiritual values but no longer unmediated. Viel thus turned his attention to mythical building and to myth as a form of speech. Similar interests are present in Jean-Jacques Lequeu's writings and drawings. While Lequeu's treatise on physiognomy was the subject of an essay in CHORA 1, Franca Trubiano's original interpretation concentrates on his more controversial *Civil Architecture*. Curious anachronisms in Lequeu's work challenge conventional categorizations in philosophy and art history, and anticipate things to come. His self-conscious, self-referential operations in language and drawing also challenge some of our deeply held assumptions about architecture and the appearance of meaning.

Relationships between urbanity and culture are considered by Henrik Reeh in his reflection on the work of Sigfried Kracauer, a significant yet unknown disciple of Walter Benjamin. Reeh's essay revisits important questions raised in previous volumes of CHORA concerning modes of participation in nineteenth- and twentieth-century cities following the demise of traditional public space and ritual. Two essays pursue spatial poetics in architecture by invoking other artistic disciplines. Irena Žantovská Murray reflects on work by the controversial artist Jana Sterbak, describing an embodied architecture that practising architects often disregard. A textual project by artist Ellen Zweig vividly demonstrates the charged poetic space created by film-makers such as Antonioni and Hitchcock, continuing the series of reflections on dramatic, cinematic, and architectural spaces that have appeared in previous volumes of CHORA. Last but not least, the present volume includes a parable in the form of a riddle, an experiment in thinking about architecture and its mimetic origins by the Swedish writer and architect Sören Thurell.

Invention as a Celebration of Materials

Myriam Blais

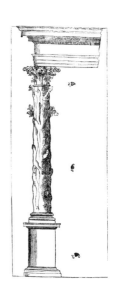

Chora

> *"l'échange, c'est de tradition, doit toujours s'accomplir au cours d'un festin"*
> (an exchange, as of tradition, always has to be performed during a feast)
>
> Michel Serres
> Hermes 1. La communication

IN THE SPIRIT OF MEANINGFUL EXCHANGE suggested by Serres, this article explores the possibility of thinking about technology as a place for celebration.[2] For that purpose, technology is defined here as the prudent use of techniques and implies a careful consideration of both thought and materials. This proposition relies on the sixteenth-century works of François Rabelais, doctor and novelist, and Philibert de l'Orme, architect, for their useful suggestions about providing a space for this celebration. Indeed, de l'Orme claimed to have contributed many beautiful and useful inventions to architecture, inventions that were supported by poetical illustrations relating to his interest in technology.[3] Rabelais was a contemporary of de l'Orme and, although not an architect, was a privileged witness of the community of spirit that characterized their time. He also discussed architecture and technology through vivid images that help situate de l'Orme's ideas about invention in a larger context.

The first part of my argument establishes the common grounds on which de l'Orme and Rabelais conceived of invention in architecture, especially by defining the "name" and the way of working of the architect. The second part studies specific images that illustrate their views of invention through technology. The third part examines the stories that de l'Orme developed to support the legitimacy of his inventions. I will follow the thread of these stories about invention as they celebrate materials, the architect's "other" in the production of a built work. Underlying all of this is the relation that Rabelais and de l'Orme believed should exist between their work and the people who will address it: "In the art of architecture, undertakings of buildings are made and pursued in hope of dwelling commodiously and maintaining our health in them, of taking pleasure from them and giving it to friends" (PT, 7r).[4]

By introducing pleasure and friendship into the realm of architecture, de l'Orme proposed that architecture should be part of an ethical situation. Relationships between buildings and people would resemble relationships between people themselves; buildings would be worth constructing if they constituted places for exchange. Accordingly, de l'Orme and Rabelais developed images of exchange and of creative encounter between thought and materials, through technology. Like many sixteenth-century French humanists, they faced an awkward situation, inheriting a copiousness of ancient works in their respective fields. To stimulate and legitimize French architecture and literature, they believed they had to determine which ancient topics were still relevant, and then find a way to translate or reactivate these materials to nourish future works.[5] They had to make a "virtuoso use" of ancient sources.[6] Virtuosity, in this sense, meant that they needed to understand these topics fully before they could produce images that would span the distance between the original sources and newly invented works. Copiousness (from the Latin *copia*, meaning abundance, plenitude) was envisaged as part of a creative approach to one's work. It prompted fruitful inventions or new propositions to be found and woven together. It also generated movements of knowledge as well as material and sensuous expressions of this knowledge.[7] In order to do so, *copia* had to be modelled after nature, which multiplies and transforms itself in abundance without ever repeating itself. In this way, *copia*-abundance was clearly distinct from *copia*-copy (or repetitive formal imitation). *Copia*-abundance worked by allusions, playful associations, and analogies, for "the feast of copious words or things [took] place under the sign of fiction."[8] This was accomplished under the patronage of Hermes, an image for the "richness of the carrier signs on which depend[ed] the fecund reception of a thought."[9]

THE NAME OF THE ARCHITECT

De l'Orme and Hermes
De l'Orme's books have been regarded mainly as technical endeavours. Consequently, their illustrations, especially the striking presence of Hermes crowning both the *Premier Tome de l'Architecture*'s frontispiece (Fig. 1.1) and one of the drawings of the architect (Fig. 1.2), have not been studied carefully in relation to de l'Orme's interest in materials. Considering his demand, stated at the beginning of the book, that one should understand "quel nom est Architecte" (what is the meaning of the name architect) (*PT*, 6v), Hermes indeed becomes a key figure.

3

1.1 Hermes, situated at the top of the frontispiece; from Philibert de l'Orme, *Premier Tome de l'Architecture* (1567) (Paris: Léonce Laget Librairie-Éditeur 1988).

Hermes generally has been presented as the gods' messenger and interpreter, the connection-maker, the friend of men in their everyday life, the god of commerce, exchange, and metaphor. He represents the possibility of a creative relationship between different parties in an exchange. Hermes is especially relevant for technology, because his myth provides an alternative to that of Prometheus. Prometheus was responsible for bringing the arts to mankind by stealing the gods' fire. However, this theft did not go unpunished, since it had been triggered by his wish to compete with the gods. Nevertheless, Prometheus was the figure that man later chose to associate with technology. This inherited concept promoted a belief in unlimited progress and a freedom to trespass boundaries. Hermes's importance, for my argument, rests in the fact that he acknowledges and respects limits and boundaries, and that he is the communication link between their different sides.[10]

1.2 The architect,
with Hermes above;
from de l'Orme,
Premier Tome, 51v.

The idea of celebration and feast characterizes Hermes and runs throughout de l'Orme's and Rabelais's works. It also implies that the architect cultivates himself for this celebration. In dealing with technology, the image of Hermes symbolizes techniques being adapted, translated, or interpreted to ensure that the encounter will please and celebrate both parties. In this sense, de l'Orme and Rabelais are concerned with the imaginative handling of distinct materials through skilful work.

The skilful intelligence that guides Hermes's abilities is called *metis*, a concept personified by the Greek goddess Metis. This conjectural knowledge is an "intellectual operation which lies half-way between reasoning by analogy and a skill at deciphering the signs which link what is visible to what is invisible."[11] *Metis* is a manner of being in the world; an acute eye and a skilful gesture enable an individual endowed with *metis* to grasp a fleeting occasion and make the best of it. *Metis* also implies a thorough technical know-how. A person with *metis* is an astute builder, a prudent craftsman who works to deliver fruitful inventions and useful constructions. *Metis* is enacted through gestures and demonstrated through effects that arouse wonder.[12] Moreover, *metis* relies a great deal on memory to resolve a difficult situation. In this sense, "memory makes possible a passage to something different, a metaphor."[13] It suggests that technology is much more than the implementation of efficient means towards an end. Since memory enables metaphors or tropes to be made, de l'Orme's use of Hermes is consistent with the "virtuoso use" of ancient sources mentioned earlier. It emphasizes the story that an architect invents to use his means in an appropriate way.

Rabelais and Messere Gaster, inventor of the arts
When Rabelais introduces Gaster, the belly, as the inventor of all the arts (*QL*, 57–62), another interpretation of the architect's "name" is put forward through Gaster's peculiar association with de l'Orme. As Rabelais imagined it, "Gaster invented the art of smashing and destroying fortresses and castles, using engines and machines of war – battering rams, stone hurlers, catapults, *the figure [drawing] of which he showed us, and which had not been well understood by the ingenious architects, disciples of Vitruvius, as the King's great architect, Messere Philibert de l'Orme, once admitted to us*" (*QL*, 61) (my emphasis).

This excerpt from the Gaster story recalls a conversation between the narrator and his fictional character, in which the truth of Gaster's statement was confirmed by de l'Orme. Rabelais used de l'Orme's opinion to account for Gaster's, so that Gaster became a sound image of the architect: Gaster and de l'Orme both understand what architecture is, while many "ingenious architects, disciples of Vitruvius" do not. A similarity is established between the way Rabelais thinks of the architect and the way an architect actually practises his art. These images of the architect, through their reciprocal collusion, acquire a mythical value. Everybody, whether architect or not, can understand and appreciate these exemplary images that illustrate and define the "name" of the architect.

Like Hermes, Rabelais is cunning and artful in doing this through wonderment. The fact – or rather the fiction – that Gaster is a belly (in Greek, *gaster* means either belly or womb, the seat of conception) establishes a resemblance between different things: a belly and an architect. This metaphor becomes a means of knowledge, and the poet is the one who discovers or invents this resemblance. Aristotle drew a comparison between the poet (with the melancholic strength of his belly's inner movements) and the archer (whose success depends on the strength of his shot). He explained that the quality of a metaphor depends on it being shot from afar with strength and success. Hitting a target from this distance, however, relies not on a law of ballistics but on a law of poetics.[14] It also provides a few interpretations of the agreement between Gaster and de l'Orme about the "figures" that were not well understood by the disciples of Vitruvius. First, as I have already suggested, technology is considered a metaphorical, inventive, hermeneutical activity. A metaphor is an act, since one has to shoot; it is also a result, since it enables us to perceive what unites two previously distant things. Secondly, Gaster's destruction of fortresses anticipates the architect's wilful use of ruins. In shooting from afar, the architect develops an eye for making a virtuoso use of ruins, relying on an architectural memory to find legitimate and worthy topics. As these images demonstrate, invention is born from those ruins or topics, which actually point to what would be worth remembering. Thirdly, Gaster's devising of engines and machines of destruction highlights the value of one's material imagination, an imagination of depths represented by the very act of destruction.[15] This suggests that the appearance of a thing should trigger one's curiosity to know what is hidden within.

This last interpretation comes full circle and meets again with the architect's *metis* as a producer of effects that arouse wonder and invite an exchange. Rabelais's Gaster story therefore suggests that the fictional story concieved by the poet-architect constitutes a conjectural truth, and that the physical and intellectual circumstances from which a work of architecture is born represent the very richness of architecture: "Thinking leaves nothing tangible at all. By itself, thinking never materializes into any objects. To manifest one's thoughts, one must use his hands. The thinker who wants the world to know the 'content' of his thoughts must first of all stop thinking and remember his thoughts. Remembrance prepares the intangible for its eventual materialization, it is the beginning of the work process, its most immaterial stage."[16]

Using one's hands (an analogue for technique) aims to materialize thought. Techniques, and consequently the thing made, "re-mind" us.[17]

It is up to the architect to look for techniques and materials that will support his thoughts. If techniques and materials exist for the sake of thought, a built work will thus be judged by inquiring whether it has been "both truly and well made."[18] On the one hand, the truly made is a form of knowledge, insofar as it is a conjectural manifestation of thought. This knowledge is metaphorical, a figure of thought that opens a new world. The well made, on the other hand, represents the architect's crafty, witty, and *metis*-like manner of working. The value of the truly and well made lies in its pleasurable agreement between the architect's ingenuity and the people who will address a work. The images that support this ingenuity therefore may be part of an ethical relationship. As the word edification suggests, it is a question of responsibility to others in constructing a building as well as oneself.[19]

IMAGES OF INVENTION

The body of the architect, the elm tree and the vine
To illustrate the "name" of the architect, de l'Orme invented a new body for the architect by grafting extra body parts (or senses of perception) and the wings of Hermes onto a human body (Fig. 1.3). The graft is the mark of one's material imagination, an imagination that gives life to a material cause.[20] An image that materializes well, that fits well to the material it adorns, makes an object's surface iridescent. Through it, one can understand its depths.

Consider the architect's winged feet. They correspond to Hermes's ability to fly, swiftly carrying himself from one place to another. Importantly, the lower members of the architect's body are what launch the flight. The transport (or metaphor) that Hermes initiates thus comes from a material foundation that is connected to the ground by the soles of the feet. Poets conceived of the wings of imagination as being located always at the feet.[21] Those wings, whose technological image is the arrow (along with the thrust that launches it), recall the Aristotelian archer of metaphor. This provides another interpretation of Gaster's and de l'Orme's ballistics of poetry, which require a humoral movement that audacious gestures convey.[22] The body of the architect manifests the exuberant experiences of his inner senses and may be regarded as a gesture, a disclosure of meaning within a world. Indeed, this gesture derives its communicative force by being connected to the body, but it

1.3 Drawing of the architect; from de l'Orme, *Premier Tome*, 283r.

achieves meaning by being situated in a particular place.[23] In this way, de l'Orme also takes the opportunity to suggest a relationship between the body of the architect and building materials, exemplified by the elm tree standing next to the architect. This suggests a play between the almost homophonic French words "homme" (man) and "orme" (elm tree), a play that would have been common at the time of de l'Orme and Rabelais. The tree was considered an image of man, and both have provided the model for the column throughout the history and theory of architecture (Fig. 1.4 & Fig. 1.5).

The architect's extra body parts and wings swirl around the body, like the vine twisting and climbing around the elm tree. Imagination and invention therefore are supported by material, the material onto which a graft is made. The body of the architect is another exemple of de l'Orme's "virtuoso use" of an important architectural topic – the human body. This body is then rethought, through a metaphorical exercise, to produce a new image: the elm tree and the vine that climbs around it. Traditionally, in the cultivation of vines, the elm tree served as a support for the vine which, in turn, had to espouse the tree in order to grow.

1.4 "D'un orme naît un homme…" (A man is born from an elm tree); form *Imaginaire végétal de la procréation* (Paris, Bibl. Sainte Geneviève, ms 2000, xiii siècle, 172r).

This procedure required an appropriate pruning of both vine and tree so that neither would smother the other. Hermes again comes to mind as an image of plenitude between vine and tree, as well as between thought and material. Hermes stands in between, where technology (as an appropriate use of techniques) seeks an imaginative reactivation of inherited sources. De l'Orme's vine and elm tree espouse each other, in the space that both unites and distinguishes them. Like Hermes, who acknowledges and respects limits, the architect works to reconcile them. He must possess the sober drunkenness that colours the spirit so that the body may turn crimson. The vine's twisting around the elm tree thus acts like a trope; its garland-like decorating effect is an image of fullness that plays between thought and material. Images growing out from what supports

1.5 The tree-column; from de l'Orme, *Premier Tome*, 218r.

them, and their celebration of this support, are of great interest to de l'Orme and Rabelais; these images invoke the hermeneutical bounds and bonds within which invention keeps itself in check. The relation between appearance and technology is thus intricate. Appearance being the proof of existence, the architect's orderly use of techniques makes this appearance manifest, so that the evidence of a building is not dissociated from the thought and the story that sustained its construction.

Rabelais's pantagruélion: the kitchen, the table, the bed, and the body
At the end of his *Tiers Livre* (49–52), Rabelais proposes another image, the "pantagruélion," a magnificent plant named after Pantagruel, the main character of his novels. It was named this way for three reasons:

first, because "Pantagruel invented it: [not] the plant, but a certain way of using it"; second, "by similitude since Pantagruel, when he was born, was as tall as the plant … and its measure was easily taken"; and third, because "of its virtues and properties," for Pantagruel was the epitome of joyful perfection and one recognizes in the pantagruélion "as many virtues, as much energy, as many perfections, as many admirable effects" (*TL*, 51). Pantagruel is Rabelais's undisputed humanist hero. He is given a philosophy, called "pantagruélisme," which accounts for his attitude towards life: a life in which wisdom, virtue, and pleasure come together. Pantagruelism makes an exchange possible, and ensures it in advance. This curious, welcoming, and understanding attitude, by which one desires to appreciate truly someone else's intentions, is characterized by a playfulness and a serenity before unexpected events. This again recalls the *metis* of the architect. Playing with life's surprises or nature's strengths aims for cultural significance, not conquest over them. The conscious exercise of art is part of that adventure. Because Pantagruel's philosophy is associated with it, the pantagruélion's soundness of name points to the validity of the image Rabelais is proposing. It is an image of Rabelais's truthful exercise of his art, and of the variety of truths that are possible, through a variety of manners and works of art.²⁴ Before describing how the pantagruélion got its name, Rabelais explained how it had to be prepared and worked, how its woody part slowly had to macerate, rest, and dry in proper temperatures in order to obtain its fibres, its most valuable and useful parts: "Those who really want to bring out its value do the same as what we have been told of the three Parcae sisters's pastime, of noble Circe's nocturnal activity, and of Penelope's long excuse to her gallant lovers during her husband's absence. In this way, the plant is brought to its inestimable virtues" (*TL*, 50).

Rabelais uses the weaving metaphor to explain this process; indeed, the Parcae sisters spin while singing, Circe sings while weaving, and Penelope for the longest time undoes at night what she has woven during the day. In this way, Rabelais emphasizes the materiality of his work and, most important, how to handle this material so that its virtues, not its properties, are made manifest. To unite the woof and the warp, or to weave, means to intertwine opposites by putting everything in its proper place. The textile object represents humanity's conscious decision making. Moreover, its very appearance always recalls the act of weaving. A textile object also combines the sensible or visible with the intelligible or invisible. It wraps the body that feels and touches it, while it displays a rigorous internal order. In a textile object, ornamental motifs are not severed from their support. Ornament and support appear together through the same procedure, as if the motifs were already dwelling within the woof. Consequently, the support is truly privileged because it helps give form to what it bears. The union of the woof and the warp suggests that there are many possible interpretations (or actual textile objects) that the warp allows the woof to generate.[25] Therefore, Rabelais suggests, truthfulness to an art lies in a patient exercise with materials; it is a truth "to" materials and not a truth "of" materials. Referring in this way to the labour of the hands, Rabelais adds a subtle refinement to the realm of technology, which our contemporary understanding seems to have forgotten. Indeed, we usually think of a technique as a *savoir-faire*, or know-how. For both Rabelais and de l'Orme, it is more precisely a *savoir s'y prendre*, or know-how-to-handle-something-in-the-right-way, with the appropriate twist of hands and twist of thought. *Savoir s'y prendre* has connotations of complete understanding.[26] It is to know how to cling to whatever one wants to understand; *savoir s'y prendre* suggests perfect grasping. De l'Orme's vine twisting around the elm tree is also an image of this idea: a proper pruning of the vine of imagination is necessary to avoid smothering the tree, and an equally adequate pruning of the tree is needed if the vine is to bear fruit at all. The vine's fate is tied to the tree's, and vice versa.

Through the image of the pantagruélion, Rabelais exposes the under-lying scaffolding of his work: "Without it, kitchens would be ignoble and tables unpleasant even when covered with exquisite meats; beds would be without delights although there was gold, silver, amber, ivory and prophyry in abundance. Without it, would not the noble art of printing perish? With it, priests are dressed and adorned, and *the whole of human nature is covered*" (*TL*, 51) (my emphasis).

Rabelais enumerates specific objects relating to basic human activities. He then encompasses the whole of human nature which, as a result of the pantagruélion, has been covered in the first place. An architect's true exercise of his art covers, adorns, and dresses nature – but not literally, as a camouflage does. The Rabelaisian text suggests that the value and utility of work rest on "a rhetoric conceived as a clothing or an orna-ment, not as a disguise and a lie."[27] The relationship that the pan-tagruélion makes possible between eating and the tablecloth, between sleeping and bedsheets, between language and paper, and between a body and its clothes, is one of celebration. Tablecloths, bedsheets, paper, and clothes establish a space of contact and exchange, suggesting that a meaningful communication is impossible without that space. Although Rabelais does not name or even describe these artifacts per se, they nevertheless come to mind very vividly as images of the virtues that the true exercise of an art will allow. By the same token, an equivalency of form and content is established between Pantagruel's philosophy and the constructed objects that provide an image of it, like a textile that recalls the act of weaving.

At the end of the same episode, Rabelais writes: "By means of this plant, invisible substances are stopped and detained visibly" (*TL*, 51). He does not merely describe how, for example, wind caught by sails or windmills can put a ship and a mill to work, the message being that technology permits an easier and more enjoyable life. There are deeper implications of the fact that invisible things are made visible because of the pantagruélion. For Rabelais, wind (and wine, the two words in French, *vent* and *vin*, being homophonic) is a symbol of imagination, hence of thought. In the true exercise of an art, "a rhetoric conceived as a clothing," a surface of contact or a resemblance must exist between the clothing and the thing that is clothed. What is thus made visible are the ways in which the architect's imagination appears.[28] This is nicely summarized by Michel Serres: "The interior of matter, as soon as one *ouvre* it (I conjugate this verb as both to open and to work) becomes an exterior."[29] The pantagruélion story, after all, may be an apology for technology, but only if technology is conceived as the thoughtful consideration of techniques. When techniques become a means to grasp things and to take the measure of the mind, they open myriad worlds that not only add to the natural one but also cover it, so that a culture may be made manifest.

THE ICONOGRAPHY AND TECHNOLOGY OF WOOD AND STONE

The wooden inventions

In 1561 de l'Orme published his *Nouvelles Inventions pour bien bastir et à petits fraiz*, a treatise describing the manners he devised for building roofs, vaults, and floors out of small pieces of wood. De l'Orme claimed that these new wooden constructions (Fig. 1.6), born from a desire to

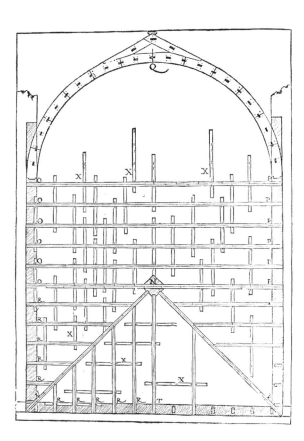

1.6a Examples of wooden inventions; from de l'Orme, *Nouvelles Inventions* (1561), 10v & 11v. Paris: Léonce Laget 1988).

cover large spaces despite a scarcity of large trees, were of his own invention: "I believe that ancient architects never thought of making such great-spanned roofs and other incredible works by means of the invention I am describing here: at least, there is nothing about it in our books on architecture" (*NI*, 34v).

We are familiar with the commonplace that an invention is born from desire and/or necessity. However, considering how de l'Orme constructed his material images (congruent with Rabelais's own poetic exercises), and considering the intentions underlying the production of his works (so that pleasure be both given and taken from them), one should examine his inventions with these two aspects in mind. As de l'Orme explains, "ancient people would have taken great pleasure in being able to cover their theaters and amphitheaters [with this invention]. They used to cover them with cloth or other things, so that the sun would not hurt people" (*NI*, 34r).

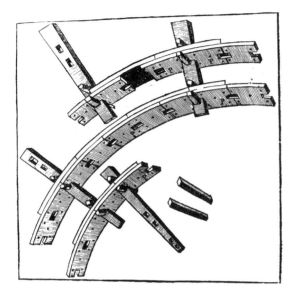

1.6b Examples of wooden inventions; from de l'Orme, *Nouvelles Inventions* (1561), 10v & 11v. Paris: Léonce Laget 1988).

Like Rabelais before him, de l'Orme turns his invention into an analogue of cloth. It is expressed rather plainly, recalling almost literally one of the uses that Rabelais had already assigned to his pantagruélion, "to cover theatres and amphitheatres against heat" (*TL*, 51). Rabelais's and de l'Orme's previous agreement on a viable way of thinking about invention is now evoked with the latter's process of invention, as an instance of the architect's true exercise of architecture. De l'Orme goes on to add that "one can use this invention as one does with stonework. There is no work or figure that this invention cannot do as long as one understands the *traits*. Because wood, according to its nature, has to behave in a different manner than stone" (*NI*, 298r).

De l'Orme's wooden inventions are the result of applying stone stereotomy – the *trait* – to wood. However, this has another implication. By reusing a technique known for another material, de l'Orme demonstrates how a careful use of techniques enables a material to behave differently without suppressing its inherent nature. Different materials may be turned, through techniques, into similar architectural elements, according to a familiar image. His use of a well-known medieval technique is significant: "it is true that wooden framework and stereotomy may be regarded as transformations of the same technique, the *art du trait*. Would one say it had not Philibert done all he could to convince us of it? Wood and stone have distinct traditions. De l'Orme made an *appareil* out of framework."[30]

De l'Orme indeed aimed to convince us of the figurative potential (through an *appareil*) of the ancient technique he chose to use anew. The *art du trait* is the art of drawing something "on" as well as "out of" materials. De l'Orme also puts a great deal of emphasis on the geometrical aspect of the *traits*. This technique, by which the architect's intentions and the materials he works with are conjoined, makes use of many learned geometrical operations. Most of de l'Orme's inventions involve them. Moreover, in de l'Orme's and Rabelais's manner (remember Hermes and Gaster), the *art du trait* is rediscovered as a metaphorical activity: the art of shooting well, that is, shooting far or from afar.[31] This may look like a circumstantial interpretation of the word *trait*, but, as a technique for working with materials (like any technique), the *trait* points to the real value and meaning of technology. In this way, technology becomes a metaphorical means that makes the surface of contact and the resemblance between different things perceptible. In a sense, the geometrical aspect of the *trait* is equivalent to its metaphorical aspect.[32] Consider again the vine growing around the elm tree; to know the material's pleats and to grasp them leads to covering and celebrating them.

De l'Orme's colomne Françoise
In his *Premier Tome de l'architecture* (1567), de l'Orme introduces yet another invention: a *colomne françoise* (a French order), or a stone column "extracted from tree trunks" (*PT,* 217r). This invention again shows how de l'Orme works to maintain the iconography of a well-known architectural element as it is translated from one material into another. This brings to mind Vitruvius's account about stone temples replacing Greek wooden temples. De l'Orme acknowledges that this way of thinking and doing is still relevant for his own practice of architecture, more than fifteen centuries after Vitruvius. With regard to his own invention, he explains that, when ancient architects built tree-columns, they wrapped metal bands around them to prevent cracking and splitting. After realizing that plants and leaves were growing between the

pour mieux parfaire tous les ordres des colomnes Françoiſes, en
y obſeruant touſiours les vrayes meſures. Ce pendant vous pour-
rez ayder de la colomne laquelle ie vous figure icy.

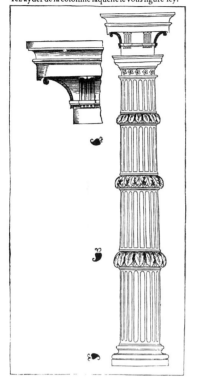
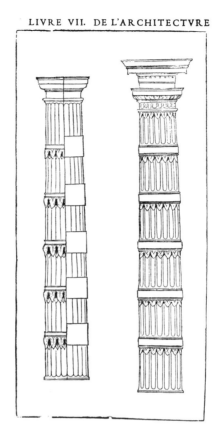

1.7 The "colomne Françoise"; from de l'Orme, *Premier Tome*, 219v, 220v, & 221r.

column and the metal bands, they carefully imitated this natural process,
inventing ornamentation for stone columns by carving leaves in the same
fashion. Similarly, de l'Orme sets out to emulate nature's copiousness
when devising a French order appropriate for French architecture.

De l'Orme's *colomne Françoise* was also born from necessity. Since it
was difficult in France at the time to construct one-piece columns, he
had to make them out of four or five stacked pieces, with carved
ornaments hiding the joints. They appeared to be one piece, resembling
the ancient wood columns with metal braces (Fig. 1.7). It has been
argued that de l'Orme's banded columns were not really new, because
similar Roman examples already existed and de l'Orme probably knew
about them.[33] Therefore, the construction of column shafts out of small

stones hardly seems to qualify as an invention. Like his wooden frame inventions, however, it is a meditation on technology's contribution to his art. Indeed, he believes that "architects who understand art and have great experience at it will find an infinity of beautiful inventions, especially when they are willing to take their topics from the nature of places, as our predecessors did: I mean the imitation of natural things, of their effect, and of Nature's processes" (*PT*, 219r).

While de l'Orme stresses that this invention imitates both ancient architects' manners and nature's processes (not merely copying their forms), his images also illustrate nature's need to be triggered by art. Remember the architect's body and the elm tree with its vine. Indeed, what would have been nature's contribution had it not been for the metal bands? De l'Orme, like Rabelais, suggests that there is an important architectural difference between the nature of materials and the celebration of materials. If metal bands are wrapped around tree-columns to prevent cracking, this seems to respond to the nature of wood. Since de l'Orme wants his many-pieced stone columns to look like the original one-piece banded wooden column, he aims to recall what they actually stood for. His stone columns are true to wood while they celebrate stone. They have been seen as a more viable type of column for French buildings because they acknowledge the nature of their supports, the small French stones.[34] However true this statement may be, it fails to give a full appreciation of de l'Orme's contribution. More than a viable building element, his *colomne Françoise* demonstrates a viable manner of invention and the logic and imagination that de l'Orme achieved when faced with both necessity and ancient architectural topics.

De l'Orme marvels at how nature blooms in strange places; he delights in anticipating, yet being surprised by, what art generates through imagination. By translating an architectural topic – the column – from wood into stone, he celebrates it as his own invention. This manner of working, a virtuoso use of inherited sources, had already brought forth his wooden-frame inventions. This does not mean that different materials are easily interchangeable. As with Rabelais's pantagruélion, it is through a thoughtful use of techniques that a material's woody part (its apparent crust) is macerated to obtain its most precious fibers (its virtues). De l'Orme's work with resemblances between wood and stone searches for intermediary images and surfaces of contact between original topics and new circumstances. This geometrical activity extracts measures from an original architectural topic and from an original building material. The appearance of ornament recalls the original process that is being reinvented. Like the textile object that recalls the art of weaving, the woof is a contingent interpretation of the unchanging aspect of the warp.

While acknowledging the inherent duality between thought and the nature of materials, an architect's inventions should turn this duality into a celebration. Materials may thus be seen as a legitimate support for thought, through technology. De l'Orme's *art du trait* has been defined as the "offspring of a misalliance between geometry and technique, which for a long time, was held to be a little contemptible."[35] As with all unlikely unions, the offspring – a grotesque body – is an image of the place where cultural significance is expressed. Because the grotesque body is in imaginary motion, it is the place of ingenuity, at the crossroads of imaginative thought and material reality. Since it is inscribed within the ethics of strange alliances, de l'Orme's technology is the revelation of the distance and the tension that exist betweeen thought and materials. Yet it provides for a way to reconcile them.

Conceived in this way, invention does not belong to the space of conquest but to the space of celebration. If architecture is to be a celebration, architects must pay attention to the techniques they use and to all the elements entering their "cuisine." The architect has to be at work in the kitchen, where the banquet is being planned and where Hermes is no stranger, for this god is also the inventor of fire, the element that binds and cements all mixes, and is the source of meaningful smells.[36] De l'Orme's and Rabelais's images for architecture imply that fecund encounters develop between an architect and materials, and later between a work of architecture and the people who will address it. It might be useful to wonder again about the current meaning of this "name" architect, especially with regard to the ethical, hermeneutical, and interpretive roles that de l'Orme and Rabelais once assigned to technology. The vine's and the elm tree's fates are still tied together.

NOTES

1 I am grateful to Alberto Pérez-Gomez and to Stephen Parcell for their careful reading of this work and their judicious comments.

2 Celebration is understood as the repeated, renewed, or even reinvented manifestation of things believed to be worth remembering.

3 See my "Enhanced Architectural Making: The Ideas and Works of François Rabelais and Philibert de l'Orme" (University of Pennsylvania, PhD dissertation 1994).

4 All translations of quotations from de l'Orme's and Rabelais's works are mine. For easier notation, the following references to de l'Orme's books are established: the *Nouvelles Inventions pour bien bastir et à petits fraiz* (1561): *NI*, and the *Premier Tome de l'architecture* (1567): *PT*; they are specified by folio, recto, or verso: Philibert de l'Orme, *Traités d'architecture. Nouvelles Inventions pour bien bastir et à petits fraiz (1561), Premier Tome de l'Architecture (1567)* (Paris: Léonce Laget Librairie-Éditeur 1988). As for François Rabelais's books: the *Tiers Livre* (1546): *TL*, and the *Quart Livre* (1552): *QL*; in Rabelais's case, references are given by chapters: François Rabelais, *Œuvres complètes* (Paris: Éditions du Seuil/l'Intégrale 1973).

5 Michel Jeanneret, *A Feast of Words. Banquets and Table Talk in the Renaissance* (Chicago: University of Chicago Press 1991), 173.

6 Terence Cave, "Copia and Cornucopia," *French Renaissance Studies 1540–70. Humanism and the Encyclopedia*, ed. Peter Sharrat (Edinburgh: Edinburgh University Press 1976), 52.

7 Terence Cave, *The Cornucopian Text* (Oxford, U.K.: Clarendon Press 1979), 3–34 and 171–82.

8 Ibid., 31–2.

9 Guillaume Budé, *L'étude des lettres* (1532). French Renaissance humanists have attributed to Hermes the all-encompassing image of humanism. He was the medium of language and eloquence and represented the figures of rhetoric that carried a thought.

10 On the relevance of Hermes for contemporary culture and technology, see Michel Serres, *Les cinq sens* (Paris: Grasset 1985), and Gilbert Durand, "Le nouvel esprit anthropologique ou le retour d'Hermes," in *Science de l'homme et tradition. Le nouvel esprit anthropologique* (Paris: Éditions Sirac 1975), 227–43.

11 Marcel Détienne and Jean-Pierre Vernant, *Cunning Intelligence in Greek Culture and Society* (Chicago: University of Chicago Press 1991), 314. Additional references to Hermes and/or *metis* can be found in Laurence Kahn, *Hermes passe ou les ambiguités de la communication* (Paris: Maspero 1978), and Michel de Certeau, *L'invention du quotidien. Arts de faire* (Paris: Gallimard 1990).

12 Kahn, *Hermes passe*, 82–3.

13 de Certeau, *L'invention du quotidien*, 126.

14 Jackie Pigeaud, "Une physiologie de l'inspiration poétique. De l'humeur au trope," *Études classiques* 46, no. 1, (1978): 23–31.

15 Gaston Bachelard, *L'eau et les rêves. Essai sur l'imagination de la matière* (Paris: José Corti 1942).

16 Hannah Arendt, *The Human Condition* (Chicago: University of Chicago Press 1958), 90.

17 A. Coomaraswamy, "A Figure of Speech or a Figure of Thought?" *Coomaraswamy. Selected papers. Metaphysics* (Princeton: Princeton University Press 1977), 13–42.

18 Ibid.

19 Edification consists of "the disciplined expansion and ornamentation of interiority" (a definition given by Ivan Illich during a lecture at the ACSA Northwest Regional Meeting, in Philadelphia on 18 October 1991, under the title "Needs, Professions and Places"). Its manifestation becomes perceptible in one's or something's appearance. Consequently, an appearance is an expression of order, "conspicuous and present in sensuous abundance" (Dalibor Vesely, "Architecture and the Poetics of Representation," *Daidalos* 25 [1987], 29).

20 Bachelard, *L'eau et les rêves*, 1–28.

21 Gilbert Durand, *Les structures anthropologiques de l'imaginaire* (Paris: Presses Universitaires de France 1963), 133.

22 Ibid., 166.

23 The four ears and hands of the architect are attributes of wisdom, which is attained by practising a trade (signified by the hands) and pondering other people's counsels (signified by the ears). Wisdom concerns man in his concrete relationship with others and with nature. The three eyes of the architect represent an interpretation of prudence, since it relies on memory and learning from the past, intelligence in ordering the present, and foresight in anticipating the future. Through prudence, art becomes the paradigm of virtuous actions since it produces tangible things. We obtain virtues and arts by exercising them, and learn by doing them. Since it accounts for a space and a time (the right space and the right moment), prudence resembles the conjectural thinking, the *metis* of a practical mind.

24 I owe part of this interpretation to Yves Délègue, "Le Pantagruélion, ou le discours de la vérité," *Réforme, Humanisme, Renaissance* 16 (1983), 18–40. In most articles and books concerned with the pantagruélion episode, the

authors attempt to find out which real plant Rabelais is talking about and ultimately interpret it as a mere praise of human work and progress. This literal approach does not do justice to Rabelais's pantagruelism. Délègue's article demonstrates an interesting concern with Rabelais's manner of exercising his art.

25 John Scheid and Jesper Svenbro, *Le métier à tisser de Zeus. Mythe du tissage et du issu dans le monde gréco-romain* (Paris: Éditions la découverte 1994); and François Dagognet, *Rematérialiser. Matières et matérialisme* (Paris: Vrin 1989).

26 The Latin *prehendere* means "to grasp" with one's hands and thought, as is implied by the verbs *apprehendere* ("to learn") and *comprehendere* ("to understand, to comprehend").

27 Délègue, "Le Pantagruélion, ou le discours de la vérité," 32.

28 René Guénon, *Le règne de la quantité et les signes du temps* (Paris: Gallimard 1945).

29 Michel Serres, "Distraction," *Le corps en morceaux* (Paris: Réunion des musées nationaux 1990), 56. The French verbs *ouvrir* ("to open") and *ouvrer* (an ancient spelling for *œuvrer*, meaning "to work") are not etymologically related. The conjugated form with which Serres plays seems Rabelaisian in spirit. As Alfred Jarry said, "when words play between themselves it is because they know their cousinship."

30 Jean-Marie Pérouse de Montclos, "La charpente à la Philibert de l'Orme. Réflexions sur la fortune des techniques en architecture," *Les chantiers de la Renaissance* (Paris: Picard 1991), 41. The French word "appareil" is translated into English as "bond." To my mind, this term does not carry all the richness of the French word: that is, something that clothes or adorns. Indeed, the verb "appareiller" (from the Latin *parare, parere)* means "to get prepared," that is, to provide something with all it needs. "Appareiller la pierre," for instance, means to cut the stones and assemble them according to a certain pattern; it is to dress the stones. This definition is also implied by the verb "to apparel," that is, to put clothes on, to dress, adorn, or embellish.

31 The noun *trait* comes from the verb *tirer*, which means also "to shoot."

32 Michel Serres, in *Les origines de la géométrie* (Paris: Flammarion 1993), explains that geometry is the result of a ruse and a detour, whose indirect road allows access to whatever goes beyond a direct practice. To measure what is inaccessible, it must be mimed or reproduced within an accessible space and time. Richard Kearney, in *Poétique du possible. Phénoménologie*

herméneutique de la figuration (Paris: Beauchesne 1984), also discusses man's intentional and creative existence. Man creates his world and himself by going beyond what is present, in time or space, and by making his way towards what is absent. Existence is a figuration (a term encompassing perception, imagination, and signification) that gives meaning to the world by making real or apparent its many possibilities. Therefore, he argues, every production is a figuration, an analogue.

33 Jean-Marie Pérouse de Montclos, *L'architecture à la française* (Paris: Picard 1982).

34 Yves Pauwels, "Théorie et pratique des ordres au milieu du XVIe siècle: de l'Orme, Goujon, Lescot, Bullant" (Thèse de doctorat, Université François Rabelais, Tours,1991). On his part, de l'Orme concludes the description of his French order in this way: "One can ornament and enrich it from Nature, and from things which this French Kingdom is most inclined to and his inhabitants most devoted to" (*PT*, 219r). Joseph Rykwert suggests that understanding the orders correctly requires us to think of them as "distilled, poetic allusions, having the force of proverbs or familiar quotations" ("The Corinthian Order," *The Necessity of Artifice* [London: Academy Editions 1982, 41]). He also suggests that "the origin of these elements is not in formal fancy ... it was a necessary, willed product of the feelings and ideas of the people who devised and used them" (ibid.).

35 Pérouse de Montclos, *L'architecture à la française*, 86. This idea seems to come from art historians's inability to see beyond the plane geometry that sustains most of the regulating lines in architectural composition. Did they fail, as the author argues, to recognize stereotomy's third dimension because its parents were unsuited to each other? In their minds, geometry had apparently married beneath its social status.

36 Serres, *Les cinq sens*, 180–1.

Sounding the Path:
Dwelling and
Dreaming

Ricardo L. Castro

Chora

> You cannot travel on the path unless you have become the
> Path itself.
>
> Gautama Buddha

PROLOGUE

Our life is marked by continuous movement through space. Standing
upright, on two legs, and looking forward contributes to our mobility
and has a significant influence on our existential condition. The act of
moving is an everyday affair that acquires a poetic dimension in creative
domains such as dance, theatre, literature, and architecture. Paths constitute the basic physical support for movement. As one of the first and
most basic communal manifestations of humankind, they also link us to
other species whose existential movements leave definite traces (paths)
on the landscape.

Following a path means following an already established order, or at
least acknowledging such an order – hence, the importance of the path
as an agent in certain myths. The idea of procession appears pervasively
in the customs of many societies, and without a path there is no procession. As a cultural construct, the path is often endowed with sacred or
mythical properties, as evident in many contemporary and ancient rites.

But there is more to the path. Throughout history, certain societies
have inhabited the path without necessarily being nomadic. They are
truly path dwellers. Their life space exemplifies the idea of "hodological
space" (from the Greek *hodos,* meaning "way"), developed by the
German psychologist Kurt Lewin in the early 1930s. According to
Lewin, hodological space is the space of possible movement.[1] Rather
than straight lines, it is characterized by the presence of "preferred
paths" that represent a compromise among several domains such as
"short distance," "security," "minimal work," and "maximum experience."[2] In this sense, hodological space is the antipode of Euclidean
space, in which a line is defined as the shortest distance between two
points.[3]

In certain ancient and modern cultures, the complexities of space are
resolved through existential movement along a path. Through their
"walkabouts," Australian Aboriginals give true meaning to the concept
of "poiesis" as they continuously recreate their world by singing. There
is a lot at stake here, for without the creative intercession of chant the

Aboriginals' world would die. In his narrative *The Songlines*, Bruce Chatwin eloquently elucidates how this remarkable cultural group apprehends its world and gives meaning to its existence. Chatwin points out that the Aboriginals' world is a "labyrinth of invisible pathways which meander all over Australia and are known to Europeans as 'Dreaming-tracks' or 'Songlines'; to the Aboriginals as the 'Footprints of the Ancestors' or the 'Way of the Law.'" He continues: "Aboriginal creation myths tell of the legendary totemic beings who had wandered over the continents in the Dreamtime, singing out the name of everything that crossed their path – birds, animals, plants, rocks, water holes – and so singing the world into existence."[4]

It is evident that the Aboriginal concept of space is inscribed in a world view that is quite different from ours.[5] Aboriginals do not own land. Instead of owning land or spatial rights, they rely on the particular knowledge and identification of a given part of the topography. By chanting the relevant myth, Aboriginals bring the land into existence. Thus they pronounce their affiliation with a particular tribal area.

Thousands of kilometres away, another extraordinary but less-known culture, the Colombian Kogi, occupy through their spatial practices another special chapter among the path dwellers. This short essay attempts to provide a succinct view of the spatial concepts that are inscribed in their fascinating symbolic and mythical world. To us, these concepts seem to be inversions of the place-bound spatial ideas to which we have traditionally adhered in the "civilized" world.

ENCHANTED PATHS

In the Sierra Nevada de Santa Marta, an unusual mountain range that rises to 5,775 metres on the northern tip of Colombia, the Kogi Indians (or Kággaba) have remained largely undisturbed by Western civilization and continue to use the physical infrastructure created by their predecessors, the now-extinct Tairona, whose highly developed culture flourished at the time of the Spanish arrival in the fifteenth century.[6] During the sixteenth century, the Spanish conquistadors, in their search for gold and slaves, practically razed the Tairona culture after inciting the native population to resist and revolt. The survivors of the Indian rebellions were suppressed brutally by the Spaniards and fled from the lowlands on the Caribbean seaboard to higher altitudes of the Sierra. Their less

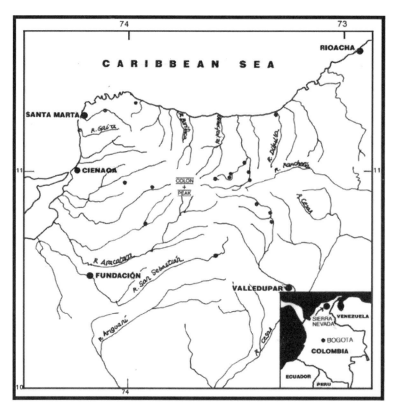

2.1 Map of the Kogi territory (Sierra Nevada). Inset: localization of the region in Colombia. Drawing by the author based on Reichel-Dolmatoff.

numerous descendants adapted their previous way of life to the more austere and demanding environmental conditions found in this new habitat. Today they still preserve many of the ancient Tairona traditions and rituals. They also maintain some of the infrastructures built by their predecessors. The Tairona *senderos de piedra* (stone paths) that criss-cross the harsh topography of this habitat in the northern slopes of the Sierra Nevada have been in continuous use since the demise of the Tairona tribe in Spanish colonial times. More than simple trails, these paths are feats of engineering, silent enchanted witnesses of past and present human dwelling.

GEOGRAPHY AND HISTORY OF THE PATHS

For the geographer, archaeologist, and ethnographer, the relatively small triangle of Sierra Nevada de Santa Marta constitutes a unique topography bounded by the Caribbean sea to the north, the alluvial plains of

2.2 Terraces in Buritaca 200.
Drawing by the author based on a photograph by Juan Mayr.

the Magdalena River to the west, and the sandy desert of the Guajira peninsula on the east.[7] As anthropologist Gerardo Reichel-Dolmatoff[8] points out, "this limited territory, apparently so coherent and easy to survey, contains a bewildering variety of natural environmental and ethnic groups with different adaptive strategies and varying human expectations."[9] Paradoxically, the uniqueness of the Sierra Nevada became evident only when accurate geographical and archaeological exploration began in the second decade of this century, and as we approach the end of the century the survey is still incomplete.[10]

Recent excavations and discoveries in the Sierra Nevada have revealed even richer examples of the Tairona's extraordinary interventions in the landscape, mediated through the construction of paths, terraces, stairs, bridges, canals, drainage conduits, reservoirs, and retaining walls.[11] Evidence of place- and path-making is abundant along the *senderos*, including those leading to Pueblito, an ancient Tairona site located near the Caribbean coast in the Tairona Park near Santa Marta, and to Ciudad

2.3 Pueblito, Sendero
de Piedra.
Photo by the author.

Perdida (Lost City), also known as Buritaca 200. Discovered only in
1976, and still quite inaccessible, Buritica is the largest ancient city found
in the Americas during this century. For the highly spiritual Kogi, who
consider their landscape to be sacred, Buritaca is their holiest ancestral
city.

Archaeological findings have demonstrated that the Tairona were
excellent engineers, potters, and goldsmiths. In 1939 Thomas Cabot, the
leader of one of the expeditions to the Sierra Nevada de Santa Marta,
pointed out: "On the northern slopes are relics of the Tairona culture,
which await archeological investigation. The Tairona race, which preceded the Arhuaco and reached its highest development perhaps five
hundred years ago, left cities built of stone, highways paved with granite
blocks, and graves filled with ornaments of gold and jasper indicating a
degree of civilization approaching that of the Mayas and the Incas."[12]

Cabot, like some of the other explorers, referred to the inhabitants of the region as Arhuaco. This term, used since the eighteenth century, is probably derived from Arawak, which commonly designated one of the cultural groups that occupied the area along with the Caribe at the time of the Spanish conquest. Today the term Arhuaco (or Arauaco) generally refers to three Indian groups currently inhabiting the Sierra Nevada: the Kogi, the Ika, and the less numerous Sanká (or Sahna), all of whom have preserved their dialects and rites. The Arhuaco are considered to be the direct descendants of the Tairona.[13] Of the three groups, the Kogi have been the most reluctant to establish permanent contacts with Western civilization, and unlike their neighbours the Ika and the Sanká, they reject commercial-trade cloth and insist on using only the textiles they craft following traditional methods.[14] This results from a profound mystic understanding of their place in the universe. For the Kogi, the spindle and loom are more than mere tools, and spinning and weaving more than simple productive activities.

SYMBOLIC PATHS

I would suggest that the spindle and the loom are sacred objects that gather tacit attributes or ideas. Two such unspoken attributes are the sense of rhythm and the notion of continuity that appear at the various experiential levels of the Kogi world and permeate all significant activities: weaving, thinking, building, planting, sewing, lovemaking, walking, and singing. In its geometry, the loom is a closed circuit of conceptual paths that can be experienced in endless combinations. Spinning and weaving are continuous processes that accompany the rhythm of the chant and set the pace for thinking. Spinning generates thoughts, and weaving intertwines them into the Fabric of Life, which is no other than a web of knowledge.[15]

The spindle and the loom are invested with important symbolic connotations. They are also mnemonic devices and conceptual diagrams of the Kogi's hodological space. Spinning and weaving are the domain of men, who provide clothing for themselves, their wives, and daughters. The spindle is a "lightly tapered rod about 50 centimeters long, which penetrates a flat disk-shaped wooden whorl of about 7 centimeters in diameter."[16] At a microcosmic level, the spindle is an analogue of the *axis mundi,* and the spindle-whorl is the earth. Anatomically they

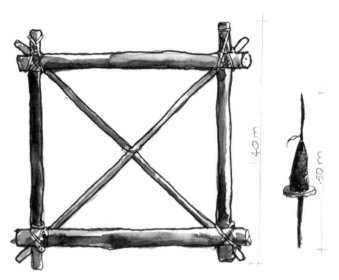

2.4 Kogi Loom and spindle.
Drawing by the author based on Reichel-Dolmatoff.

symbolize the male and female elements; architecturally, the "circular temple floor is a whorl, and the near vertical sunray that falls upon its centre on the equinoxes at noon, is the spindle."[17]

The Kogi loom is a simple device consisting of a square frame made of wooden poles, each about six centimetres in diameter. The frame is reinforced by two diagonally crossed poles. There are, of course, other complementary elements used in weaving.[18] However, it is the quincunx arrangement of the loom that I want to concentrate on since it constitutes the primary icon of Kogi religious thought.[19] Numerous analogies can be made with the loom since it functions interchangeably as a map, a chart, and a plan, ranging from the cosmic through the geographic to the micro-cosm of the human anatomy. It should not come as a surprise that the four corners of the loom represent the four major Colombian or "west-ern" cities delimiting the Kogi territory (Santa Marta to the northeast, Riohacha to the northwest, Fundación to the southwest, and Valledupar to the southeast), but the loom also represents the sunrise and sunset points during the solstices and the sun's meridian position during the equinoxes. At another level, the crossbars of the loom represent the pre-established paths that a person's soul must travel in the afterlife. The Kogi call these trails "pathways of the souls," and they are important elements in their model of the Beyond.[20] Agricultural fields and planting also have direct associations with the loom and the act of weaving. For the Kogi, planting and gathering crops is their way of "weaving society's food."[21]

WOVEN ARCHITECTURE

The loom and the act of weaving colour many other facets of the Kogi's existence. The woven walls of their houses and the pervasive interlacing of structural elements and connections speak unquestionably of an architecture that has been woven physically and conceptually in a true Semperian way.[22] The round Kogi house, maximum four metres in diameter, is made of wattle-and-daub. Its conical roof, thatched in mountain grass, terminates in an apex formed with vertical sticks knitted together and topped with inverted cooking ware. The deliberate "knitting" of sticks and wares carries various symbolical connotations.

Kogi temples are like houses but larger, sometimes reaching almost nine metres in diameter and often built on platforms. They always have two opposite doors, usually aligned east-west. Although a central post is commonly found in the building practices of similar cultures, the Kogi temple has four posts with a specific orientation that divides the interior space with geometric precision. During solstices and equinoxes, the sun's movement along virtual paths in the temple turns the building into an astronomical observatory. Like the Roman Pantheon, the Kogi temple acts as a gigantic "camera obscura" whose pinhole at its apex projects the trajectory of the luminous disk onto the sacred floor. The sun thus weaves the floor of the temple. I believe that a corollary spins off from this fact: the function of the temple as a celestial observatory is linked with night-walking. We have to remember that, in an environment in which electrical lighting is totally absent, the most favourable time for night-time travel is during the full moon. Visibility is best at this time. And incidentally, the moon, the Sun's wife, occupies an important place in Kogi cosmology, along with "the shadows." For the *mámas*, as the priests are called, and especially for those aspiring to become priests, this is relevant since much of their daily activity occurs at night.[23] I would speculate that the temple serves also to observe the lunar cycles, another important rhythmic event among the Kogi.

The direct correlation between loom and temple architecture is more than coincidental. The temples are small-scale models of the cosmos. They include constructive details that echo those of the loom, as well as the loom-like frames that provide structural stability to the Kogi's buildings. The various structural elements of the temple – posts, beams, rafters, and cross-sticks – also have specific symbolic connotations. Even

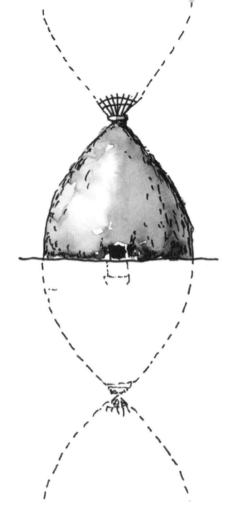

2.5 The Kogi temple and its
conceptual inversion.
Drawing by the author based
on Reichel-Dolmatoff.

the interior roof poles represent the "paths or ways of the soul" moving
towards heaven.

Another important analogy relates temples and houses to mountains.
In the interchangeable analogical system of the Kogi, temples, houses,
and sacred mountains continue underground in an inverted form. The
principle of inversion among the Kogi is also manifested in other aspects
of their life, as we shall see. Some mountains recall the form of a built
temple and are considered to be temples as well. They are holy land-
marks within the Sierra Nevada, a sacred terrain that is regarded as a
female body, a symbol of fertility. Footwear is forbidden among the Kogi,
since they believe that only bare feet should touch the delicate skin of
the Earth-Mother. In contrast, the contemporary Western mind seems

committed to the creation of innumerable barriers that increasingly detach our bodies and lives from the living earth on which the Kogi dwell.

Like the loom, temples and, to a lesser degree, houses function as instruments of memory and teaching. Kogi society gives special importance to the *mámas*, who are carefully selected at an early age to undergo a rigorous training that ideally lasts eighteen years. The priesthood is exclusively a male domain. Entrance to the temples is granted only to initiated men and to the *mámas*. At first, the role of women in Kogi society seems more circumscribed than that of males, but this is probably not the case. The feminine presence pervades the Kogi universe.[24] Men and women live apart, collaborate in strictly prescribed tasks, and occupy separate spheres of activity. Women also have special temples where they gather to perform rituals such as dancing and singing. There, they also carry out one of their most significant activities: the manufacture of carrying bags, called *mochilas*, an Indian word now used commonly in Colombian Spanish to designate shoulder bags.

WEAVING AND WALKING

I believe that the *senderos de piedra* are more than mere infrastructure works or feats of engineering. These ubiquitous spatial supports enable significant symbolic and domestic activities to be carried out. In the Kogi universe, similar propositions acquire resonance in every realm of action and thinking. The knitting of *mochilas* is one such endeavour.

The Kogi women's manufacturing of *mochilas* is the counterpart of the men's privileged spinning and weaving. Their "knotless netting" technique is symbolic, since the *mochilas* represent the womb of the Mother and are associated with fertility. In a society for which analogy is a fundamental concept, it is not surprising that the act of sewing the *mochilas* represents the twenty-eight-day lunar cycle, which in turn is associated with female fecundity. The incessant netting by the women also reinforces the belief in the continuity of cycles. Reichel-Dolmatoff observes that "all day long the women, when not occupied with other menial tasks, can be sewing these simple objects which have many uses, especially since the Kogi have practically no basketry, and netted bags are their principal carrying utensils ... Even when nursing her baby or while walking over steep mountain trails a Kogi woman will continue

2.6 Kogi man with Mochilas and lime gourd.
Drawing by the author based on Reichel-Dolmatoff.

her work; in fact, a woman's reputation as a wife and as a mother depends in part on her dedication to this activity."[25]

The various kinds of *mochilas*, given their symbolic and functional characteristics, are an integral part of the Kogi's attire. Cabot points out: "Both men and women usually carry several hemp bags slung over the shoulder bandoleer-fashion. For heavy loads they use a larger bag suspended from the forehead. The babies are carried on their mothers' backs in bags shaped like a chair. Still larger bags are used to pack animals. The bags are made by knotting hemp twine into a fine net-like crocheting without a needle. The women work at this whenever their hands are free, even when on the march."[26]

Initiated Kogi men carry two *mochilas*, one made of cotton yarn and another made of agave fibers. The former serves to carry sacred objects, including toasted coca leaves contained within a small bag, and a *poporo* (lime gourd) with a stick. The latter contains non-sacred objects such as food, matches, and a pocket knife. The long strap handles of the *mochilas* are meant to be crossed over the chest and back. Here, as in many other circumstances, the Kogi demonstrate their obsession with the symbol depicting the X-like intersection of two diagonals.[27]

SPATIAL INVERSION

The extraordinarily rich symbolic universe of the Kogi counterpoints their limited material culture. This austerity has shocked many Westerners who have come into direct contact with them.[28] Few manufactured components exist in the Kogi culture: "There are hardly more than thirty individual elements, apart from such features as a house, a bridge, a hearth, or a loom."[29] I would strongly argue that the path is another significant element in this category. In the Kogi universe, many things are symbolic: material elements; some topographical features such as caves, mountains, rivers, and boulders; natural phenomena such as thunder, rain, and seasonal cycles; and everyday activities such as chewing coca, spinning, weaving, and planting. The Kogi exploit this symbolic dimension by using analogical processes. Through analogy they are able to explain all existential aspects of their world, thus enabling them to dwell perennially and actively.[30]

The cycles of sun, moon, planting, harvest, fertility, birth, and death are intimately tied into the net of the world, gathered together, and made manifest. The Kogi's continuous engagement with the world is enhanced by the rhythmic act of walking that occurs symbolically along the paths of life. It also occurs physically, I suggest, along the *senderos de piedra*. This recalls Osip Mandelstam's description of Dante's opus: "The Inferno and especially the Purgatorio glorify the human gait, the measure and rhythm of walking, the foot and its shape. The step, linked to the breathing and saturated with thought: this Dante understands as the beginning of prosody."[31]

Rhythms find their counterparts generated by walking, weaving, singing, procreation, and the bodily patterns of breathing and pulse. The staccato of steps, the flow of water, and the hiatus of landings and

2.7 Stone bridge along the Sendero de Piedra to Pueblito. Photo by the author.

terraces strung along the path evoke continuity, event, and memory. And is this not one of the reasons why the Kogi have preserved the ancient Tairona tradition of building terraces, paths, stairs, and bridges?

The ubiquity of the *senderos de piedra* throughout the Kogi environment is the direct result of their unorthodox inversion of hodological space. The Kogi build villages without a precise plan but adapt them carefully to the topography. However, they do not actually inhabit their villages on a day-to-day basis but use them instead as nodes for collective meetings and significant events such as ceremonies and feasts. [32] Today the maintenance and repair of the Tairona-Kogi paths is undertaken by a large segment of the tribe. It also involves the spiritual sweeping carried out by individual tribal members.[33] Thus, for the Kogi, the path itself is the usual destination, and the village at the end of the path is a deviation from it. In 1934 the explorer William Seifriz noted the Kogi's remarkable spatial inversion.[34] Several decades later, Reichel-Dolmatoff elucidated the puzzle by pointing out that "these villages ... are not permanently inhabited; most if not all Indians live in scattered homesteads in their fields, at several hours distance. A single family may own as many as

2.8 Stone stair along
the Sendero de Piedra
to Pueblito.
Photo by the author.

four or five houses, each of them surrounded by small garden-plots and
situated at different altitudinal levels, over a range of almost 2,000
meters. This pattern of occupying a vertical scale of mountain slopes
allows them to participate in many different ecological systems ... The
villages, then, are simply gathering places where neighbours come
together periodically, perhaps twice a month, to exchange news, discuss
community matters, perform some minor rituals, or to trade with the
visiting Creole peasants."[35]

The Kogi's extraordinary symbolic drive turns what otherwise would
be just an adaptive function into an important element of their mythical
fabric. The loom, which can be many things (a garden plot, a rack, a
spider's web, the whole Sierra Nevada, and so on), thus becomes the
mountainside. On its slopes, all the vertical displacements along the
paths are called "weavings."[36] Moving along the paths is a choreo-
graphic analogy to the pattern of a fabric.

Walking along the ancient Tairona-Kogi paths, one is sensitized to the
possibility of wondrous architectural encounters. Tunnelled passages

through large rock formations are common along the paths. The tunnels have been made by displacing and repositioning gigantic slabs. Often, specific segments of a path are paved with large slabs that are perfectly balanced and permit a slight tilting and repositioning. The weight of an individual walking on them is sufficient to cause them to tilt and hit a strategically placed supporting slab. The distinct sound that is produced resonates audibly throughout the thick tropical jungle. It is generally believed that the purpose of this lithic sound-making device was to mark the arrival of intruders. But could there be a less pragmatic interpretation? Can the path be conceived as a true living sacred entity, one that uses sound to engage the body of the traveller? Is it not possible to grant the path its acoustic dimension? The "singing path" enchants the passer-by. Suffice it to recall that the action of enchantment, from the Latin *incantare*, originates in the song, the *canto*. Thus, it would seem that the common thread that weaves through the songlines, the sacred ways, and ultimately the *senderos de piedra* is to be found in our existential make-up. The Kogi's hodological space, now threatened by innumerable pressures from the Western world (narcotic traffic, tourism, government apathy, and guerrilla activity) offers us an opportunity to reflect on our existential condition. Ultimately, on the Tairona-Kogi's *senderos de piedra*, thinking, singing, weaving, and dreaming come together and give meaning to the act of dwelling.

NOTES

1 Kurt Lewin, "Der Richtungsbegriff in der Psychologie. Der spezielle und allgemeine hodoligische Raum, *Psychologische Forschung* 19 (1934): 286.

2 Christian Norberg-Schulz, *Existence, Space and Architecture* (New York: Praeger Publishers 1971), 22.

3 Kurt Lewin, in his *Principles of Topological Psychology* (New York and London: McGraw-Hill 1936), 41–58, expanded the concept of hodological space so that, instead of simply meaning the space of possible movement, it includes the space of free movement. Unlike the former, the boundaries of the latter depend on specific psychological processes or regions which may be of a physical, social, or conceptual nature.

4 Bruce Chatwin, *The Songlines* (New York: Penguin Books 1987), 2.

5 It is a perception, incidentally, that adequately corroborates the Barthesian notion of myth being a form of language. See Roland Barthes, "Myth

Today," in *A Barthes Reader*, edited and with an introduction by Susan Sontag (New York: Hill and Wang 1982), 93–149.

6 During the Spanish conquest the term Tairona was used to designate the inhabitants of the Buritica valley, a small region on the northern slopes of the Sierra Nevada. Reichel-Dolmatoff, "The Great Mother and the Kogi Universe: A Concise Overview," *Journal of Latin American Lore* 13. no. 1 (1987): 75n.1, points out: "Eventually (and erroneously) the name was applied to almost all Indians, prehistoric and early historic, of the Sierra Nevada de Santa Marta ... This archaeological culture covers, sporadically but quite recognizably, much of the entire sierra massif, and is in no way limited to the Santa Marta-Pueblito-Buritica area. The name *tairona* , in spite of modern romanticizing folk etymologies, is derived from Kogi, Ika, and Sanká roots referring to concepts of virility. The Kogi call the ancient Tairona language *téizua* and still use it in certain ritual contexts."

7 The region is a triangle with each side measuring less than 150 kilometres. The Sierra Nevada is indeed overpowering even for the layman. Griffith Taylor, "Settlement Zones of the Sierra Nevada de Santa Marta," *Geographical Review* 21, no. 4 (1931): 539, for instance, points out: "In few parts of the world are to be found mountains rising 17,000 feet above a coast; and when this occurs in a tropical latitude as is the case with the Sierra Nevada de Santa Marta of Colombia, whose snowy crest is only 23 miles from a tropical sea, a very special environment results. On the slopes of the Nevadas [*sic*] behind the town of Santa Marta there is a mantle of tropical jungle flung over the entire slope almost from sea level up to 10,000 feet. Above the jungle is a zone of grasslands, paramos, while the uppermost zone is capped with eternal snow which feeds a few small glaciers. The entire series is visible from the Caribbean, and nowhere in the world is an exact parallel to be found."

8 To date, the late Gerardo Reichel-Dolmatoff is undoubtedly the anthropologist who has produced the most important work on the inhabitants of the Sierra Nevada and particularly on the Kogi Indians. The following material by him will be cited throughout this essay: *Colombia* (London: Thames and Hudson 1965), 142–68; "Training for the Priesthood among the Kogi of Colombia," in *Enculturation in Latin America: An Anthology*, ed. Johannes Wilbert (Los Angeles: UCLA Latin American Center Publications 1976), 265–88; "The Loom of Life: A Kogi Principle of Integration," *Journal of Latin American Lore* 4, no. 1 (1978): 5–27; "Some Kogi Models of the Beyond," *Journal of Latin American Lore* 10, no. 1 (1984): 63–85; "The Great Mother

and the Kogi Universe: A Concise Overview," *Journal of Latin American Lore* 13, no. 1 (1987): 73–113; *Los Kogi: Una tribu de la Sierra Nevada de Santa Marta*, 2 vols., 2nd ed. (Bogotá: Procultura 1985); *The Sacred Mountain of Colombia's Kogi Indians* (Leiden, New York, Kobenhavn, Köln: E. J. Brill 1990).

9 Reichel-Dolmatoff, "The Great Mother," 75.

10 Exploration of the area in the 1910s, 1920s, and 1930s brought about the publication of significant documentation. The first professional anthropologist to visit the Sierra Nevada was Konrad Theodor Preuss, whose publications in the late 1920s, particularly *Forschungreise zu den Kágaba: Beobachtungen, Textaufnahmen und sprachliche Studien bein einem Indianerstamme in Kolumbien, Südamerika*, 2 vols. (Vienna: Antropos Verlag 1926–27), became the basis for further anthropological studies of the area. The first descriptions of the Tairona were made by J. Alden Mason in the following publications: "Archaeology of Santa Marta, Colombia: The Tairona Culture, Part I. Report on Field Work," Field Museum of Natural History, *Anthropological Series* 20, no. 1 (1931); "Archaeology of Santa Marta, Colombia: The Tairona Culture, Part II. Section 1. Objects of Stone, Shell, Bone and Metal," Field Museum of Natural History, *Anthropological Series* 20, no. 2 (1936); "Archaeology of Santa Marta, Colombia: The Tairona Culture, Part II. Section 2," Field Museum of Natural History, *Anthropological Series* 20, no. 3 (1939). Additional relevant sources are: Thomas D. Cabot, "The Cabot Expedition to the Sierra Nevada de Santa Marta, Colombia," *Geographical Review* 29, no. 4 (1939): 587–621; William Seifriz, "The Sierra Nevada de Santa Marta: An Ascent from the North," *Geographical Review* 24, no. 3 (1934): 478–85; Griffith Taylor, "Settlement Zones of the Sierra Nevada de Santa Marta," *Geographical Review* 21, no. 4 (1931): 539–58.

11 Leonardo Ayala and Pablo Gamboa, "Los Artifices de la Tierra y el Mar," *Historia del Arte Colombiano* 2, nos. 20, 21, 22 (1975): 387–440.

12 Cabot, "The Cabot Expedition," 594.

13 Ayala, "Los Artifices," 398.

14 Reichel-Dolmatoff, "The Loom of Life," 5.

15 Before a Kogi man weaves a new garment he chants a tune: "I shall weave the Fabric of my Life; / I shall weave it white as a cloud; / I shall weave some black into it; / I shall weave dark maize stalks into it; / I shall weave maize stalks into the white cloth; / Thus I shall obey divine Law." See Reichel-Dolmatoff, "The Loom of Life," 12–15, for a thorough analysis of the tune.

16 Ibid., 6.

17 Reichel-Dolmatoff, *The Sacred Mountain,* 14–15.

18 A full account of the device and its operation is found in Reichel-Dolmatoff, "The Loom of Life," 6–8.

19 Reichel-Dolmatoff, *The Sacred Mountain,* 16.

20 For a complete description and analysis of this complex model, see Reichel-Dolmatoff, "Training for the Priesthood," and particularly "Some Kogi Models." Also relevant are "The Loom of Life," 15–19, and *The Sacred Mountain,* 14–17.

21 Reichel-Dolmatoff, *The Sacred Mountain,* 16.

22 See Gottfried Semper, *The Four Elements of Architecture* (Cambridge: Cambridge University Press 1989), 101–11.

23 For an extensive discussion of the various aspects of the priesthood, see Reichel-Dolmatoff, "Training for the Priesthood."

24 See Reichel-Dolmatoff, "The Great Mother."

25 Ibid, 17.

26 Cabot, "The Cabot Expedition," 612.

27 The scope of this essay makes it impossible to provide further details here. For the persistence of the X symbol among the Kogi, see Reichel-Dolmatoff, "The Loom of Life" and "The sacred Mountain." For relevant observations regarding another South American Indian group that employs similar symbols, see Gail Silverman-Proust, "Weaving Techniques and the Registration of Knowledge in the Cuzco Area of Peru," *Journal of Latin American Lore* 14, no. 2 (1988): 207–41. Also relevant is Stacey Schaefer, "The Loom and Time in the Huichol World, "*Journal of Latin American Lore* 15, no. 2 (1989): 179–94.

28 Mason considers them "weak, inveterate Coca chewers, sedentary, who shun contact with the outside world." See J. Alden Mason, "Coast and Crest in Colombia: An Example in Contrast in American Indian Culture," *Natural History* 26 (1926): 31–43, cited in Seifriz, "The Sierra Nevada," 482. Cabot, in his report, says: "My own view is that these Indians are a decadent race and that there has been both an excess of deaths over births and an emigration to the lowlands by the mission-educated youths." He is referring to one of the Capuchin missions established early this century in the village of San Sebastián. Later he remarks on the inefficiency of the Arhuaco as farmers and their lack of native enterprise as a factor deterring the development of the region. He suggests that this is largely due to their consumption of coca leaves: "It is asserted, but not proved that cocaine adds endurance to the

Indians. It certainly causes partial stupefaction. One cannot say to what extent it has contributed to the decadence of the race, but I doubt whether there are more than 1500 Arhuacos left." He concludes with a sweeping statement: "All the Arhuacos seem to be diffident, unemotional, suspicious of strangers, and lacking in ambition." Cabot, in a typical imperialist vein, considers that "the most promising use for this great region to the outside world is as a playground ... And when the resort is established, I want to be one of the first visitors!" See Cabot, "The Cabot Expedition," 598–615. Luckily for the Kogi and for us, Cabot's vision of the area's future was not realized, but there are dangers nonetheless. Shortly after the discovery and exploration of Buritica, I remember reading and hearing about an outrageous project to build a cable car to provide easy access to it from the coast.

29 Reichel-Dolmatoff, "The Loom of Life," 10.

30 For a more detailed account of this aspect, see Reichel-Dolmatoff, "The Loom of Life," "The Great Mother," and *The Sacred Mountain*.

31 Osip Mandelstam, *Conversations with Dante,* cited in Chatwin, *Songlines,* 230.

32 Ayala, "Los Artifices," 398.

33 Reichel-Dolmatoff, *Colombia,* 142–68.

34 William Seifriz, "The Sierra Nevada," 482. This is his account: "Some sixty or seventy huts grouped closely together with neat open spaces between them constitute the village of San Miguel – room enough to house fully a hundred people, yet when we entered not a person was in sight. The village is used only as a gathering place. Every Indian has his one, two, or three small farms some distance away, where he has built himself a hut as comfortable as the one he owns in town. Here he goes with his wife, children, pigs, chickens, and dog to care for first one crop and then the next. In the higher altitudes he grazes his cattle and plants potatoes and arracacha. Near the village, or slightly lower, plaintains, sugar, cane, corn, cotton, coca, and tobacco are grown. In the hot lowlands he raises yuca, bananas, and some few other fruits."

35 Reichel-Dolmatoff, *The Sacred Mountain,* 2.

36 Reichel-Dolmatoff, "The Loom of Life," 22.

Surface and Appearance in Guarino Guarini's SS. Sindone Chapel

Janine Debanné[1]

3.1 Virgin and Child with two Angels, Baouît, Egypt (fifth or sixth century); from Jean Clédat, "Le Monastère et la Nécropole de Baouît," *Mémoires publiés par les membres de l'Institut français d'archéologie orientale du Caire*, vol. 12, plate XCVI.

AN EARLY CHRISTIAN FRESCO in a chapel near Baouît, Egypt, contains an intriguing depiction of the Madonna and Child, flanked by two angels. The fresco, contained in a half-circle motif, is damaged in parts, and bare stone shares the surface with the solemn faces of Byzantium centred in their halos. A prayerful image, its iconography is typical in every way, except that the Virgin is not holding a child in her arms. Rather, she is holding an *image* of the child on a rigid oval disk.[2] The ambiguities of this representation are manifold: with the Christ child appearing twice removed, on a surface within a surface, the image collapses two different times, transposing the timelessness of Christ, achieved as an adult in the Passion and Resurrection, to his infancy. The Virgin of the Baouît fresco therefore holds a prophesy in her arms, a child that will never leave her again, since he is already projected beyond the realm of mortals.[3] As an emphatic statement of the presence of God in the human world, it fulfils the primary purpose of a religious image, yet the spirit of the fresco remains ambiguous: is the Virgin sadly presenting the icon as a reminder of her son's Passion, or is she reassured to be holding a thing more enduring than human flesh, and more eternal

3.2 Antonio Tempesta, View of the Castello and Piazza Castello during the exhibition of the Holy Shroud (1613); from Biblioteca Reale Torino.

than a child? In either case, the Christ-in-image of the fresco presents us with a poignant expression of the dilemma posed by the dual nature of Christ: his bodily presence in the world, and his absence from it.

It is the very paradox of the Incarnation that Guarino Guarini faced in 1667 when he was commissioned to take charge of the design for a chapel to house the piece of linen (*sindone*) purported to have wrapped the body of Christ while it lay in the tomb. The SS. Sindone Chapel already had been under construction for ten years when Guarini was appointed engineer to the project by Duke Carlo Emanuele II, in response to concerns about the Chapel's structure.[4] This work would be the primary focus of the latter part of Guarini's life.[5] Like all Christian representations, the SS. Sindone would reflect on the notion of *logos* becoming "flesh," in reference to John 1:14, "The Word became flesh and lived for a while among us," and would attempt to give a tangible "image" to the fleeting corporeal essence of the divine – a task rendered all the more delicate by the subject at hand: the complex events of the death and Resurrection of Christ, and the precarious moment of emptiness contained between them.[6] This representational pursuit has always been accompanied by conflict, as testified by recurring debates between iconoclasts and iconophiles regarding imagistic reminders of the Incarnation. At the centre of this debate is the very surface of the sacred image – the site of profound disagreements as to the nature of the impulses it generated in its viewers. Specifically, did the image lead to the veneration of God or was it a path to idolatry?[7] The iconoclasts believed that "pictures are loathsome" and "we become loathsome when we love them,"[8] and the defenders of images maintained that representation was permissible – even warranted – because God himself had taken on matter, form, and body and become representable, as John of Damascus had argued in the eighth-century version of the debate.[9] Guarini was interested in these questions by virtue of his vocation as a member of the Theatine order, a Counter-Reformation order of priests whose part in the debate on the "veneration of relics and legitimate use of images"[10] is well recorded. Although the twenty-fifth session of the Council of Trent preceded Guarini's life by almost a century, it remains significant that Charles Borromeo (instigator of the SS. Sindone Chapel through his personal eagerness to venerate the Shroud) and Guarini's Theatine Order were directly involved in its formulation.[11] The SS. Sindone Chapel in turn finds itself at the heart of this debate owing to its architect, its historical context, and, of course, its relic.

Relics are organized on a range of proximity and distance from the body: as actual body parts of saints or as objects that have simply touched a saintly body. The Shroud is an intermediary relic that stands on the cleft between body and icon.[12] By its lesser degree of figuration and by its divine origin, it could be promoted by the Counter-Reformation as a relic more reliable than a mere body part and as a "true" image coming from direct contact with Christ, in a climate where authentic origins were being avidly sought by the Church of Rome in response to the challenges of the Reformation. Although Calvin and others had vehemently attacked the cult of relics in the sixteenth century, denouncing its many irregularities[13] and urging the removal of images from churches, in Guarini's day the Shroud remained a relic of relics.

The burial cloth of Christ belonged to that special category of contact relics, "true images" that relate miraculously to the body; it was the trace of *logos* incarnate – its fibers brushed over and imprinted with the figure of the divine. Whether it is described traditionally, as a miraculous *acheiropoïton* relic,[14] or in contemporary terms as a "luminous index"

3.3 Sixth-century
bas-relief on ivory
depicting the Holy
Sepulchre.

of the absent body of Christ,[15] it is a perennially dual sign: vestige of
bodily presence and reminder of absence, tangible and yet invisible. The
"burial strips" of Christ and the headpiece, mentioned in each of the
gospels in the contexts of the deposition and the discovery of the empty
tomb, are associated with the beginning of belief in the Resurrection;
this sign of absence triggered belief in presence. As it wavers between
logos and flesh, the shroud signals the end of the Incarnation and the
decline of the figural, and inaugurates a new phase in the relationship
between humans and God.[16] In turn, the strong semantic association of
the Shroud and the Incarnation is evidenced in an early Christian icon-
ographical theme, in which depictions of the Shroud laid flat on an
empty tomb are inserted anachronistically into Nativity scenes.[17] As for
the mode of production of the image, quite aside from ongoing debates
about the Shroud's authenticity, sindonologists generally agree that its
stains are unfolded flat projections of the four sides of a body onto the
plane of the cloth, and that this geometric imprint is an unlikely image.[18]
Given all of the Shroud's characteristics, the building to house it was
liable to be a poignant expression of the theological tension between
logos and flesh.

This tension not only exists at the core of the SS. Sindone's architecture but is also a prevalent theme in Guarini's writings. In a series of treatises in Latin and Italian, Guarini wrote on numerous subjects, including geometry, fortifications, philosophy, and architecture.[19] These writings comprise an important counterpart to Guarini's architectural works, and contain insights that can enlarge conventional readings of his work, in particular with regard to the modality of appearance in the SS. Sindone Chapel. Indeed, existing scholarship on Guarini often describes the SS. Sindone dome as an attempt to create an "impression of unlimited space"[20] or as a perspectival illusion of infinity.[21] Such comparisons, although accounting for a contemporary experience of the Chapel space, tend to relegate the dome to the realm of the purely visual, and in this way they fail to convey adequately the "world of the work." This optical emphasis is in keeping with dominant rationalist interpretations of Guarini's work but remains difficult to ratify in light of the architect's own words.[22]

Guarini's treatise on architecture and his philosophical work are rooted in a concern for mediation between invisible and visible realms. The primary aim of the posthumous publication *Architettura Civile* (Turin 1737) was to show how to materialize geometry into stone through the art of stereotomy, and the broad strokes of his earlier Scholastic work, *Placita Philosophica* (Paris 1665), inquire into the relationship between spirit and matter. This conceptual framework is most helpful in an understanding of a building (and its enigmatic dome) that is not simply visual but unquestionably dialectical in theme, in program, and in experience, and that cannot be understood in isolation from its relic.[23] In seeking the terms with which to describe the SS. Sindone Chapel, we must ask the questions: what kind of vision is assumed in Guarini's writings and architecture, and how is the relation of "appearance" to "surface" to be understood?

While the word "appearance" refers to something that we see, "image" has theological connotations because of its association with the scriptural statement that "God created man in His own image" (Gen. 1:27). An appearance would then function as an image when it refers to a spiritual object, whether by analogy or by projection. Just as the "appearance" of the icon becomes an "image" of God in heaven, its appearance may seem to advance "forward" from the surface while its image recedes "back" from it, both in space and in time. In this sense

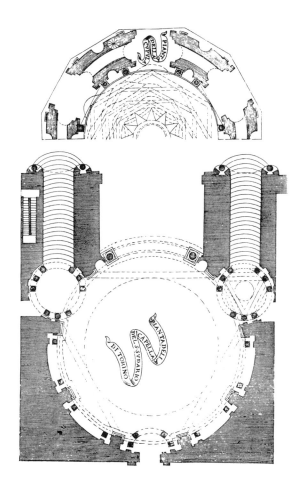

3.4 Plan of the SS. Sindone Chapel, from *Architettura Civile* (1737 ed.).

the image completes the appearance, endowing it with spiritual reverberations. Constructions that waver between light and matter, such as the high spaces of Gothic cathedrals, tend to evoke an experience of transcendence by fixing an image of the "un-imageable." The Chapel's dome will be central to this discussion about "image" because it oscillates ambiguously between the solidity of stone and the intangibility of light, appearing and disappearing simultaneously, prompting comments by numerous architectural historians.[24] It is fitting that *Architettura Civile's* famous litany, headed by the title "Architecture should not be as permissive as perspective," should contain an intriguing statement about surface and appearance: "Perspective, because it fools the eye and *makes the surface of a body appear,* obtains its end, and achieves what it sets out to do; hence even an unruly architecture can achieve its end,

3.5 Left: Distant view of the SS. Sindone dome from a distance (author).

3.6 Right: The SS. Sindone dome, exterior view. Photograph from Paolo Portoghesi, *Guarino Guarini 1624–1683* (Milan: Electa Editrice 1956), 21.

receiving the praise of all. But architecture cannot achieve its end of pleasing the eye without *true symmetries,* its ultimate end being not to fool the eye."[25] This unusual statement suggests that, in representations of architecture, surfaces of architecture should be kept from appearing completely and that a deferral between the full three-dimensional surface and its manifestation to the viewer was for Guarini somehow desirable. One has to ask why this is so, and then examine how Guarini aspired to carry this out in architecture.

Certainly the "surface" is a dominant concern for Baroque architecture in general, and this is all the more true in the SS. Sindone Chapel, which is primarily an internal space. Located at the intersection of the Royal Palace and the San Giovanni Duomo of Turin, the Chapel is accessible only from inside these buildings.[26] Its exterior expression is limited to a windowed wall in the Duomo provided for the draping of the Shroud, a portal in the *piano nobile* of the Royal Palace (Fig. 3.4), and a "woven dome" that emerges from the building complex. As a

3.7 Transition from embedded to detached orders in anterooms. Photograph from *Guarino Guarini e l'Internazionalita del Barocco* II: 30 (Torino: Accademia delle Scienze 1968).

result, the importance of the interior surfaces is heightened throughout. The approach from the Duomo to the Chapel furthers the modulation of surface by orchestrating a slow progression from obscurity into light, underlined by a lightening of the stone in the upper levels of the section and by a radical transformation of surface texture that takes place in the course of the procession to the reliquary.

One ascends to the Chapel via one of two long staircases clad entirely in polished black marble with fluted pilasters embedded in the walls and intumescent shells and friezes in the shallow vault of the ceiling. In this telluric realm, all the architectonic elements fuse, and one has the sense of being fully absorbed into a "deep surface." For every element that recedes from the surface, another emerges forward, as with the heart-shaped accretion beneath each of the stair's wall niches. The stairs lead to the Chapel proper through circular anterooms at the level of the *piano nobile* of the Royal Palace. In the two anterooms associated with the Duomo (a third one leads to the Royal Palace) the floors are indented

3.8 View of reliquary and dome (author).

by the last three treads of the stairs; in turn, two undulating steps overflow onto the circular plan from the raised Chapel. It is here that a dialogue of surface and distance is launched by the introduction of a detached Corinthian order juxtaposed with the embedded order of the stairs, foretelling the dialogue of distance and proximity, and emptiness and fullness, that will be played out in the reliquary Chapel: just beyond these half-lit anterooms rises the domed rotunda, perched atop pendentives and a ring of serlianas, suffusing the space with light from above and dissipating the density of the surface texture. Below, the grey and white stones of a radially patterned floor are worn unevenly, and inlaid bronze stars swell slightly above them. A low balustrade circumscribes the Chapel's centre, with its inescapable occupant, a massive reliquary elevated four steps above the floor. Beneath a dome that seems to evaporate vertically, the reliquary advances as an insisting presence. Bronze rays extend vertically from it, towards a dove in the lantern of the dome.

Geometrical delays and plays of distancing, such as the delay of the dome by the insertion of the pendentives and serliana ambulatory, recur

3.9 SS. Sindone dome "weave" of light and stone (author).

throughout the architecture and are largely responsible for the Chapel's shimmering quality. The spacings introduced between architectonic elements invest the Chapel's surfaces with a temporal content. This is especially true of SS. Sindone's dome, where the relationship between stone and light is the most ambiguous. The dome is constructed with a set of twelve external buttresses and an internal weave of thirty-six elliptical arches layered vertically such that each one springs from the keystone of the arch below. The relinquishing of the mass between the buttresses leaves behind a weave of stone that challenges the very definition of domical structures and places this structure in a category of its own, at the mid-point between dome and oculus, oculus and lantern, covering and aperture. Structural investigation further demonstrates this intermediate state, revealing that the deep load is carried by the twelve external ribs, enabling the inner weave to be dedicated solely to modulating light. To this end, elongated pairs of apertures are set deeply into the space beneath each of the dome's arches. This sinuous stone weave effectively supports only itself – the load of its own "skin."[27] The peeling apart of surface and depth is finally revealed in the oculus, where ovaloid

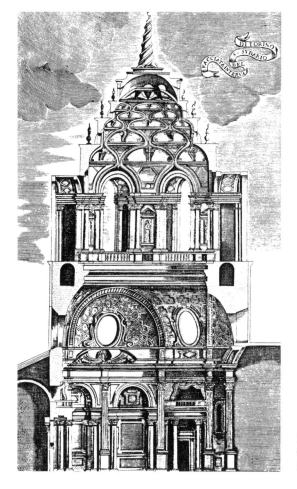

3.10 Section of the SS. Sindone Chapel, from *Architettura Civile* (1737 ed.).

windows perforate the outer shell to backlight the twelve-pointed-star cut-out at the apex of the dome. This delicate relationship between stone surface and "appearance," where the epiphany of the Chapel's appearance comes from *behind* the surface, suggests that Guarini's concern in the dome was not merely to proffer an optical illusion of depth but to challenge the depth of the surface itself by endowing the dome with a diaphanous quality and the capacity to waver between stone and light.

The diaphanous weave takes on its full meaning in relation to the section of the Chapel. There exists a clear relationship of projection between the floor of the Chapel where the relic sits and its dome. The entire impulse of the architecture seems to be to express, slowly but surely, the process that leads one to the other. Delays and distantiations are introduced throughout the section as it progresses upward from the order of nine in the rotunda to the triad of the pendentives, to the hexagonal geometry of the dome. These divisions and multiplications

3.11 Above: SS. Sindone anteroom floor. Photograph from Paolo Portoghesi, *Guarino Guarini 1624-1683* (Milan: Electa Editrice 1956), 28.

3.12 Below: SS. Sindone anteroom ceiling. Photograph from Paolo Portoghesi, *Guarino Guarini 1624-1683* (Milan: Electa Editrice 1956), 27.

(by two or by three) of the respective geometries of the constructional tiers ensure geometrical continuity. However, in the course of sectional transformation, certain elements are left behind (such as three of the pilasters from the first order which are not carried into the pendentives); other architectonic elements become latent in the walls before reappearing at an elevated point, and geometries that are merely implied in lower zones become explicit higher up.[28] Notably, the implied (invisible) triangle in the ground floor plan becomes the dominant (visible) geometry of the pendentive realm. Similarly, an implied hexagon in the ground-floor plan reappears as the structure of the dome, multiplied six times. Through such elisions, a powerful temporal sense is introduced into the architecture. The dome is a future version of the plan. In the same way, the anteroom floor pattern (a circle with alternating elongated and equilateral triangular rays) is repeated in the stone cut-out below the dome's oculus, and the Chapel floor and pendentives both bear the same

ARCHITETTURA
CIVILE

DEL

PADRE D· GUARINO
GUARINI

CHERICO REGOLARE

OPERA POSTUMA

DEDICATA

A SUA SACRA REALE
MAESTÁ.

IN TORINO, M.DCC.XXXVII.

Appreſſo Gianfrancefco Mairefe all' Infegna
di Santa Terefa di GESU'.

3.13 *Architettura Civile*,
frontispiece (1737 ed.).

Greek cross and hexagon pattern. In this way, the stones of the floor appear to have re-emerged three-dimensionally in the cupola, raised above the reliquary through stereotomic operations. It is as if the embedded geometries of the Chapel were in gestation in the anterooms, yet to be raised. This, of course, leads to Guarini's theory of parallel projection, *ortografia*.

Indeed, Guarini's treatise has much to say on the creation of an "appearance" in stone. The first question in *Architettura Civile* is how to give form and consistency to the complex geometrical entities that resulted from the undulation of the classical orders. After all, *ortografia*, Guarini's theory of parallel projection, is intended to be used in stereotomy.[29] It is expounded in the third and fourth books of the treatise: "Della Ortografia Elevata," which is concerned with frontal projection and the representational idea of elevation, and "Della Ortografia Gettata," which develops projections proper and shows how to unfold three-dimensional curves in plan and section with a view towards stone-cutting in vault and dome construction. It is in these pages that the term *proiectione* first appears.[30]

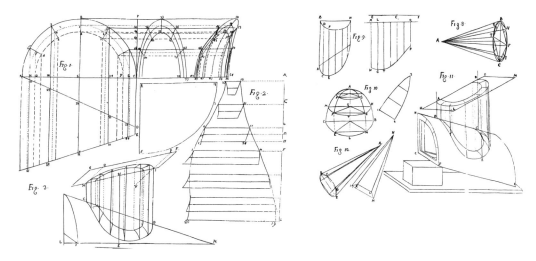

3.14 Left: Extending the surface of a barrel vault intersected by a semi-cylinder and an inclined plane, from *Architettura Civile* (1737 ed.), Lastra IV, Tratt. IV (detail).

3.15 Right: Geometrical methods for the intersection of a barrel vault, a cylinder, and an inclined plane, from *Architettura Civile* (1737 ed.), Lastra I, Tratt. IV, Fig.11 (detail).

As for *ortografia*, "the architect should know two kinds: one that presupposes a plan and raises a drawing from it; and another that does not, but is drawn in suspension and then thrown into plan."[31] While it seems clear that the first refers to the raising of an elevation, *ortografia gettata* is more complex; it is a section in search of its unfolded plan. Indeed, Guarini explains that the former is the opposite of the latter in both title and mode of operating. With *ortografia elevata*, "plane surfaces are projected with perpendicular lines to give them body and form the *fabbrica*," and *ortografia gettata* casts "bodies which are suspended above" back down into plan "in order to extend their surfaces."[32] In other words, even if one knows the curve in section, whether concave or convex, one must still determine the stretched area from which the stones are to be cut and bevelled, so that when set together, the roundness of the original three-dimensional shell is recovered, as shown in the illustration plates pertaining to the problem of a semicylinder intersected by an inclined plane at one extremity and by an inclined cylinder at the other. What is striking in the definition of *ortografia* is the portrayal of geometry as the tool with which such "suspended bodies" could be

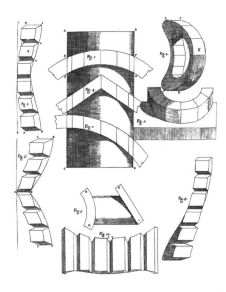

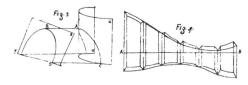

3.16 Left: "Method of uniting the inner and outer surfaces of a cylinder segmented obliquely," from *Architettura Civile* (1737 ed.), Lastra III, Tratt. IV.

3.17 Above: *Ortografia Gettata* applied to stone cutting, from *Architettura Civile* (1737 ed.), Lastra V, Tratt. IV.

ushered into the material realm – moved towards embodied *fabbrica,* as it were. This movement is the focus of the plates that accompany *Architettura Civile,* which often show the unfolded plan "peeling off" the orthogonal plan, as in the problems of a hemispherical dome intersected respectively by a triangle and a pentagon. The vault is a perceivable entity in stone but is also related through *ortografia* to an immaterial (suspended) entity that eludes perception. The simplest example of this relationship is found in the problem of "how to throw round or oval surfaces into plan, given an angle of inclination": the method of dividing the original circle with lines, carrying them to a slope in section, dropping the intersecting points into plan, and reconfiguring the circle in a compressed (oval) state relies on temporarily dissolving the circle into a number of points.[33] The semantic structure of Guarini's geometrical method ("throwing" from section to stretched plan) includes a moment of parenthesis and loss of form that is appropriate to an architecture that deals with the mystery of the Incarnation.[34] Much like the image on the Shroud, "*Ortografia* is none other than an impression, termination or vestige recorded in the perpendicular plane of a surface."[35]

While Guarini prefers parallel projection to create and represent the "true symmetries" of architecture, his treatise also includes instructions on optical corrections.[36] In fact, this demonstrates an important aspect of Guarini's world-view: his belief that geometrical truth and human

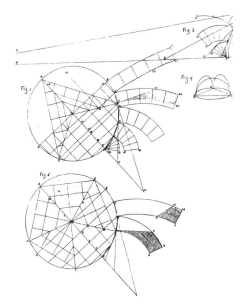

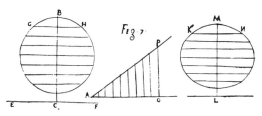

3.18 Left: Determining the stone-cutting plans (hatched areas) for a dome intersected with a triangle (Fig. 5) and a pentagon (Fig. 6), from *Architettura Civile* (1737 ed.), Lastra XII, Tratt. IV (detail).

3.19 Above: Illustration for the problem of throwing a circle onto an inclined plane, from *Architettura Civile* (1737 ed.), Lastra I, Tratt. IV, Fig. 7 (detail).

perception (in particular, optics) are ontologically distinct.[37] Guarini's delicate sequencing of architecture – "nonetheless an art of flattery" – with mathematics, reason, and pleasure[38] begins to align with his suspicion of perspective. When Guarini conveys instructions on optical-correction methods in *Architettura Civile,* he insists that they should always be used not to "expand" the visual experience, but to compensate for the limitations of vision and to ensure that the other senses are not deprived. "Because the end of architecture is to please the senses, if the senses are mistaken, which happens often, judging a straight object as curved, an upright one as slanted, a large one as small, it will be necessary to supplement the senses with what seems to be missing, even though it is not really missing, adding not more than is right, but just enough."[39] It is in the spirit of restraint of this statement that the elongated section of the dome, a conoid rather than a hemisphere, must be understood: hemispheres have a tendency to appear "shallower than they are."[40] Guarini's concern is not to give the dome an illusion of *more* depth than it actually has, as is frequently argued, but rather to ensure that its appearance is *not less* than its geometrical reality.

As a general rule, *Architettura Civile* advocates optical corrections to restore the proper perceptual appearance, the "competent distance," in situations where one is too close to the object of vision or where optical rules distort the parallelism and "true symmetries" of architecture.[41] The

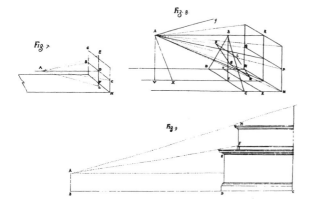

3.20 The proper viewing distance: twice the width of the object or four times its height (Fig. 7); perspectival visual cone (Fig. 8); method of lifting the reveals when viewed from a close point (Fig. 9); from *Architettura Civile* (1737 ed.), Lastra III, Tratt. III.

problem of increasing the depth of an overhang and the elevation of a cornice to make it "reappear" when viewed from a close point – the subject of the twenty-second chapter of the third book – is therefore crucial; the façade of a building is the interface of the idea and the sensuous world, and the collapse of its three-dimensionality implies the loss of the idea itself. The illustration for this part of the text is a section of a building façade and a visual cone; it is placed just beneath a sectional perspective that is meant to be read as a "scene inside the eye"[42] (Fig. 16). In other words, the order of the building is liable to be lost in the very same way that parallelism is lost in vision. Here we may recall Guarini's odd admonition against perspective in *Architettura Civile*, because it accelerates the appearance of the "surface of bodies." Perspective is deemed overly "permissive" and unable to convey the "true symmetries" of architecture. Throughout the treatise, Guarini thus privileges parallel projection as a tool for design and representation. Implicit in this approach is the idea that parallel projection enables the preservation of a precious "distance" between appearance and surface.

Guarini writes in *Architettura Civile* of a preference in painting and sculpture for that which is sketchy and rough over that which is "totally finished."[43] This attitude towards representation is enmeshed in a historical context that cannot be ignored: the late seventeenth century was preoccupied with decoding the rules of optics and fascinated with optical illusion. Practices of *inganni* were extremely popular during Guarini's lifetime.[44] Illusions proffered a marvellous effect for the viewer by conjuring a point at which visual rays and geometrical lines coincided; however, by being perspectival and convergent, such representations necessarily distorted the order of the architecture by shedding parallelism and measurability. In perspective, there is a presupposition that parallel lines converge at a point at infinity, and that the perspectival image rises out of it, its final veil. Significantly, Guarini does not acknowledge this infinite point, nor that this frontal image is born from a convergence there.[45] The corollary, that visual lines eventually become parallel at a distant point, is refuted with equal vehemence; what is more, Guarini finds "the idea frustrating and the supposition absurd," arguing that an image emanating from infinity would be so diminished by its transit that it would be invisible. The singular point from which a perspectival illusion is revealed implies the end of the appearance. In other words, perspective accelerates the "appearance of the surface of things" and results in the hemorrhaging of vision's temporal nature. A distinction between surface and appearance is necessary to avoid such a trauma of the surface.

Another weakness of the perspectivist paradigm is its self-referential content, or, in Guarini's words, that which perspective "liberally invents for itself,"[46] for it is a function of the position of the viewer in relation to the object. The "appearances" it generates are the result of intersecting a picture plane and an individual's visual cone (a precarious entity), and these appearances are liable to be dispersed by a mere shift of the gaze, as forcefully demonstrated by, for example, a painted illusionistic dome on a flat ceiling. Guarini's preference for Euclidean geometry and *ortografia,* both of which operate with parallel lines, is based on their ability to safeguard the order of the plan and section and hence to preserve a space of revelation on the frontal plane. Because of its parallelism, the projection enables a shimmering appearance to rise forth from a distance behind the surface.

In this context, Guarini's writings on optics in *Placita Philosophica* should be briefly examined.[47] In his presentation of the "marvelous architecture of the eye," which draws from a blend of medieval and Renaissance anatomical knowledge, Guarini points out the limitations of visual experience with terms that recall his criticisms of perspective. In attempting to understand how vision is formed in the eye, the crucial question of how the eye interprets distance is posed. To explain why some objects appear closer than others, Guarini resorts to a qualitative rather than mechanical account of vision: it is the "vivacity" of the image in the eye *(specie),* a tactile sense, that allows one to understand distance;

DISPVTATIO VI
DE ALTRICI ET
AVCTRICI FACVLTATE.

POST generatiuam facultatem, ex Arist.1.de anim. c. 4. tex. 48. se-
cundas obtinet sedes altrix potentia & auctrix. Eius tractatum priori de generatione annectimus. At quia altricis operatio in nutri-
tione consistit, & ad hanc perfectiùs explicandam, suppetiæ ab
Anatomia sunt petendæ ; hinc est, quòd aliquas Figuras Anatomicas , tum
ad hanc disputationem , tum ad animam sensitiuam spectantes , hic exhi-
bemus.

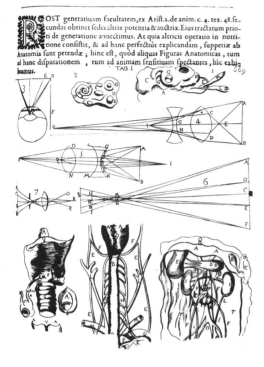

3.21 Anatomical plate showing visual cone and lens refraction diagrams, from *Placita Philosophica* (Paris: Denys Thierry 1665), 669.

furthermore, if vision often fails to convey a perfect expression of the object, it is because this *specie* is like a reflection in a mirror; however, unlike a reflection in marble, it loses its "opacity" while the latter retains it.[48] The inherent contradiction in the fact that one judges size and distance based only on a tiny image in a remote eye is overcome by vision's haptic content.

Guarini's sense of the "incompletion" of optical phenomena is indissociable from his disdain for oblique lines; for, indeed, a marked preference for parallel lines pervades his optical theory.[49] This suggests that his account of vision still relied on the notion of a medieval visual cone

– in which the image is created by the rays that hit the surface of the eye perpendicularly, the oblique rays being too weak to enter the eye and have an impact on vision – rather than on the theory of rays refracting within the eye's crystalline lens.[50] This is also implied in the plates of the treatise, in which lens-refraction diagrams and a medieval visual cone are depicted separately. Obliqueness is hence responsible for the failure of the picture to convey the perfection of the object. Once again, the strange notion of a distance between the object and its surface arises: "These *species* reflect things extremely obliquely, expressing the object *not distanced from itself,* but rather, *integrated to its own surface.*"[51] The integration of the object and its image is a hindrance to proper vision. With this, the main flaw of perspective as put forth in *Architettura Civile* - that makes "the surfaces of bodies appear" – is reiterated vividly: "obliquation," just as perspective, reveals too much, too quickly. In contrast to the momentary brilliance of a fireworks display or an optical trick, an enduring appearance is infiltrated with distance.

"Even if Architecture depends on Mathematics, it is nonetheless an art of flattery, which by reason does not wish to offend the senses."[52] Guarini's memorable litany on subordinating reason to the senses offers a corollary to his disdain of perspective; architecture should bring delight to the senses but must not deceive the eye. It will come as no surprise to find further on in the treatise that this delight is a function of the surface. The first mention of "projections" in *Architettura Civile* involves *ortografia elevata* – an art which, "as all arts, has certain principles through which it composes and forms its ideas ... and these principles are generally different kinds of overhangs called *proiectiones*, and other reveals, which advance out of the building face and fold themselves into other forms, bringing delight to the work."[53]

The importance of sectional "prominences" is best illustrated in the SS. Sindone pendentives, whose surfaces are strikingly activated despite the fact that they are structurally unnecessary.[54] This final "visible" layer of the Chapel is extensively coffered with Greek crosses and squares, and the large interstitial shells of the arches are carved with hexagonal and six-pointed-star patterns.[55] Because the pendentives span from a shorter arc on the first cornice to a longer arc above, their rising surfaces need to cover more area and seem to "stretch," as if made of fabric.[56] Their geometrical motifs are thus charged with a revelatory role, for they allow the invisible work of geometry to appear on the surface of the stone.

The star-and-cross patterns on the pendentives and inter-pendentive arches are also found on the Chapel floor, suggesting that the floor has been raised vertically.

A key to understanding the rapport between light and matter in the Chapel is afforded in the relationship between pendentives and dome. In preparing to receive the dome, the pendentives arc towards the constricted cornice, on their way to forming a dome themselves. The trajectory of the pendentives is then halted by the cornice, untraceable in the ambulatory and the ring of serlianas above, from which the dome springs. An evocative reciprocity exists between the two: the pendentives are truncated to enable the dome to rise; in turn, the dome sheds light onto the pendentives and brings shadows to the coffered texture of their surfaces. As the coffers fill with light and shadow, they begin to "advance out of the wall," becoming "prominent," as Guarini would say, and thus acquire an appearance beyond their surface.[57] Here, the otherwise restrained and sober Chapel shares in the more typical exuberance of Baroque expression, in which matter overflows into space through folds and creases, fulfilling the primary Baroque quest to mediate between a "lower" and an "upper" world through the senses.[58] The perforated dome allows light into a space that would otherwise disappear into darkness, and, conversely, the undulations of the stone surface allow light to be registered and become "incarnate." Light and stone mutually create an "image."

In a remarkable passage about vision in *Placita Philosophica,* Guarini writes about the meeting of light and matter in the creation of an image for the eye, and once again, the importance of material density is emphasized: for an object to register an appearance, it must have "thickness."[59] He expounds upon the qualities of translucency, opacity, and the diaphanous with regard to the relationship between light and matter. Three dialogues are dedicated to diaphanous substances. In describing light "coming out of an object and leaning toward another," Guarini stresses the need for some kind of material resistance for the recording of an image.[60] What is completely translucent cannot be imprinted by images, since they would pass right through it. In turn, what is completely opaque does not reflect *specie,* or images, because "for matter to capture light" or "for light to become a subject," the environment must have a diaphanous quality.[61] This was seen earlier in Guarini's optical theory, in which vision is given partly through the clarity of a mirror and partly

PLACITA
PHILOSOPHICA
R. P. D.
GVARINI GVARINI
MVTINENSIS
CLERICI REGVLARIS,
Vulgò Theatini,
SACRÆ THEOLOGIÆ PROFESSORIS,
PHYSICIS RATIONIBVS, EXPERIENTIIS, MATHEMATICISQVE
figuris oftenfa : quæ ficut facræ Theologiæ leniùs obfequuntur , ita à
principiis aliarum fcientiarum obftinatiùs non abhorrent fimulque
Vniuerfæ Philofophiæ Thefes felici pede percurrunt.

CVM DVOBVS INDICIBVS,
Altero Difputationum; Rerum altero.

PARISIIS,
Apud DIONYSIVM THIERRY , viâ Iacobæâ, ad infigne Ciuitatis
Parifienfis.

M. DC. LXV.
Cum Priuilegio Regis, & Superiorum Permiffa.

3.22 *Placita Philosophica,*
frontispiece (Paris: Denys
Thierry 1665).

through the opacity of marble. The importance of thickness and opacity in the conservation of light and appearance is a recurring theme in the treatise. It is interesting, then, to consider the diaphanous quality of the dome in relation to Guarini's emphasis on matter as a "conserver" of the image of light, and to envisage the dome as the place where these two entities combine. A comment in *Placita Philosophica* regarding the need for the diaphanous to be white in colour – saturated colour being opposed to the diaphanous quality – sheds an interesting light on the meaning of the progression from black to whitish stone in the Chapel.[62] However, all of Guarini's writings seem to be preoccupied with the mediation between the invisible and the tangible, and a similar discussion about "imprinting matter" with light is found in the seventh book of *Placita Philosophica,* which deals with metaphysics.[63]

Placita Philosophica takes on questions posed by Aristotle and later by Thomas Aquinas and other nominalist Scholastic philosophers regarding the issue of mediation between visible and invisible things and the question of how corporeal and non-corporeal substances are organized in creation (Fig. 3.17). This is interesting in the context of the SS. Sindone Chapel, whose relic itself asks the question of how matter is imprinted with spirit as it pertains to its own image, and whose thematic program considers the hinge-point between *logos* and flesh in the death and Resurrection of Christ. The dialogue "On Separated Substances" considers the relationship between spirit and matter in a series of riddles of High Scholasticism, which Guarini poses and then proceeds to answer. The question of whether "separated spirits" (beings that have shed their body) can move freely through the world without a mediator is answered negatively, in keeping with Aristotle's ideas on motion.[64] This strongly recalls the need for "thickness" to preserve light and allow appearances to happen in the sensory realm, discussed in relation to Guarini's theory of vision.

Following an insistence that spirits need a medium of some density in order to move or to cause "subtle corporeal motion," light is identified as one of the possible substances that could serve as a medium of transference: "In order to move bodies, separated spirits produce a subtle corporeal operation such as light, but they cannot move by their own volition."[65] This is of interest in relation to the role of light in the Chapel. The diaphanous quality of the dome becomes an expression of the spiritual dwelling in matter. After all, the light from the dome enables the *detti proiectiones* to advance out of the Chapel's walls, and the dome's shimmering surface to have an appearance in the world of the senses.

Elsewhere in the treatise, Guarini compares the notion of the soul imprinting itself onto humans to the notion of visible images imprinting themselves onto matter: "Visible images *(species)* certainly cannot imprint themselves onto matter, or in thick organic substance: because their opacity and thickness is to this purpose inept. Neither can the spiritual soul imprint itself into humans: because their aspect is corporeal."[66] Guarini proposes that a mediating substance, "neither spiritual nor thick," is needed in order for the soul to imprint itself into the body. This substance would neither support the images *(species)* nor transmit them; as an intermediary, it would enable passage between spirit and body.[67] The visual analogy is potent: just as opaque matter obstructs the passage of light, spirits are inhibited by matter and require a mediating entity by which to make their way into the sensory realm. The diaphanous modality is once again evoked: the notion of something that is neither opaque enough to impede light nor clear enough to let it through without registering an appearance accurately describes how the SS. Sindone dome intertwines light and stone as it hovers above the reliquary.

The structure of the relic, an image of divine light fixed into the weave of cloth, is thus repeated in the architecture. The geometrical method responsible for the dome and its diaphanous quality therefore emerges with a new meaning by analogy with the metaphor of Incarnation. *Ortografia* is the means by which the invisible takes form and becomes perceivable. It is vested with a dual quality and begins to resemble the *substantia media,* "neque spiritualis, neque crassa,"[68] that is needed to impress spirit onto matter (stones, in this case). This re-enacts by analogy the fixing of the stain into the weave of the Shroud.

The SS. Sindone Chapel was the fruit of fifteen years of labour and of a lifetime of reflection on the relationship between the tactile and the invisible. The tool that served to make the Chapel, *ortografia,* had the capacity to safeguard a distance between the appearance and the surface and to create a vision that cannot collapse into illusion – indeed, an enduring "image" in the theological sense. It was thus with *ortografia* that this architect of the late Baroque managed to commemorate divine passage through our mortal coil.

Guarini's SS. Sindone Chapel architecturally organizes, around its relic, an experience of passage through embodiment and through absence, and expresses the ushering forth of *logos* into matter, from a distant place. The parenthesis of *ortografia* and the delays between elevation and plan are re-enacted in the architecture's sequencing of spaces and modulations of light, from the thick space of the stairs to the inscribed surfaces of the pendentives and to the diaphanous stone-and-light "mixture" of the dome. It is not likely that Guarini thought of the dome not as an illusion of infinity but rather as an intermediate diaphanous substance that could transfer spirit onto matter in the manner described in *Placita Philosophica*. The geometries of the Chapel surfaces, *grafia,* are the material expression that contact has been made, that non-corporeal substance has been imprinted into matter. The SS. Sindone thus may be seen as an emblem of the *logos* suspended, hovering above matter and awaiting incarnation once again. The projective operations of *ortografia* are destined to make stone swell outward from the face of the wall, leading the idea towards tangible presence, and, ultimately, to guide the architecture of a diaphanous "image."

Finally, it must be said that the space between the appearance of perceived things and their own embodied surfaces – a space repeatedly insisted upon in both *Architettura Civile* and *Placita Philosophica* –

bespeaks a mystical distance. This gap between appearance and recognizability recalls Christ's appearance to the disciples after the Resurrection, when "[their eyes were opened] and they recognized him; and he became invisible from them."[69] The trauma of an image disappearing from sight the moment it is recognized is poignantly summarized by the qualities of the *sindone* relic and the Chapel. Here we find ourselves in the realm adumbrated by the Byzantine icon itself. Both *ortografia* and the icon operate within a logic of projection, and their power is sited in the veiled nature of their disclosures; the relationship of their content to their surface is abstract, kept from appearing completely: the surface of the SS. Sindone must also remain *remotum a se*, at a distance from itself, just as "God's true image" eludes the icon. Georges Didi–Huberman has pointed out that the "effectiveness of Christian images," beyond their representational and symbolic value, has to do with the fact that they come to us from far away: "the recoiling of the body of Christ before us, in a kind of refusal to remain visible."[70] Therein lies their enduring captivation. Emmanuel Lévinas has written something similar about the human face: "The face is abstract ... its wonder holds to the elsewhere from whence it comes, and to which already, it pulls away."[71] So, too, are *ortografia elevata* and *ortografia gettata* related to each other in space and time, each a "vestige" of the other, to use Guarini's term. Both rely on a moment of distance, receding just far enough from the surface to create a space for revelation and appearance, and advancing into mass just close enough to touch us. The SS. Sindone Chapel offers an answer to the iconoclastic debate by creating an image that is always double, wavering between a screen of recognizability and an other-worldly point beyond. In this light, the Baouît fresco resurfaces in its sadness and mystery: as a projection, the child remains an enigma, even to the woman who beholds him. In their distance, they are ever near.

NOTES

1 This article is drawn from my M.Arch. dissertation, "Guarino Guarini's SS. Sindone Chapel: Between Reliquary and Cenotaph" (McGill University 1995). I wish to acknowledge gratefully the following individuals for their comments: Alberto Pérèz-Gómez, Lily Chi, and Kenneth Hayes.

2 This chapel and fresco, dating from the fifth or sixth century, are documented in Jean Clédat, "Le Monastère et la Nécropole de Baouît," *Mémoires*

publiés par les membres de l'Institut français d'archéologie orientale du Caire (Cairo: Imprimerie de l'institut français d'archéologie orientale 1946), 12, plate XLI.

3 The tradition of the oval *clipeus* image of a Christ who has already died and come back is discussed in André Grabar's exhaustive study on reliquaries and martyria, *Martyrium – Recherches sur le culte des reliques et l'art chrétien antique,* 2 vols. (Paris: Collège de France 1946), 1:176–9. The Baouît fresco is reproduced therein as plate LIV.

4 Guarini's work continued that of the Castellamonte (first the father and then the son) and by Bernardo Quadri (whose design had been put into execution as of 1657). H.A. Meek, *Guarino Guarini and His Architecture* (New Haven: Yale University Press 1988), 62–7. A detailed history of the Chapel's construction is also found in Nino Carboneri, "Guarini ed il Piemonte," *Guarino Guarini E L'Internazionalita Del Barocco,* 2 vols. (abbrev. *GGIB*) (Turin: Accademia delle Scienze 1970), 2:347.

5 Guarino Guarini, 1624 (Modena) – 1683 (Milan).

6 At this moment of *kenosis* when "He made himself into nothing" (Phil. 2:7). A much earlier structure based thematically on this moment is of course the Holy Sepulchre *(Anastasis Rotunda),* built by Constantine in the fourth century (Fig. 3.3).

7 This was customarily resolved by distinguishing between levels of veneration: *latria,* which was appropriate only to God, and *dulia,* which could be offered to saints. The centrality of the iconoclastic debates in Baroque architecture is clearly delineated in Christine Poletto's analysis of Jesuit scenography. See *Art et pouvoirs à l'age baroque – crise mystique et crise esthétique aux XVIe et XVIIe siècles* (Paris: L'Harmattan 1990).

8 A. Karlstadt, "On the Removal of Images" (1521), in D. Mangrum and G. Scavizzi, *A Reformation Debate – Three Treatises in Translation* (Ottawa: Dove House 1991), 20n.2.

9 *On the Divine Images – Three Apologies Against Those Who Attack the Divine Images (circa* 787), trans. D. Anderson (New York: St Vladimir Seminary Press 1980), 23.

10 "On the Invocation, Veneration, and Relics of Saints, and on Sacred Images" (1563), in *Canons and Decrees of the Council of Trent,* trans. H.E. Schroeder (London: Herder 1941), 214–17.

11 On this point, see A.D. Wright, *The Counter Reformation* (London: Weidenfeld and Nicolson 1982), 103–91, and Paul Kunkel, *The Theatines in the History of Catholic Reform* (Washington: Catholic University of America

Press 1941), 35–8, 155–9. On the influence of Charles Borromeo on the Council of Trent see R. Wittkower, *Art and Architecture in Italy, 1600 to 1750* (Harmondsworth, U.K.: Penguin Books 1985), 21–5.

12 In this, the Holy Shroud represents a synthesis of Latin and Byzantine notions of hallowedness. Indeed, whereas the Latin church had a preference for bodily relics as objects of devotion, the Greek church had a marked preference for icons, and it was precisely this divergence that caused the division between the two churches in the fourth century. See Grabar, *Martyrium*, 1:43, 2:357.

13 One such irregularity was the number of relics of a given saint adding up to more than one body, as revealed in his critical inventory of relics claimed to be owned by the churches of Europe. See Jean Calvin, "Traité des reliques ou avertissement très utile …" (1523). This treatise is included in Collin de Plancy's later version of the inventory, *Dictionnaire critique des reliques et des images miraculeuses* (Paris: Guien et Compagnie 1821).

14 The term *a-cheiro-poïton* ("not made by [human] hand" or "god-given") is found in the New Testament in reference to the Jerusalem Temple and to a house (1 Cor. 15:45–7, 2 Cor. 5:1) and is used to describe miraculous portraits of Christ. On this topic, see Ewa Kuryluk, *Veronica and Her Cloth: History, Symbolism, & Structure of a "True" Image* (London: Basil Blackwell 1991), 29, and A. Grabar, *Martyrium*, 2:347.

15 Georges Didi-Huberman, "The Index of the Absent Wound (Monograph on a Stain)," *October* 29 (1984):41. The French biologist Paul Villon's turn-of-the century term "vaporograph," which refers to the idea that the stain was caused by vapours of burial ointments in combination with bodily fluids, also comes to mind. R. Drews, *In Search of the Shroud of Turin: New Light on Its History and Origins* (Totowa, N.J.: Rowman and Allanheld 1984), 4–5.

16 Paul Ricoeur's analysis of the narrative of the Empty Tomb in the Gospel of Mark, which identifies a "progressive disappearance of the body throughout the Passion narrative" and an "increase of the word," is noteworthy. See "Le récit interprétatif – Exégèse et Théologie dans les récits de la Passion," *Recherches de Science Religieuse* (Paris: Aux Bureaux de la Revue 1985), 73:1, 37.

17 Grabar, *Martyrium*, 2:158.

18 "A first, essential condition for what is visible on the Shroud has to be that the position of the cloth was relatively flat over the body." Peter Wilson, *The Shroud of Turin* (New York: Doubleday 1978), 246. In other words,

the Shroud must have been pulled taut, like a screen over the body and on the sides, to receive the stains as frontal projections. This was also the conclusion of research conducted at NASA with a "VP-8 Image Analyzer." R. Drews, *In Search of the Shroud*, 99, 123n.4.

19 Notable works that examine Guarini's architecture alongside his writings, in particular *Placita Philosophica*, are Mauro Nasti, "Il sistema del mondo di Guarino Guarini," *GGIB*, 2:559–78, and Bianca Tavassi La Greca, "La Posizione del Guarini in Rapporto alla Cultura Filosofica del Tempo," the *Appendice* to the re-edition of Guarino Guarini's *Architettura Civile* (abbrev. AC) (Milan: Edizioni Il Polifilo 1968), 439–59. Marcello Faggiolo has drawn analogies between astronomical diagrams in Guarini's *Caelestis Matematica* (Turin 1683) and the SS. Sindone plan, in "La Sindone e l'enigma dell'eclisse," *GGIB*, 2:205–27. Other writings include a play entitled *La Pieta Triunfante* (Messina 1660), *Modo di Misurare le Fabriche* – a handbook for architects and builders (Turin 1664), *Euclides Adauctus et Methodicus* (Turin 1671), *Trattato di Fortificazione* (Turin 1676), and *Compendio della Sfera Celeste* (Turin 1679).

20 S. Giedeon, *Space, Time and Architecture* (Cambridge, Mass.: Harvard University Press 1963), 125.

21 It has even been described as a "forced perspective." See especially E. Robison, "Optics and Mathematics in the Domed Churches of Guarino Guarini," *Journal of the Society of Architectural Historians (JSAH)* 50, no. 1 (Dec. 1991): 384–401. The illusionism argument is also found in Meek, *Guarini*, 75.

22 In the only English-language monograph on Guarini, H.A. Meek refutes the symbolic dimension of Guarini's work, citing Giulio Carlo Argan's remark that "no one more than Guarini has affirmed the non-symbolic, non-allegorical, non-metaphorical character" of the architecture. See Meek, *Guarini*, 108, 149, 154, and G. C. Argan, "La Tecnica del Guarini," *GGIB*, 1:36.

23 The intimate rapport between the SS. Sindone Chapel and the Shroud is underlined by Jacqueline Gargus in her analysis of the Chapel's section. "Geometrical Transformations and the Invention of New Architectural Meanings," *Harvard Architecture Review* 7 (1989): 123–8. Through a study of dynastic and sacred symbolism in the Chapel's iconography, John Beldon Scott also presents the Chapel as a conversation with its relic. See "Guarino Guarini's Invention of the Passion Capitals in the Chapel of the Holy Shroud, Turin," *JSAH* 54, no. 4 (Dec. 1995): 418–45.

24 Many have identified the suppression of the interstitial mass between the outer buttresses of the dome as being Guarini's most important architectural innovation. See, for example, S. Kostof, *A History of Architecture* (New York: Oxford University Press 1985), 519, and Meek, *Guarini,* 53. As to possible origins of the perforated dome (such as mozarabic influences), see A. Florensa, "Guarini ed il mundo islamico," *GGIB,* 1:639–65; Paolo Verzone, "Struttura delle Cupole del Guarini," *GGIB,* 2:401–13; and Juan Antonio Ramírez, "Guarino Guarini, Fray Juan Ricci and the 'Complete Salomonic Order,'" *Art History* 4, no. 2 (June 1981): 180.

25 The quote continues as follows: "Perspective is not concerned with the solidity and soundness of the work, but only with delighting the eye. Architecture on the other hand is concerned with the soundness of the work, and it follows that it cannot liberally do what Perspective invents for itself." *AC,* 19–20. This and all subsequent translations are by the author; assistance with Latin translations was received from Léo Laberge O.M[di], Raymond Tremblay C.SS.R., and Michel Debbané.

26 This hinge-point location of the seats of spiritual and temporal powers established the SS. Sindone Chapel as a palatine chapel. See E. Battisti, "Schemata nel Guarini," *GGIB,* 2:136n.2. On the role of the Chapel in the consolidation of Turin as a sacred capital, see Martha Pollak, *Turin 1564– 1680* (Chicago: University of Chicago Press 1991), 137–8, 160–4.

27 A structural analysis of the dome is found in Meek, *Guarini,* 75–6. In this context, Eva Kuryluk's remark that, in the Scriptures, "light, skin and garment are often used as synonyms" is most interesting. *Veronica and Her Cloth,* 179–98.

28 Mario Passanti's analytical term "geometrical concatenation," which refers to the fact that the "traces (of some geometries) disappear" in vertical development, is useful in this context. "La Poetica de Guarino Guarini," *GGIB,* 2:89, and *Il Mundo Magico di Guarino Guarini* (Turin: Toso 1968), 165–93.

29 It is noted that the treatise considers only the geometrical aspect of this question; Werner Müller is correct in saying that Guarini never deals directly with the "actual working of the stones." See "The Authenticity of Guarini's Stereotomy," *JSAH* 27, no. 3 (Oct. 1968): 203.

30 It appears in italics and is preceded by the word "detti," suggesting that it was an unfamiliar term. *AC,* Tratt. III, 113. In fact, the term is not found in most period dictionaries.

31 Ibid.

32 "Perché là dove in quella le superfizie piane s'innalzano con linee perpendicolari, per dare a loro corpo, e formare la fabbrica, questa per lo contrario i corpi in alto sospesi con linee perpendicolari riduce in piano per istendere la loro superficie." *AC,* Tratt. IV, 288.

33 *AC,* Tav. XXIX, fig. 7.

34 Guarini's *ortografia* is certainly related to the *trait géométrique* of Philibert de l'Orme, outlined in *Le Premier tome de L'Architecture* (Paris 1567) as a method of casting geometry into tactile and volumetric configurations in stone. In addition, a conceptual similarity is intimated by the fact that both writers were preoccupied with the question of embodiment and fascinated with medicine.

35 "La Ortografia non è altro … che una impressione, terminazione, o vestigio notato nel piano di una superficia ad esso normale, la quale circondi un'altra elevata dal detto piano." *AC,* Tratt. IV, 289–90.

36 *AC,* Tratt. III, 243–59. On the opposing positions of Guarini (who accepted optical correction) and Claude Perrault (who dismissed it), see A. Pérez-Gómez, *Architecture and the Crisis of Modern Science* (Cambridge, Mass.: MIT Press 1983), 31–2.

37 The distinction between "vision as concrete fact" and "geometric representation" is clairvoyantly insisted upon by Corrado Maltese, "Guarini e la Prospettiva," *GGIB,* 1:560. This is also argued by A. Pérez-Gómez, who advances that it was precisely the fact that Guarini distinguished between optics and geometry which fundamentally set him apart from Girard Desargues. *Architecture and the Crisis of Modern Science,* 91, 100.

38 *AC,* Tratt. I, 10.

39 Ibid., 17.

40 *AC,* Tratt. III, 259.

41 Ibid., 242.

42 Ibid., 251 and Fig. 8, *AC,* Tav. XI (plate number from *Il Polifilo* edition).

43 *AC,* Tratt. I, 18.

44 For an enlightening account of seventeenth-century Jesuit *quadrattura* fresco painting, as well as other practices of the art of *fingere,* see Françoise Siguret, *L'Œil Surpris* (Paris: Biblio 17 1985).

45 This is argued at length in *Euclide Adauctus et Methodicus* (Turin: B. Zapata 1671), Prop. II conc. ii, cited in Maltese, "Guarini e la Prospettiva," 560. Guarini refutes the existence of a point at infinity in the physical world; infinity remains a metaphysical notion. See "De Infinito," *Placita Philosophica* (abbrev. *PPh*) (Paris: Denys Thierry 1675), 267–73.

46 *AC,* Tratt. I, 20. On the notion of seventeenth-century perspectivism turning "back on itself," see Fernand Hallyn, *The Poetic Structure of the World* (New York: Zone Books 1990), 169.

47 Guarini's visual theory is expounded in two parts of *Placita Philosophica*: the dialogue "De Luce," *PPh,* 397–468, and in a chapter of "De Vita," *PPh,* 711–24. It contains references to a broad range of optical theories, including those of Aristotle, Galen, Alhazen, Witelo, Aguillon, Vesalius, and Kepler.

48 Ibid., 721. Guarini's account of vision implies that it is in the balance of the clear and the opaque that proper vision can happen. An intellectual component – which Guarini refers to as "imagination" in *Architettura Civile* and as "judgement" (*vi iudicativa*) in *Placita Philosophica* – also plays a role in the correction of optical phenomena. See *AC,* Tratt. III, 255 and *PPh,* 721.

49 For example, "Sed radii obliquissimè, ex Perspectivis, debilissimi sunt." *PPh,* 721.

50 Ibid., 720. The opinion that Guarini may not have understood the lenticular function of the eye is also expressed in Maltese, "Guarini e la Prospettiva," 559. On the medieval visual cone, see D. Lindberg, *Theories of Vision from Al-Kindi to Kepler* (Chicago: University of Chicago Press 1976), 74–5.

51 "Quae species obliquissimi reflectunt obiectum *non remotum à se,* sed *in ipsâ sui superficie* exprimunt." *PPh,* 721, my italics.

52 *AC,* Tratt. I, 10.

53 *AC,* Tratt. III, 113.

54 The contradiction of the pendentives, which make a transition from a circular drum to a circular dome (rather than from a square to a circle, as is traditional), is pointed out by Wittkower, *Art and Architecture,* 408, and Meek, *Guarini,* 71.

55 This non-figural iconography is an additional facet of the mozarabic quality of the dome that is often commented upon, and the notion that the Chapel synthesizes Greek and Latin mysticism (see note 12). The Greek cross is also the centrepiece of the Savoy coat of arms. See John Beldon Scott, "Guarino Guarini's Invention," 438.

56 On Guarini's renovation of classical syntax, see Paolo Portoghesi, "Il Linguagio di Guarino Guarini," *GGIB,* 2:9–34. Gargus compares the cofferings to "a membrane pulled taut, almost to the breaking point." See "Geometrical Transformations," 125.

57 *AC,* Tratt. III, 113–14.

58 This refers to Gilles Deleuze's hermeneutic of "the Baroque fold." The projections of marble into space are like "folds between matter and soul." *Le Pli* (Paris: Editions de Minuit 1988), 138–63.

59 "De Luce," *PPh,* 397–468.

60 "Nam lumen, quod à quocumque corpore egreditur, debet illud nobis estendere: in id enim institutum est. Quae vero translucida sunt, visum non terminant, & maximé si de summa transparentia agatur." *PPh,* 418.

61 "Lux, ad sui conservationem, diaphano medio indiget, ad hoc ut sit tan quam subiecto." Ibid., 417.

62 Ibid., 418.

63 Ibid., 794–826.

64 "In order to move bodies, separated spirits produce a subtle corporeal operation, such as light, but they cannot move by their own volition." Ibid., 823. On the question of angels and the motion of the heavens in *Placita Philosophica,* see Mauro Nasti, "Il Sistema del Mondo di Guarino Guarini," *GGIB,* 2:575. It is noted that this portion of the treatise is subtended by questions regarding the fate of the body after death that are much more reminiscent of Augustine's and Thomas Aquinas's meditations on the topic than of the philosophies of the late seventeenth century.

65 *PPh,* 823.

66 Ibid., 637–42.

67 "Quid sunt spiritus? & an in omni vivente reperiantur?". . . Prob. Secundo specialiter deanimalio. Quia species visibiles certè non possunt imprimi in materia, & in substantia organica crassiori: quia eius opacitas et crassitudo, est ad id muneris inepta. Sed nec anima spiritualis in homine: quia species sunt corporeae. Ergo debet dari aliqua *substantia media,* quae neque sit spiritualis, neque sit crassa. Quod autem substantia haec opaca & crassior, non sit apta ad suscipendas species, & eas transmittandas. . . ." Ibid., 637 (my italics).

68 Ibid.

69 Luke 24:31.

70 Georges Didi-Huberman, *Devant L'Image* (Paris: Editions de Minuit 1990), 220.

71 "Le visage est abstrait ... sa merveille tient à l'ailleurs dont elle vient et où déjà elle se retire." Emmanuel Lévinas, *Humanisme de l'autre homme* (Paris: Fata Morgana 1972), 63.

Human and Divine Perspectives in the Works of Salomon de Caus

Katja Grillner

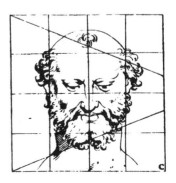

Chora

> The sense of the world must lie outside the world ... If there
> is a value which is of value, it must lie outside all happening
> and being-so ... It is clear that ethics cannot be put into words.
> Ethics is transcendental (Ethics and Aesthetics are one).[1]
>
> Ludwig Wittgenstein

THESE LINES FROM WITTGENSTEIN'S *Tractatus logico-philosophicus*
acknowledge the human desire to step outside one's world in order to
find a neutral viewpoint which has always been impossible to attain.
Wittgenstein valued the experience of art because it enabled man to
contemplate the world as a limited whole – to see the world from the
viewpoint of eternity, *sub specie aeterni*.[2] He considered the controlled
experiment and the fictional proposition important to questions of ethical and aesthetic value. Through the experience of art, man might learn
to live and act as an ethical being. Only by showing, and never through
saying, could ethical considerations be conveyed. This central part of
Wittgenstein's philosophy echoes an almost religious concern, yet he
lacked the most important element in religion – God.

The works presented in this article belong to a world very different
from Wittgenstein's. In the early seventeenth century, God was still
present and looked upon as the ultimate "eye of eternity" – the viewpoint
that Wittgenstein longed for. At that time, the work of art played a
crucial role as mediator between human and divine perspectives, guiding
man through life towards his end in God. While the major part of this
essay focuses on the seventeenth-century architect and engineer Salomon
de Caus, I would like the reader to reflect also upon the problems
surrounding possible modes of action in our present time. In spite of the
differences, there are some quite interesting parallels to observe. In
creating a historical platform, this study seeks to open up some new
perspectives on our view of knowledge and the human artefact – something that is needed at a time when universal values have disappeared.

De Caus's architectural constructions are regarded here as "built fictions," in the sense that they were imaginative manifestations of divine
truths put forward to man through matter. De Caus was a faithful
Christian who believed that truth existed in God and in Him only.
Absolute truth could never be known fully by man but it might be
glimpsed through the artisan's materialized interpretation. As will be
shown, de Caus emphasized that human knowledge had its necessary

limitations and that our scientific theories would always remain imperfect interpretations of divine truth. His garden machines were illusionistic wonder-works that brought man to a space between dream and reality. His whole body of work – artefacts and treatises – provided only *instruments* or *tools* for man to use on his journey from human corruptibility to divine eternity; in themselves they gave no conclusive answers.

RENAISSANCE MAGUS AND CALVINIST TEACHER

The post-Renaissance, pre-scientific world of northern Europe in the early seventeenth century was a time of transformation characterized by many conflicting ideas. Characters contemporary with Salomon de Caus, such as Francis Bacon, Johannes Kepler, and Robert Fludd, each demonstrate a complex body of apparently contradictory thoughts.[3] Two characteristics are crucial to my reading of de Caus's work: his Protestant background and the magico-mystical atmosphere at the royal courts where he practised.

Salomon de Caus was a French Calvinist who was born in Normandy in 1576 and died in Paris in 1626.[4] His family moved to England in the 1590s and he spent most of his life outside France, working in various European courts as "architect and engineer" – as he called himself – designing and constructing gardens and garden machinery. His designs were influenced by Italian Renaissance gardens, which he is known to have visited, as well as by Dutch and English garden styles. Not much is known of de Caus's formal education but his texts show that he was familiar with classical authors such as Hero of Alexandria, Vitruvius, Pliny, Euclid, and Boethius, as well as contemporary writers on mechanics and music theory such as Jacob Besson, Augustin Ramelly, Pontus de Tyard, and Gioseffo Zarlino.

De Caus was a writing practitioner, something that had not been common until the end of the sixteenth century. He wrote four treatises: on perspective (*La perspective avec la raison des ombres et miroirs*, London 1612), machines (*Les raisons des forces mouvantes*, Frankfurt 1615), music (*Institution Harmonique*, Frankfurt 1615), and sundials (*La pratique et demonstration des horloges solaires*, Paris 1624).[5] These books are interesting in that they combine two different kinds of discourse. As technical handbooks they provide "recipes" for the practitioner; as theoretical discourses they aim to give a thorough understanding of their science.[6] Theory and practice were thus related and interdependent in his work. When the first three were written, de Caus was employed by the English courts of Queen Anne and Prince Henry (1607–13) or by the Palatinate court in Heidelberg of Frederick V (1613–19). In the course of their construction his palace gardens in Heidelberg became known throughout Europe as the "eighth wonder of the world."[7]

As an artist employed by the Protestant courts in England and Heidelberg, de Caus was part of the neoplatonic hierarchy that dominated these courts at the time.[8] The king was regarded as God's representative on earth, and the artist was employed as a "magus" who would follow the principles of natural magic to ensure good influences from the macrocosm.[9] The work of the artist – whether a painting, a sculpture, a building, a garden, or even a musical or theatrical performance – was believed to connect the macrocosm of the divine momentarily to the microcosm of man, and to bring a glimpse of the immaterial divine to mortal man.[10] By imitating the macrocosm, the work of art had the power to convey knowledge of the world as a divine creation. Gardens played an important role in this context. They were sites for royal masques, theatrical performances in which the king often participated as the link to the divine, and they contained intricate grottoes with automata (moving statues) and waterworks that re-enacted classical myths. Gardens also expressed the desire to recreate the Garden of Eden on earth, a prevalent dream for the Protestants of the sixteenth and seventeenth centuries.

In his treatises de Caus demonstrated that he was a faithful Christian. Calvinism, like other Protestant and humanist movements, criticized authoritarian structures and proclaimed man's power to change his situation. In his *Institutes of Christian Religion* (1536), John Calvin emphasized the duty of each individual to seek and spread the knowledge of God by studying the three testimonies to his eternal presence: *man*, *nature*, and the *holy scriptures*. For the Calvinist, seeking true knowledge was no longer a privilege but every man's duty, and the sources were no longer limited to classical texts but now also included nature herself and man as the image of God. De Caus always focused on the relationship among himself as a maker, nature as a provider of material, humanity for whom he worked, and God towards whom his works pointed. He regarded himself as a humble servant, fully aware that he was only "playing" on the instruments provided by God through nature and human reason.

Traditionally, the Christian God had been above and *beyond*; he was goodness and truth, while man was effectively a fallen creature. However, the Protestant movement and a growing interest in hermetic magic began to modify this view in the Renaissance, particularly with regard to man's ability to change his own situation. Suddenly man could dream of recreating paradise on earth. Despite being bound to matter, man could move his spirit as close as possible to God. Since man was created in the image of God, he should aspire to live up to that honour: "All men should be educated fully to full humanity ... in order to make men as like as possible to the image of God ... to unite them with God by true religion."[11] Man had the power to make the world better, to lift it up towards divine goodness, but for him to succeed, knowledge had to be spread to all.[12] This religious ideal was the driving force behind the movement for universal learning and an important factor in the early development of modern science.[13]

Many aspects of de Caus's works can be explained by his Calvinist outlook, including his ambition to make his knowledge accessible outside the "profession" and his selection of topics dealing with John Calvin's three principal sources for knowledge of God – nature, man, and the divine itself. His treatise on machines disclosed the reasons behind the forces of nature, his treatise on perspective revealed a geometry of human reason, and through music and shadows cast by the sun he displayed the traces of divine presence on earth. De Caus believed that it was his duty to spread this knowledge through all of the means available to him: the text, the drawing, the machine, and the magical events devised for the gardens. His treatises constitute a large encyclopedia with a coherently planned structure. According to the Vitruvian tradition, the field of architecture incorporated many different arts and sciences within what was referred to as the "Encyclopaedia." This universal frame of knowledge was regarded crucial to the aspiring architect since it assisted the difficult process of acquiring mastery of the profession.[14]

John Dee was the first to bring passages from Vitruvius's and Alberti's writings into the English language. With his preface to the 1570 edition of Euclid's *Elements*,[15] Dee initiated among the artisan class a deep interest in Vitruvius's theories, which remained strong at the time when de Caus was working for the English court.[16] However, Dee filtered Vitruvius's work through his own Elizabethan world-view and slightly altered the focus of those ancient ideas. While Vitruvius had seen *architecture*

4.1a Frontispiece to *Les raisons des forces mouvantes* (1615). From facsimile edition by Uitgeverei Fritz Kunf B.V., Amsterdam, 1973.

as the chief art comprising all others, Dee believed that this role belonged to the art of *archemastrie*, which brought to *actual experience* what all other mathematical arts proposed. *Archemastrie* still included architecture among its possible applications, yet it also included a broad range of other fields. The *archemaster* was not only familiar with the teachings of each particular art and science, but also knew how to *apply* them in order to *convey* them in "complete experiences."[17] Only through human experience could theoretical knowledge be productive, by being materialized and brought into the human soul.[18]

Both de Caus and Inigo Jones, his colleague in the English court, emphasized the importance of human experience in their work. While de Caus applied his technical skill to garden machinery, Inigo Jones focused on theatrical illusions. Both used similar mechanical and hydraulic principles. In his practice, de Caus effectively synthesized the knowledge that is presented separately in his treatises. His play between *theory*,

4.1b Frontispiece to
*La perspective avec la raison
des ombres et miroirs* (1612).
From original edition by
courtesy of the Canadian
Centre for Architecture,
Montreal.

as explained in his treatises, and *practice*, in which knowledge from all
fields was applied to specific situations, also constituted a dynamic play
between the *specialization* needed to gain theoretical knowledge and the
synthesis of that knowledge demanded in practice. The applied works
portrayed in his treatises, as well as his own writings, aimed to present
the order of nature and the divine through the human experience of
wonder and beauty. True knowledge of these sciences could be conveyed
only through *appearance*. For this de Caus relied on the immutable
principles of Nature, the root of human perception and understanding,
and God, the eternal provider of light and motion. In Dee's terminology,
Salomon de Caus would have been a true *archemaster*. As a whole, de
Caus's work was a life-long educational project. Like many others, he
aspired to move humanity closer to God. Progress was not yet conceived
as linear and infinite; instead, it was seen as but motion towards a point
in harmony with nature and God.

THE DIVINE SCIENCES

Salomon de Caus distinguished the sciences according to their relation to
nature, man, and God. This is evident in the three different frontispieces
for his works on machines, perspective, and music. The frontispiece was
the emblem for entering each book, and it enabled the reader to situate
himself in relation to the knowledge embodied in the work. Examining
the frontispieces in a sequence from *Les raisons* to *La perspective* to
Institution Harmonique, one detects changes in the viewpoint from *looking down* at the mechanical laboratory in *Les Raisons*, to *looking straight*
at the theatrical stage in *La Perspective*, and finally to *looking up* at
Apollo's muses in *Institution Harmonique*. Even before entering the treatise, the reader has his vision directed towards the site of its subsequent

studies: the surface of the earth, the theatre of worldly appearance, or the spheres of the heavens. While machines were based on natural principles of the four elements and matter, and perspective was based on geometrical principles of human reason, music and astronomy, unlike the other sciences, were founded ultimately on God rather than on material nature or the human world. The *truth* of these latter sciences, which de Caus called "divine," was absolutely out of reach for man. Nevertheless, he considered their *application* on earth – for example, in the performance of music – to be the most efficient way to approach the divine and to gain knowledge of God from our human perspective.

De Caus argued that it was impossible ever to gain a complete knowledge of the divine sciences. His arguments were based on theological premises and empirical observations. Theologically, he emphasized the inevitable difference between God and man, His image, and warned man not to attempt the transgression of this invisible boundary. Empirically, he argued in favour of recent empirical observations demonstrating that neither the harmonic musical scale nor the heavenly motions could be described perfectly through numerical proportions, which traditionally had been considered divine.[19] De Caus explained this position most clearly in his treatises on music and sundials, *Institution Harmonique* and *La pratique et demonstration des horloges solaires*. His argument was rooted in the radical transformation of the theory of music that took place during the Renaissance.

During the Middle Ages, music was part of the *quadrivium*, along with the other exact sciences, arithmetic, geometry, and astronomy. However, as a traditional liberal art, the theory of music was distant from its practice. It was not until the Renaissance, when polyphonic compositions originated, that a firmer connection between theory and practice was demanded.[20] This prompted a radical change of the traditional Pythagorean model. The practitioners had long known that the Pythagorean proportions neither accounted for all musical consonances in use nor represented them with the exact proportions that they actually had when played.[21] Using their musical sense, the instrument maker and the musician had always adjusted the proportions a little, to make them just right. But in music theory, the traditional model had remained intact.

According to the Pythagorean tradition, musical proportions corresponded to the proportions of the heavenly spheres. In Plato's *Timaeus*, both the elemental visible world and the invisible world-soul were structured according to geometrical proportions that corresponded to the musical consonances discovered by Pythagoras. This theory of correspondence provided a theoretical basis for all human making. All artificial creations were expected to reflect this "original" divine harmony, conveying a benign influence on man. Of all forms of human composition, music was considered the most influential, since it was brought to the senses through air, the medium in which the spirits travelled. By imitating the stars, the performance of music was believed to have the power to move man towards God.[22] When confronted with the unpleasant observation that musical harmony could not be described through simple harmonic ratios, the traditional cosmology was threatened. Could this deviation be explained away by noting the fallibility of the human senses, or must the divine proportions be declared invalid?

De Caus managed to defend the capacity of the human senses in *Institution Harmonique* without really threatening the old cosmology and its connections between music and the divine. In fact, he reversed the traditional argument:

The Divine power, having created the world, and all which it contains, wished that there would be a variety of movements proportioned on Him, as much in the firmament and planets, as in the sea with its ebb and flow ... Now, to return to our harmonic proportions, I say, that the natural consonances and intervals, as the Divine providence has ordered them, are not more precisely known to us than the celestial movements, and similarly cannot be comprehended with our numbers, as can be seen in the preceding proposition. And the fault comes, as I have said, from that God does not want to allow man the knowledge of his perfect works, as there is nothing perfect in us, also this science could not be called Divine, as it has been judged, if we could have a perfect knowledge of its proportions.[23]

Here de Caus does not question the traditional analogy between celestial movements and harmonic proportions. However, instead of seeking the signs of divine truth in their perfect regularity (the traditional argument), he saw God's greatness in their actual complexity. This unknowable complexity, he writes, is the truly divine, since God could not possibly want man to have immediate and perfect knowledge of His works. To know the truth of these proportions would be to know the secret of the world's creation, and with this knowledge man would become the Creator himself. De Caus also claims that God wishes man never to stop perfecting the sciences, "in order that we shall always know our ignorance."[24] There is, for de Caus, no human science or endeavour that could not be made more perfect. Life is thus a constant process of perfecting and refining whose outcomes are always doomed to deviate, if ever so little, from their divine original.

How, then, could God hide his secret proportions from man? De Caus argues that God must have his own numbers: "But some pedant of a musician could say that numbers are just and the ear faulty: because what is right to the judgment of one's ear is not right to another's. Which is very true: But he would then have to find other numbers than ours ... Which demonstrates that Nature does not at all use our numbers in what she prescribes, and that she has other [numbers] of which we have no knowledge."[25] He also writes that all works "organized" (*ordonné*) by God have ratios that appear irrational to man.[26] De Caus thus complicates the Pythagorean position, advocated fifty years earlier by John Dee in his preface to Euclid's *Elements*, which claimed: "All thinges (which from the very first originall being of thinges, have bene framed and made) do appear to be formed by the reason of Numbers. For this was the principall example or patterne in the minde of the creator."[27] On the one hand, de Caus still believes in a well-ordered divine structure, probably based on numbers, but on the other hand, as we have seen, these numbers were not *human* numbers. One could speculate about the relationship de Caus conceived between these two kinds of numbers: the human and the divine. Perhaps it was analogous to that between the human mind, *nous*, and the divine mind, *mens*; the human mind and its numbers were only imperfect reflections, allowing man an understanding that would never be complete.

IMAGE AND ORIGINAL

This question about the human and divine numbers points to a fundamental aspect of representation, which began, according to Alberti, with Narcissus: "What else can you call painting but a similar embracing with art of what is presented on the surface of the water in the fountain?"[28] Narcissus's mistake was that he could not distinguish between representation and original. His mirror-image belonged to another level of reality, yet he fell in love with it. In Pimander, the Hermetic account of Genesis, the fall of man is blamed on Narcissistic self-love; man saw his reflection

4.2 Narcissus gazing at his reflection in one of the grottoes at de Caus's garden in Heidelberg. From facsimile edition of Salomon de Caus, *Le jardin palatin* (1620) by Les Éditions du Moniteur, Paris, 1981.

in nature, fell in love and "came to inhabit the irrational form."[29] After the fall, man became an imperfect representation of God. He was the reflection in the rippled surface that God saw when looking down. However much God loved man, He could not embrace him. Man could only try to make himself as perfect a representation as possible, to come closer but never to unite. God and man existed on different planes; the material and the divine world could never mix.

In arguing for the existence of numbers "irrational to man," De Caus distinguishes between different levels of reality and points out the importance of looking at things from the right point of view. Thus it is not unexpected that man cannot find perfect regularity in God's creation. God created the world from His own perspective, not from man's. However, this does not mean that man sees nothing from his own oblique viewpoint. De Caus still uses numerical proportions to establish his musical scale, but he also adds "imperfect" or "artificial" consonances to achieve a smooth harmony. By combining reason, which establishes the initial numerical proportions, and hearing, which adjusts the tones to suit his judgment, man can make music that brings the spirit closer to God. Human numbers thus provide a necessary framework for the irrational, yet sensitive, judgment of the ear. In de Caus's world, the senses are no longer just a source of corruptibility and evil. Through the senses, especially the sense of hearing with its spiritual medium of air, divine inspiration could be brought to the makings of man.

De Caus even regarded geometry, as defined in Euclid's *Elements*, as a human, rather than a divine, science. This is mentioned in the dedication to the French Cardinal Richelieu in de Caus's book on sundials. As with musical proportions, he confesses that the course of the sun cannot be demonstrated as rigorously as Euclid's propositions on geometry. By now, we are familiar with de Caus's explanation: while the heavenly motions were ordered by God, geometry emerged from human reason and was thus perfectly intelligible to man. De Caus worked during the transition period between the essentially Pythagorean geometry of Renaissance metaphysics and the transcendental geometry of the Baroque.[30] Even though he believed that numbers had a divine significance, he regarded both arithmetic and perspective as lower in rank and dependent on geometry.[31] Geometry was the order of the human mind, and de Caus organized his books according to its principles. Through the frame of human reason, constituted by the principles of geometry, divine wisdom could be sought. For de Caus, however, geometry was not a direct manifestation of divine truth but a necessary filter for revealing the traces of divine presence on earth.

This emphasis on the mediation of knowledge through the senses also distances de Caus from Pythagorean cosmology. The first English translation of Euclid's *Elements* (1570) clearly states that geometry, as a science dealing with objects perceived by the senses, must be considered *lower* in rank than arithmetic, the science dealing with numbers, which falls under no sense but is considered only by the mind. Geometrical objects

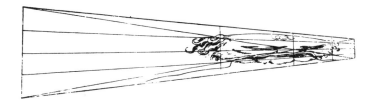

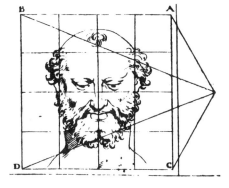

4.3 Anamorphic perspective: demonstration of "how to foreshorten a head so that one cannot recognise it unless one does not see it from its point of view." From Salomon de Caus, *La perspective avec la raison des ombres et miroirs*, Book I, ch. 28. From original edition by courtesy of Canadian Centre for Architecture, Montreal.

were regarded as things of the senses, while numbers were intellectual.[32] De Caus expressed the opposite opinion: for him, geometry was the *source*, and arithmetic its product. Man could never become independent of his senses. Only through them could he understand the world.

MAN AS MAKER

From God's perspective, man was only His imperfect reflection, but man himself could also assume the role of maker. Like God, he could make images based on himself. *Human* numbers and geometry would then become the first law, the point from which everything in the man-made world could be explained. Amidst these divine, human, and man-made worlds, anamorphic perspective acquired a metaphoric role. In his treatise on perspective, de Caus teaches this "other method of foreshortening." It makes the represented object appear to be "out of its nature ... but nevertheless, if seen from its own point of view it represents the foreshortened thing as natural."[33] The resulting anamorphic representation would be incomprehensible if regarded from a position other than the predetermined point. Arriving at that point probably gave the viewer a certain sense of satisfaction and reassurance, since what had seemed an irrational composition suddenly became perfectly ordered. God's creation, of course, did not always appear as rational, good, and perfect as one might have wished. Experiencing this leap from disorder to perfection, through anamorphic perspective, made it easier to believe in the existence of a point, somewhere in the universe, where the world would appear to be beautiful, rational, and infinitely good. From this eternal point, truth and justice would prevail.

De Caus's treatise on sundials is thorough and instructive, using fold-out figures to help the reader understand the geometrical operations necessary for constructing solar clocks. A modern-day reader of the treatise is struck most by how this art appears as an exercise in elevating oneself to an exterior viewpoint on the world. The solar clock had to be imagined as a model of the universe while, at the same time, it was used as an instrument to determine the exact position in space and time of a body on the surface of the earth. The first definition demonstrates what the "centre of the world" is for the maker of sundials: "[Here] it is necessary to show that even if all the clocks that exist in the whole world each has a centre of the world, each of those centres is imagined to be in the middle of the firmament: which is not so [in reality], because the true centre of the firmament is a point in the centre of the earth, as apprehended by the intellect; but wherever we are on earth, by the apprehension of our senses, it always seems to us as if we were in the middle of the firmament."[34]

De Caus distinguishes between the intellect's comprehension of the actual facts and the senses' adaptation to the appearance of things, and he notes the importance of using the imagination in order to situate oneself on earth. Without using the sundial, as a model of the universe that brought the external viewpoint of the sun down to earth, man would never be able to find his own position. This, I would argue, is when the instrument also becomes a fiction – a fiction that planted man's body on earth but lent him an eye in heaven. From that position, perhaps he could also hear the heavenly tones.

De Caus writes about the sun as if it were actually the divine point of view. In the sixteenth and seventeenth centuries it was not uncommon for the sun to be considered divine. Apollo, the sun-god in ancient mythology, was often related to Christ. Light symbolized wisdom and truth. De Caus wrote, "This light coming from the Sun is the first and principal light of all which is natural, always shining with the same strength, because the Sun does not receive any alteration ... The sun thus is the one light which illuminates the whole world, that is, the earth and the sky, because the world is all."[35] When de Caus defines the four elements in his treatise on machines, he gives fire a particular importance. Fire is of two kinds, one "material" and the other "elementary."[36] The elementary fire stood above all other elements because it nourished all other activity. De Caus believed that the elemental fire "is the heat of the Sun, since all other fire or heat is subjected to nourishment and perishing, thus the heat coming from the body of the Sun is the only elemental fire ... The Sun ... is the true natural light."[37] He observes that nothing would be produced by the earth if it were not heated by the sun.[38] In these simple statements, de Caus emphasizes man's dependency on an external, nourishing force. God had not just ordered the world at the beginning and then left it alone; He was forever watching over and maintaining it, and He would continue to do so until the end of the world.

De Caus did not believe it possible for man to create perpetual motion. He argued that this was possible only for God, who "had neither beginning, nor end" and who was the only one to be attributed with the words "without end" or "endless." Pushing aside "those words," de Caus demonstrates a machine that "acts on its own," but only "if it is maintained by the four elements from which it is composed."[39] He emphasizes that this machine may appear to provide perpetual motion, but in reality it must be maintained by its maker: a change of water every fortnight. This particular machine is a simple thermometer, but its design could be applied in principle to other, more complicated inventions of de Caus – for example, his water clock. Within this theological argument, the machine is a metaphor for man and nature, suggesting our ultimate dependency on God.

Other machines by de Caus embodied the divine force of the sun, the "elementary fire," in a more poetic way. Problem thirty-five in *Les raisons des forces mouvantes* taught the reader how to make "an admirable machine, which is at the base of a statue, sounding when the sun rises or when the sun sets so that it seems as if the statue made the sound."[40] De Caus refers to the Egyptian statue of Memnon, the son of Eos or Aurora, which was said to have sounded at dawn. However, the statue de Caus presents is not Memnon, but probably Hercules, wearing a loincloth and holding a club in his right hand. He makes the sound of a tambourine, an instrument of warfare. Thus, in de Caus's garden, the virtuous hero wakes up each morning, is strengthened by the first rays of the sun, and goes out to wage war against evil. Later in the treatise,

4.4a Drawing on the story of the Egyptian statue of Memnon, de Caus designed this "admirable machine, which is at the base of a statue, sounding when the sun rises or when the sun sets, so that it seems as if the statue made the sound." By referring to Hercules, the statue calls the reader's attention to the virtues of an active life. From Salomon de Caus, *Les raisons des forces mouvantes* (1615), Book I, Problem 35. Facsimile edition by Uitgeverei Fritz Kunf B.V., Amsterdam, 1973.

the statue appears on top of an artificial mountain with a pyramidal shape, constructed to allow "a better view of the parterres"[41] (Fig. 4.4a–b). The automaton thus marks the dawn from the top of an Egyptian pyramid. Through art, Salomon de Caus transformed the heat of the sun into music and revealed the divine source of his marvels. By this he demonstrated that this divine gift, if wisely used, could guide man towards a virtuous life.

Considering the time period, de Caus's occupation probably put him at risk in the eyes of the church. The "wonder-works" he demonstrated could well be misused by ignorant people who wished to proclaim their God-like creative powers by abusing de Caus's "magic" designs. To prevent this, de Caus continually emphasized the essential ignorance of man with respect to God. He also reminded the reader, through proverbs and myths, of the dangers of hubris. For example, he uses the fable of Apollo and Phoebus – concerning the dangers of a mortal's desire to

4.4b Placed at the top of a pyramidal mountain, the statue will be struck first by the rays of the morning sun, and his "song" will announce the beginning of a new day. From Salomon de Caus, *Les raisons des forces mouvantes* (1615), Book II, Problem 10. Facsimile edition by Uitgeverei Fritz Kunf B.V., Amsterdam, 1973.

make God's work – to demonstrate how to make a wall-painting in *La Perspective*.⁴² As long as one realized that the machines one had made or the perspectives one had drawn utilized principles that God originally created – that man would be nothing without Him – these arts and sciences would remain true to de Caus's own religious conviction.

It must be emphasized that de Caus's creations were not intended to demonstrate man's mastery of nature. Instead, they were celebrations of God's creation. Automata, perspectives, and musical performances were all metaphoric compositions. For only a brief moment, they provided man with a glimpse of the divine perspective on the world. They both "filtered" the divine to make Him visible to human eyes and "mirrored" man and nature to enable them to be contemplated. As metaphoric models, they were vehicles for the imagination, providing alternate perspectives on man and the world. For once, the imaginative man could move effortlessly among various spheres of represented reality. Yet he did not float. He knew his place very well, and he also knew the destination of his life.

ART AND INTERPRETATION

Today, living in a pluralistic age dominated by mass media, we may seem to be floating hopelessly among represented realities.[43] Our time is, of course, distant from that of de Caus. We have indeed departed from the ground that was laid out in his treatises. The four elements have multiplied and are now thought to interact within thermodynamic chaotic systems. God has long since been declared dead by philosophers and scientists, and it becomes more and more difficult to imagine a position from which to "contemplate the world as a limited whole." Many contemporary thinkers have either lamented or celebrated our state of "rootlessness" – Nietzsche, Heidegger, Derrida, and Baudrillard among others – but only a few have discussed the consequences of this condition and whether it is possible to learn how to live with it.[44] From an oblique angle this article wishes to contribute to that discussion.

At the beginning of this essay I hinted that one might find parallels between our present situation and de Caus's time. As we have seen, man in the early seventeenth century regarded his knowledge and corporeal nature as imperfect and distinctly separate from God's. Although absolute truth existed, it was never present as a totality on earth. To reach such an understanding, man depended on mimetic representations to reveal the divine traces hidden in nature. This dependency was acknowledged; to consider other possibilities would have been heretical. Existence and knowledge in the material world were bound to be ephemeral and – to paraphrase the introductory quotation – the sense of the world thus lay outside the world, in the eternal divine. Today Western culture is in a similar situation after having concluded that absolute truth is not to be found among us. Moreover, we have lost our earlier innocent belief in the existence of a divine perspective. In one respect, we are in the same problematic situation as de Caus: trapped in our momentary, ever-changing existence, but wanting a fuller grasp of the whole. However, the goals of *our* actions differ radically from those of de Caus: while he assisted man to find the *right* way of life that would lead to God, we might encourage an individual to act responsibly towards other people on the grounds of his or her *own* ethical convictions.

By making this limited comparison, we might better understand possible alternatives to our contemporary modes of action. I have particularly emphasized the role of metaphor in the early seventeenth century. Metaphoric compositions helped the experiencing subject to comprehend something far greater than the work at hand by enabling that work to appear both in its *actual* physical manifestation and as an *image* of something else. As Paul Ricoeur has noted, a major function of metaphoric compositions is to "redescribe reality."[45] By connecting what was once separate, the metaphor is able to establish new logical boundaries within language while breaking down others. Ricoeur connects the notions of metaphor, fiction, and model. They all seek to illuminate something that would be too complex to grasp without them, and they all function as *tools* for the imagination.

Throughout this essay I have referred to "vehicles," "tools," and "instruments" when discussing de Caus's works. These nouns all refer to something "through which another thing is made, as a hammer, a saw, a knife ... are organs through which a work is put to perfection," to use de Caus's own words.[46] By employing these terms I have wished to emphasize that the essential *meaning* of his works is not to be found in their actual physical form but rather has to be sought in the *effect* their appearance was believed to have on man's understanding of the divine creation. The work to be perfected by de Caus's tools was man himself – perfected and lifted up towards God.

Today, most art no longer tries to lift us up towards the divine. Instead we find ourselves immersed in a transitory reality where there is no ultimate ground to be found. Understanding this reality demands a momentary suspension of it, making possible temporary interpretations. Attempting to grasp the life we are living is a necessity for acting responsibly. If architecture, as an art form, still has a role to play, it might be precisely this: to embody in matter imaginative interpretations of reality which may assist the experiencing subject in seeing for him/herself the world as it appears. Just as man in the early seventeenth century did, we also depend on metaphors and models to understand our situation. On the basis of what is there in front of us, we must *interpret* the world and ourselves. Through fictional propositions, we may imagine other worlds, gain access to an external point of reference, and momentarily *look down* on the real world as we inhabit it.

NOTES

1 Ludwig Wittgenstein, *Tractatus logico-philosophicus* (London: Routledge and Kegan Paul 1957), × 6.41, 6.42 and 6.421.

2 Ibid., × 6.45.

3 Thomas da Costa Kaufmann, *The Mastery of Nature* (Princeton: Princeton University Press 1993), 190; and Paolo Rossi, *Francis Bacon – From Magic to Science* (Chicago: University of Chicago Press – Midway Reprint 1978), xii.

4 Biographical data on de Caus are assembled from various secondary sources: mainly C.S. Maks, *Salomon de Caus* (Paris: Jouve and Cie 1934); Roy Strong, *The Renaissance Garden in England* (London: Thames and Hudson 1979), 72–112; and Frances Yates, *The Rosicrucian Enlightenment* (London: Routledge and Kegan Paul 1972), 11–14.

5 *La perspective, Les raisons,* and *Institution Harmonique* were originally published by Jan Norton. *Les raisons* was translated into German and published as *Von Gewaltsammen bewegungen* by A. Pacquart in Frankfurt 1615. An extended version of *Les raisons* was also published by two different publishers in Paris 1624: Charles Sevestre and H. Drouart. H. Drouart also published *La pratique et demonstration des horloges solaires* in the same year. Of these, at least two are available as reprints of their first editions: *Institution Harmonique* (New York: Broude Brothers 1969); and *Les raisons des forces mouvantes* (Amsterdam: Uitgeverei Fritz Kunf B.V. 1973). De Caus also published a book on the Heidelberg gardens: *Hortus Palatinus* (Frankfurt: T. de Bry 1620). It was published simultaneously in Latin, German, and French. A facsimile of the French version, *Le Jardin Palatin,* was published in Paris 1981 by Les Éditions du Moniteur.

6 For a discussion on the emergence of these kinds of technical handbooks see Paolo Rossi, *Philosophy, Technology and the Arts in the Early Modern Era* (New York: Harper Torchbooks 1970), 41.

7 Lily Fehrle-Burger, "Der Hortus Palatinus als 'achtes Weltwunder,'" *Ruperto Carola Mitteilungen der Vereinung der Freunde der Studentenschaft der Universität Heidelberg* 14 (1962): 106–19.

8 For extensive studies of the philosophical ideas dominating the Protestant courts, see Vaughan Hart, *Art and Magic in the Court of the Stuarts* (London: Routledge 1994); Eustace M.W. Tillyard, *The Elizabethan World Picture – A Study of the Idea of Order in the age of Shakespeare, Donne and Milton* (New York: Vintage Books 1943); and Frances Yates, *The Occult*

Philosophy in the Elizabethan Age (London: Routledge and Kegan Paul 1979), 23–48, 79–108.

9 Natural magic was believed to operate via the interconnecting paths running among various parts of the cosmos. For example, Marcilio Ficino argued that music could bring benign influences of the stars down to man by carefully imitating celestial movements. See Marcilio Ficino, *The Book of Life* (Irving: Spring Publications 1980), 160.

10 Hart, *Art and Magic,* 33.

11 See Johann Amos Comenius, *Pampaedia* in *Selections* (UNESCO 1957), 98.

12 See, for example, Francis Bacon, *The Advancement of Learning* (1605); Johann Amos Comenius, *The Great Didactic* (1627) and *Pampaedia* (1650) (both published in *Selections,* UNESCO 1957); and Tommaso Campanella, *Civitas Solis* (1623). See also Yates, *The Rosicrucian Enlightenment.*

13 Rossi, *Philosophy, Technology and the Arts,* 64.

14 I refer here to the passage in Vitruvius, *Architecture ou Art de bien bastir,* Book I, ch. 3, fol. 4 (Jean Martin's translation, published in Paris 1547, facsimile edition by Gregg Press Inc., Ridgewood 1964), which states: "It could seem strange and marvellous, to people with little experience, that a normal man could learn and keep in his memory such a large number of doctrines. Nevertheless, when they come to consider that all the arts have a certain affinity and communication between each other, they can easily believe that it is feasible and possible; and also seeing that the Encyclopaedia (or the circular doctrine) is neither more nor less than a body, composed of all its members: and from this follows that those who are instructed in diverse sciences from a young age, recognise from only a few characters the elements of all the doctrines, and through this more easily reach the understanding of things" (translation from the French by the author).

15 Euclid, *The Elements of the most auncient philosopher EUCLIDE of Megara* (London 1570).

16 See Frances Yates, *Theatre of the World* (Chicago: University of Chicago Press 1969).

17 John Dee, *The Mathematicall Praeface* (1570) (New York: Science History Publications 1975), in section on "Archemastrie" (reprint of the preface to the 1570 edition of Euclid's *Elements*).

18 Katja Grillner, *Automata, Perspective and Music: Poetic Instruments in the Written Garden of Salomon de Caus* (Stockholm: Institutionen för Arkitektur och Stadsbyggnad 1995), 16–20.

19 In experiments performed by Vincenzo Galilei in the latter part of the six-teenth century, the Pythagorean musical proportions were proven to be quite mistaken. See Claude V. Palisca, *Humanism in Italian Renaissance Musical Thought* (New Haven: Yale University Press 1985), 275–6.

20 Ibid., 20.

21 This meant that the tones produced by the instrument would, if tested in comparison with a monochord, be found to have a different proportion from the pythagorean proportion suggested to correspond with it.

22 Ficino, *The Book of Life*, 160.

23 De Caus, *Institution Harmonique*, Proposition 23. This and all subsequent quotations from de Caus's texts have been translated from the original French by the author.

24 Ibid., 1.

25 De Caus, *La Pratique*, in discourse on proportions, section on musical proportions.

26 Ibid., in dedication.

27 Boethius, quoted and translated by Dee in *The Mathematicall Praeface*.

28 Leon Battista Alberti, *On Painting* (New Haven: Yale University Press 1966), 64.

29 Quoted in Frances Yates, *Giordano Bruno and the Hermetic Tradition* (Chicago: University of Chicago Press 1964), 24–5.

30 On geometry as a source of transcendental truth, see also Alberto Pérez-Gómez, *Architecture and the Crisis of Modern Science* (Cambridge, Mass.: MIT Press 1992), 87–127.

31 De Caus, *La pratique,* Introduction.

32 Euclid, *The Elements*, fol. 183.

33 De Caus, *La perspective*, ch. 26. Salomon de Caus was among the earliest to present the technique of constructing a perspective with its vantage point in an extreme position. See also Jurgis Baltrusaitis, *Anamorphic Art* (New York: Harry N. Abrams Publishers 1977).

34 De Caus, *La pratique*, Def. 1.

35 De Caus, *La perspective*, Book II, Introduction.

36 De Caus, *Les raisons*, Part I, Def. I. (*"Il y a de deux especes de feu, l'un eslementaire, lequel n'est subiect à corruption, lequel ie croy estre la chaleur du Soleil ... la seconde espece de feu est le materiel, lequel est dit ainsi, à cause qu'il est nourii & maintenu de matiere corporelle."*)

37 De Caus, *Les raisons*, Part I, Def. I.

38 Ibid., Part I, Theorem I.

39 Ibid., Part I, Problem 12.

40 Ibid., Part I, Problem 35.

41 Ibid., Part II, Problem 10.

42 De Caus, *La perspective*, Book II, ch. 10. In the same treatise (Book I, chs. 30 and 31) de Caus uses the proverbs "*Cognois toi-mesme*" and "*Songe avant que de parler*" to demonstrate the principles of optical correction for inscriptions on monuments. They both allude to the importance of contemplating oneself before acting, and according to Calvinist doctrine this was one of the three sources of divine wisdom. De Caus probably found it important to emphasize this message along with the teachings of natural and anamorphic perspectives. For a more thorough discussion, see my *Automata, Music and Perspective*, 41–3.

43 For a discussion on the philosophical implications of mass media, see, for example, Gianni Vattimo, *The Transparent Society* (Baltimore: Johns Hopkins University Press 1992).

44 Gianni Vattimo has concentrated on this issue in his book *The End of Modernity* (Baltimore: Johns Hopkins University Press 1991).

45 Paul Ricoeur, "The Function of Fiction in Shaping Reality," *Man and World* 12 (1979): 134. This essay has also been published in *A Ricoeur Reader: Reflection and Imagination*, ed. Mario J. Valdez (Toronto: Harvester Wheatsheaf 1991), 117–36.

46 De Caus, *Les raisons*, Book III, Introduction. In this part on the making of musical organs, de Caus introduces the subject with a general discussion on the history of the organ, including the original sense of the word. See also my *Automata, Perspective and Music*, 97–103.

Demas: The Human Body as a Tectonic Construct

Maria Karvouni

Chora

5.1 The "Goddess of Myrtos," the great-grandmother of Athena (Goddess of Weaving). The jug-like artefact becomes the embodiment of the female Goddess and of her traits. The allusion to motherhood is hard to miss, an astonishing example of the "blurring" between artefact-human body. Early Minoan IIB Settlement of Myrtos. Courtesy of the Museum of Hagios Nikolaos, Crete, Greece. Photograph by author.

NAMES, ACCORDING TO PLATO, ARE INSTRUMENTS that help us distinguish and teach the essence of things.[1] With a similar notion in mind, many of us architects wonder from time to time about the meaning and origins of our architectural expressions. Tracing back terms to their origins offers a way to reach an initial, and perhaps authentic, state of things, to rediscover threads of continuity and to reaffirm their importance.

Words such as "architect," "architecture," "tectonics," "technology," "technic," "dome," and "domicile" are among many architectural terms of Greek origin. Among all these technical terms one can also find the oldest (known) Greek word for the human body: *demas*. This indicates that a bond between body and building is built literally into the language. Such an intriguing connection may be of particular significance for our times, when architects seem so preoccupied with visual representation and so little concerned, if at all, with embodiment.

In this article, I will address the likely kinship between tectonics and the human body by investigating a larger set of building terms in their original (Greek) setting. In doing so I hope to reveal some of the shades of meaning and association that are still lurking in our current architectural vocabulary. Yet we should also keep in mind that even Plato, who declares that language holds the key to many interesting discoveries, warns us of the risks that such an inquiry involves: "One who follows names in the search after things and analyzes their meaning is in great danger of being deceived."[2]

In the Greek language, two etymological families provide the vocabulary for building: one based on the root *tek-* and the other based on the root *dem-*. Accordingly, two verbs describe the act of building: *tektaino* (or *tektainomai*) and *demo*.[3] Both verbs are used by Homer and each belongs to a group of technical terms, most of which can be found unchanged or slightly modified in the Greek language from Mycenean times to the present. The former belongs to the group that *tekton* and later *architekton* (architect) and *architektonike* (architecture) come from. The latter is the core word in the family of terms that includes *domos* (house), *doma* (room or terrace), *dome* (structure), *oikodomo* (build a house, or, simply build), and *oikodomike* (the art of building – architecture).

It is often believed that a *tekton* was a carpenter, a joiner working in wood.[4] Evidence shows that this was not always the case and definitely not in Homeric times. Although a wood-joiner was probably always a *tekton*, a *tekton* was not always a worker in wood. *Tekton* comes from the Indo-European root *tek*[5] which generally signified "to work with an axe, to fashion."[5] However, the Greek equivalent of an axe, the *pelekys*, had been used for working in both stone and wood since prehistoric times.[6] Therefore, it seems more accurate to define a *tekton* as an artisan who used strong tools to fashion hard materials. Many ancient references confirm such a view. The ancient lexicographers point out that a stone worker was also a *tekton*.⁷ Students of Greek building terminology also consider *tekton* an artisan working in hard materials, mainly wood and stone.⁸ An inscription at Eleusis calls *tektones* the artisans who fit the plinths.⁹ In an excerpt from *Basileia B* that describes the building of David's palace, workers in both wood and stone are called *tektones*: "*Tektones xylon* (wood-tectons) and *tektones lithon* (stone-tectons) were sent to build (*okodomisan*) David's house (*oikon*)."¹⁰ In Homer, *tektones* are both the shipbuilders and the house-builders since, as Polydeukis had observed, Homer uses *tektones* to refer to masons as well.¹¹ Later, and especially in Hellenistic times, a *tekton* was mainly a woodworker and especially a roofmaker, but this was not the original meaning of the word.¹²

In summary, a *tekton* was originally an artisan who, *pelekys* in hand, shaped hard materials. His work proceeded by cutting and joining. Therefore, it was his way of working, more than the material used, that defined his *métier*.

A *tekton* cuts and joins, divides and connects. Dividing and composing are also the two main modes of operation by which an art (*techne*) proceeds, according to Plato.¹³ Surprisingly, the *tekton* is the only artist-artisan who shares with *techne* the common root **tek-*.¹⁴ This suggests some very interesting implications for the original meaning of art (*techne*) and its close connection to constructing.

A *tekton*'s mode of working requires a tool (the axe), unlike work done with bare hands, such as molding (*platto*, to mould, is related to *palame*, palm, hand). Whereas molding involves continuity, tectonics is defined first by the discontinuity of cutting and then by joining. Tectonics deals with the arrangement of "distinct units" that the tecton first shapes with his tools and then places and joins together.

This dual, seemingly antithetical, activity is what defines tectonics. Since tectonics is literally at the root of architecture (*archi-tektonike*), this dual mode of operation is also at the core of architecture. "The division (*diairesis*) and synthesis (*synthesis*) of wood (or stone)" is an expression found in ancient building inscriptions.¹⁵ The work of an architect consists of *diairesis* and *synthesis*. "The *synthesis* and *harmonia* (fitting) of the pieces of stone and wood is nothing else but the genesis of the *eidos* (kind) of a house," says a scholiast.¹⁶ This dual operation is also found in cosmogonic myths, in mathematical accounts, in philosophical speculations, and in the discussion and definition of art in general. In the Greek mind, "coming into being" seems to be similar to the "tektonic process." This basic pair of operations is reflected in the two major cosmogonic forces of most myths of creation: the force of dividing and the force of bringing together.[17] It is also evident in basic mathematical operations: dividing (*diairesis*) and adding (*prosthesis*).[18] In prescientific Greece, numbers had ontological significance and numerical operations expressed plurality and becoming. Numbers, therefore, could illuminate the process of genesis and change in the microcosm and macrocosm.[19] The word *diairesis* (division) describes both a mathematical and a tectonic operation.

The same two forces of separation and connection, portrayed as Strife and Love, are found operating in the whole universe in Empedokles' philosophy. Love is the force that brings things together while Strife is the force that keeps them apart. The joining force is also called *Harmonia* and this brings to mind *Harmon*, the father of *Tekton* in the Homeric personification of building and harmony.[20]

The two basic operations of a *tekton* seem to epitomize the basic principles of genesis and change. On the other hand, no word in the Greek vocabulary defines the artist-artisan comprehensively. Only *tekton* seems to comes close. The Greek language suggests that *tekton*, in its most general sense, is the person whose occupation is *techne* (art). And in the ontological world of ancient Greece it is the most corporeal of the arts that serves as a prototype for understanding the "workings" of art. This understanding of art is so strong that it is found even in music. In ancient writings on music, musical composition is described in terms of spatial arrangements and assembling.[21] T. Georgiades, stressing this "corporeality," explains how Greek rhythm is built up from sound-bodies as if they were building blocks joined and placed together.[22] Similarly, a poet is called *rapsodos* (from *rapto*, to sew, and *ode*, song, poem, ode), and a dancer is called *betarmon* (literally "step-joiner," from *bema*, step, and *armozo*, join-fasten). When a poet is called *tekton epeon* (builder of epic songs) or *tekton hymnon* (builder of hymns) the language is less metaphorical than we may think. Furthermore, when the word "architect" first appears, it is attributed to the Muse: *Tectonarchos Mousa* (chief-builder Muse).[23]

The tectonic process, therefore, underlies both artistic creation and the Greek understanding of creation in general. In addition, *tekton* and *techne* seem to have something in common with *tikto*, to bring into the world, to beget. They sound suspiciously close and etymological connections have been suggested.[24] The analogy between "dividing-connecting" in tectonics and "separating-bringing together" in myths of creation favours a possible association. Furthermore, this association is made explicit by Plato, who remarks that there are two ways to bring things to life. One way is by being a parent; the other way is by being an artist. Plato, of course, uses art in its more general, Greek sense. It is not difficult to guess which type of parenthood Plato prefers. For him, no natural parent can be compared to Homer or Hesiod and their "offsprings." The point that interests me here is that art is perceived as a way of begetting and thus as a striving towards immortality.[25] Plato's analogy, I believe, echoes notions of earlier times when *tekton*, *techne*, and *genesis* were closely bound together.

One may conclude that, in its most basic sense, *tekton* refers to a person who applies *techne* (art) in manipulating any material. *Techne*, on the other hand, is the ability to divide and connect. This requires delimitation (assigning limits, measures, proportions) and synthesis (joining, composing, assembling). In doing so, the *tekton* imitates the cosmogonic operations of bringing things into existence.

In tectonics, thinking is imbedded in making. *Tektainomai* from its early beginings (Homer) meant both to "devise" as well as to "construct." A *tekton* both conceives and brings to life. This supports the suggested etymological connection between *tektaino* and *tikto* (to give birth), which also presupposes conception.[26] Indeed, in some of its earlier uses, the word *tekton* is feminine. Both Aeschylus and Euripides refer to a female *tekton*.[27] On the other hand, when Zeus is named *Tekton Phules* (builder of the race), he is understood as a father.[28] It seems that in the ancient world people perceived parallels between tectonics (artificial making) and *tokos* (natural making), as well as between *tektones* (builders, constructors, authors) and *tekountes* (natural parents). The image of the *tekton* who, axe in hand, contributes to creation brings to mind the birth of Athena from Zeus's head. Hephaistos's axe splits open Zeus's head and Athena emerges. Interestingly, both Hephaistos and Athena are Gods of the arts, and this "unnatural" birth is assisted by an axe, the tool and symbol of a *tekton*-builder.

If in *tektaino* the art of making is considered a genesis, in *demo* the outcome of this making is understood as a body. However, before analysing this term, a few technical aspects should be mentioned.

Demo, etymologists believe, signifies building in equal superimposed layers; it refers particularly to wall construction and things of similar nature.[29] Although it is usually assumed to involve masonry-construction, the Mycenean *naudomo* (shipbuilder)[30] and the Homeric *mesodme* (the central beam of a boat)[31] caution us against such a generalization. *Demo* was also used in maritime construction where it would have been performed by a *tekton*. As with *tektaino*, the emphasis in *demo* is also on the way of making rather than on the material used. It stresses building in layers and usually from the ground up.[32] Furthermore, *tektaino* and *demo* are not mutually exclusive but rather complementary; they can even be used interchangeably at times. In Homer a *tekton* both *tektainei* and *demei*: he builds ships, houses, halls, walls, courtyards, and so on.[33]

The Homeric poems are not the first texts in which these two terms appear. In tablets of the deciphered syllabic linear B script, dating from Mycenean times (*c.* 1300–1200 B.C.E.), the following names have been found:

TE KO TO NO (*tekton*): builder
NA VO DO MO (*naudomos*): builder of ships
TO KO DO MO (*teichodomos*): builder of walls
E TE DO MO: builder of?[34]

From this early age, *tekton* qualifies a person working in a specific way and it stands by itself. -*Domo*, on the other hand, exists only in composite form and indicates a way of making that is inseparable from the object that is made. In the various -*domo* composites, the maker, the way of making, and the final product are all combined in one single word. -*Domo* points towards conclusion, towards the fulfillment of the act of building, by defining the completed artefact.

While *tekton* stresses the "how" in making, -*domo* emphasizes the "what." This is supported by the various composites that the two terms generate: *tekton* defines an artisan with no need for further qualification. It is rarely found in composite form, apart from the well-known exception: *archi-tekton* (chief builder). In its few composite forms it always indicates the material that the *tekton* is working with: for example, *siderotekton* (iron-tekton), *chrysotekton* (gold-tekton), *laotekton* or *lithotekton* (stone-tekton).[35] Therefore, a *tekton* can be associated with the material he is using but never with the final product of his effort. This is apparent even in the Homeric *phreno-tekton*: someone who constructs with his *phrenes* (mind).[36] Once again it is the "material" that is emphasized.

In contrast, -*domos* (a person who builds) appears only in composite form, as in *oikodomos* (housebuilder), *teikhodomos* (wall builder), *naodomos* (temple builder), *pyrgodomos* (tower builder); the reference is to the built artefact, and the emphasis is on the completion of the work. There is no reference to the builder independent of his built product. This notion remains evident in the Mycenean *tokodomos*, in the *oikodomos* of Classical, Hellenistic, and Christian times and even in the *oikodomos* of modern Greek. From the start, the builder must have in mind the goal of his making, an image (however vague) of the wall, the house or the temple he is going to build. In this act of making the future product is already envisioned and the whole operation is expressed in a single word that acknowledges the builder, the built artefact, and the way of making. For example, *teikhodomos* is a builder who constructs a wall by superimposing and binding together layers of built material. The argument that *demo* emphasizes completion is also supported by the fact that the verb never appears in the future tense and rarely in the present tense. It is almost always used in the past tense, which denotes the act completed.[37]

The emphasis on completion suggested by the composite forms of -*demo* may be strengthened by an additional and, perhaps, unexpected connection: among the many derivatives of *demo* (*domos, doma, dome*, and others)[38] that relate to construction, one also finds *demas,* the earliest known Greek word for the human body. This "coexistence" has a dual significance. On the one hand, the realization that a linguistic bond once existed between body and building may lead to other possible connections between them. On the other hand, one may wonder why the human (and animal) body is understood as an artefact, and furthermore, why it is the art of building that provides the first term to capture the human body as a totality. Why is the living body expressed by a derivative of the verb "to build" and in particular the one (*demo*) that suggests completeness and totality? This last question is extremely important, since scholars have doubted that the human body was perceived as a unity in early Greek thought. Snell, for example, was convinced that the notion of the human body as a whole does not exist in Homer. It is never the human body, he says, but a part or parts of it that participate in action or suffer consequences, and the same may be said for feelings and thoughts. He concludes that the Homeric body is fragmented.[39]

On the contrary, I would argue that the existence of the Homeric *demas*, the human body as a built artefact, suggests the exact opposite. The very fact that the human body is called *demas*, a derivative of *demo* (the building term that implies completion and unity), demonstrates that the body was understood as a unified construct.

The word *demas* appears mainly in Homer and occasionally in the lyric and tragic poets. In later years it fades away and is replaced by *soma*. In Homer it is used to denote the living human body in its overall structure, form, and substance. It is also used in an adverbial form to indicate likeness.[40] "From the bath he stepped, in body like the immortals (*demas athanatoissin homoios*)," says Homer about Telemachos and later about Odysseus (*Odyssey* 3.468, 23.163).

Demas expresses the physical composite that is recognizable as a distinct individual. In the *Iliad* (13.45), Poseidon "takes on the likeness of Calchas, in bodily form (*eisamenos Kalchanti demas*)." When Athena disguises herself as Mentor, when she draws near Telemachos "in the likeness of Mentor in demas and in voice," she does not simply look like Mentor, she assumes his body, she embodies him (*Odyssey*, 2.268). This is the kind of likeness that the adverbial *demas* denotes: "in the build of something else, in a similar 'bodily structure'".[41] It is a metaphor in the original sense (*meta-phero*, carry over): "to be like something else," implying "to be able to stand in its place," "to fit in its form and assume its substance," thus to embody it. It is of great significance, I believe, that it is *demas* (the body), a derivative of *demo* (to build), that expresses this type of analogy.

All recent etymological and general lexicons agree that *demas* is the living body (primarily the human one) and that it comes from *demo* (to build), yet no further discussion is offered to account for this connection.[42] Older lexicographers also render *demas* as the human body,[43] and although they offer more than one alternative for its etymological origins, their etiological explanation is, I believe, of great importance. In the Etymologicon Magnum the following explanation is offered: "*Demas*: the body; from *deo: desmeuo* (to bind, tie, fasten, fetter) because the soul is tied to the body; because the body is the bonds and the fetters of the soul; or from *demo: oikodomo* (to build, to build houses) since the body is the structure built around the soul and the place of its dwelling."[44] The scholiast, unable to decide the origin of this word, associates the human body both with "binding together" and with "building."

Even though the derivation of *demas* from *demo* may be the most accurate (as modern etymologists insist), the intention of the older scholiast to associate the body with a sense of binding is not without merit. In *demo*, the notion of "binding" elements (building blocks) together is always present. Consequently, *demas*, as a derivative of *demo*, comprises not only a sense of the body as an artefact built up from individual "building members," but also the notion of the human body as a totality, as a tightly fitted and firmly bound whole. Its various parts are held together by a force or power (*phrenes, thymos*?) that guarantees a unity in action, in feeling-thinking, and in form. When the power that holds everything together is gone, the body is no longer a *demas* (built-up unity), but a *soma* (a corpse). Its parts disintegrate and the unity is dissolved.

The affinities among *demas* (body), *demo* (build), and *deo* (tie) suggest that a body composed of parts needs an element to bind its parts together into a totality. According to the scholiasts, the binding element for the living body is the soul. In a work of art this is achieved with *harmonia* (actual fastening)[45] or with "proportions." Proportions are the invisible bonds (*desmoi*) that hold units together, whether they be artefacts, the human body, or even the whole world.

Bruno Snell's thesis, that the body as a totality does not exist in Homer, has been refuted by many scholars on various grounds. Yet, to my knowledge, it has never been pointed out that the Homeric *demas* itself is the best refutation of Snell's assertion.[46] Norman Austin argues for the existence of a "unity in multiplicity" by comparing multiplicity in Homeric accounts of time and space to multiplicity in the Homeric language for the body.[47] He points out that in Homeric thought, the individual, the harmoniously integrated community, and the constructed artefact all have a composite structure. "Man is the sum of his parts. What happens to one part affects the whole."[48] Austin believes that Homer is a poet who thinks in terms of structural relationships and imposes unity through these relationships.

Although never mentioned by Austin, the Homeric *demas* provides a strong confirmation of this "unity in multiplicity." Its etymological connections with construction realized by fitting and tying provides a vivid image of the body as a structural composition that is properly secured and unified by the "binding" of its elements.

The Greek technical vocabulary indicates the ability of the Greek mind to oscillate between the concrete and the abstract. It also shows a tendency to pair (and compare) artificial making with natural making (*tek*) and built artefact with living body (*dem*), as if each could help explain and illuminate the other. These connections are not only suggested by the etymology but are also encountered in many ancient texts, including both Homer and Plato. One simply has to listen to their imagery.

Homer conceives of the human body in its parts and its totality as a well-constructed artefact. Body, soul, and mind were not yet distinct categories. "I have my eyes, ears and both my feet and a *noos* (mind) well constructed (*teucho*) in my chest," he says.[49] Organs, body-parts and even the *noos* (mind-spirit-soul) are fabrications that depend on good "craftsmanship." The individual is a larger structure in which parts must "fit well together" (*ararisko*). *Phrenes* (mind-feelings)[50] is something that can be built (*tektainetai*); a prudent person is one "well fitted" in his *phrenes* (*phresin ariros*).[51] *Phrenes* resemble the work of a *tekton* and its good construction depends on how its pieces are put together (*ararisko*, to fit well, and *harmonia*, means of fastening, harmony, come from the same root, *ar**). Homer uses the same epithet, *isos*, to refer to a properly built boat and a virtuous human being; both are *isoi*, "well balanced in construction."[52]

Limbs (*melea*) can be "unloosed" (*lyo*),[53] *harmonia* (the actual fastening in a construction) can be unloosed, and so can a wall.[54] In building phraseology, the expression "to unbind a wall" (*lyo to teikhos*) or "to unbind its harmonies" means to demolish it.[55] Building a wall (*demo*) was understood as a kind of fastening (*desis* or *syndesis*). "He built a bridge by tying (*deo*) the stones" says Herodotus.[56] To bind (*deo*) the stones or the planks, and to fasten (*deo*) the joints (*harmoi)* are common expressions. In addition, the means of connecting the stones in a wall were called *desmoi* (bounds-fetters again, from *deo*, to tie). *Harmoi* and *harmoniai* were the joints of a construction (usually a stone structure and often a wall). In Homer, *harmoniai* were one of the means of fastening planks in the construction of a ship.[57] Once more the terminology shows that the act of building (*demo*) includes an act of fastening (*deo*).[58]

A similar notion is evident in Homer's references to the body not only as a well-crafted artefact but also as a well-bound compound held together by some powerful "fastening" element. The precariousness of the human condition is well reflected in this powerful image. Once the "string" is let loose, the cohesion and coherence of the whole are destroyed. It does not take much for the "edifice" to collapse. As in a wall, external forces or internal conditions (inadequate fitting) may cause collapse, but the better the "construction," the greater the resistance. Good construction requires tight fitting and fastening. This is why a person "well fitted" in his "mind-feeling" (*phrenes*) is prudent. When *phrenes* are gone, the limbs are "unloosed" and the whole bodily structure becomes unfastened and in danger. Homer uses the same verbs for the construction of a wall or a boat and for the making of the body. The proper fitting and "fastening" of the parts guarantee the competent function of the whole. *Demas,* the only word that Homer uses to refer to the human body as a whole, clearly reflects this notion, since *demas* comprises both the notion of building (*demo*) and that of fastening (*deo*).

Homer does not tell us which means of "fastening" are involved in the "construction" of the human body: that is, how it becomes a *demas,* a well-bound and well-built whole. However, he gives us some clues as to when this unified construction disintegrates: when it is struck at a vital point or when it is subject to violent emotional shock such as fear,[59] then *noos* can "flow together," collapse, and lose its shape. When the "*phrenes* are taken away" (by Ate for example), the limbs "will be unloosed." It is obvious that *noos* and *phrenes* are pivotal for the integration of the whole body. They play an active role by providing the necessary binding. On the other hand, it is clear when the body ceases to be a *demas:* when there is no life in it, the *demas* becomes a *soma* (a corpse). Since *phrenes* in Homer is, among other things, the seat of life or life itself,[60] *phrenes* may well provide the "live bonds" that keep the body alive, that make it a *demas.*

Listening to Homer, one becomes aware of a language in which the concrete and abstract notion of a word are part both of its sense and of a way of thinking in which a reciprocal relationship between the natural and the artificial is maintained.[61] In the Homeric world, the living body is conceived as an artefact, and at the same time an artefact can embody a living thing. *Harmonia* is the means of fastening the planks of a boat (a concrete notion) yet also an agreement between human beings, an invisible bond that keeps them together (an abstract notion).[62] *Tektones* can build houses but they can also construct thoughts. This makes it easier to accept that "to build" (*tektaino*) and "to beget" (*tikto*) may be transformations based on the same root "*tek*."[63]

Homer initiates (or records) a relationship that was gradually transformed into the body-building analogy in architectural theory. Before it appears in architectural writings, this analogy is articulated by Plato. In *Timaeus*, Plato describes how the world came into being. He portrays God as a *tekton* and his artefact, the universe, as a living being modelled out of the human body.[64] Although the Pythagorean influences on Plato's account have been discussed repeatedly, especially his love for portioning material and shaping forms through numerical and geometrical analogies, Homeric influences are almost never mentioned. Yet it is in Homer that the first (written) cross-references between body and building are developed.

As in Homer, Plato's imagery is revealing: the making (*poesis*) of the world is a construction and God is a *Demiourgos*, an artisan.[65] He is also referred to as *tektainomenos* (acting like a *tekton*). He works by using the living body as a model, his work is therefore a *mimesis*, like any other work of art.[66] This divine artificer proportions his materials and uses *symmetries* (proportions) like any other good artisan.[67] God *tektainei* (builds, joins), *harmozei* (fits), and *oikodomei* (builds houses or simply builds).[68]

The "building up of *phrenes*" in Homer is equivalent to the "building up of the soul" in Plato (*psychen synetektaineto*).[69] As in Homer, the eyes were "constructed" (*synetektenato*), and, within the head, organs (eyes, ears, and so on) were "fastened" (*enedesan*).[70] God had "built" (*etektinato*) a perfect (*teleon*) universe, giving it its appropriate shape (*schema*).[71] He had "joined together and constructed the heaven."[72] Everything was "structured" (*to pan synetektaineto*).[73] Everything was made with skill and knowledge, thus with art (*ek technes*). The gods "built" the human body around the soul, "working with lathe and chisel around it" (*peritorneusan*). After finishing the mortal body, they "built" (*pros-okodomoun*) a mortal soul inside it.[74] Finally, a three-part soul "was housed" (*katokistai*) inside every mortal. The building imagery continues.

In Plato, as in Homer, the members of the living being (*kosmos*) are "fitted together" (*harmotousin*). Various elements and body parts are joined and built up (*tektaino-oikodomo*) like parts of a house. Any living being, either the whole universe or an individual human, is made perfect and complete with the use of *analogiai* (proportions), which Plato calls *desmoi* (means of fastening, bonds). These numerical *analogiai* guarantee harmony (*harmonia*) in the universe, in the soul, in music, and in any artefact. The binding notion of *harmonia* that is found in Homer is also present in Plato, where it is transformed into mathematical proportions.

The Homeric *harmonies* – the means of fastening a structure, a human body, or even a human relationship – gradually became the Platonic (and Pythagorean) *harmonies*, the metaphorical means of "binding" the movements of a soul or the movements of the stars reflected by the soul. Plato's *harmonies* also have musical connotations, yet one should remember that even musical *harmonies* depend on some kind of fastening: for example, on the tuning of the strings of the musical instrument.[75] Harmony is one of those wonderful words that, in the Greek mind, could assume simultaneously a tectonic, musical, and abstract (mathematical) character. At the same time, harmony is what keeps the human body together and guarantees its good "tuning" and "fitting."[76]

According to Plato, both the universe and the individual human being were made according to the same model, the same materials, and the same rules of "construction" used in the making of a well-adjusted house. This well-adjusted house-body is what Homer calls *demas*. Plato's *Timaeus* is a commentary and a development of this basic notion, expanding the house-body relationship to incorporate the whole universe. Body, house, and universe are all made up by similar rules. Each one has been set in order (*dia-kosmethe*) by division and arrangement.[77] Each one is a *kosmos*, an order, and an embellishment. When Plato attempts to understand the making and working of the cosmos, he resorts to the art of building to provide analogies and mediating tools. The living body was the model for cosmos. Furthermore, the body (of the universe, or the individual being) is "fashioned like a house" and the tectonic process serves as a paradigm that explains life in its making.

Homeric and Platonic images present the body and its functions "as if" the body were an artefact. Art seems to mediate and explain life. Their use of technical terms probably reflects those of the artisans of their times. On the other hand, the art of tectonics appears as the art of

5.2 Clay model of a shrine. The wall-shrine is a representation of the Deity and also a cult scene. We see a woman leaning over a tall pithos making offerings. In the wall-shrine which is surmounted with a bull's head, protuberances suggesting breasts are clearly visible. The wall-shrine is a built aniconic image of Deity. The built-artefact embodies Her. Cyprus Museum Nicosia. Published by permission of the Director of Antiquities and the Cyprus Museum.

embodiments. Homer first and Plato later present us with the notion of a reciprocal relationship between body and building. And yet this notion, as the artefacts show, was of much greater antiquity. After Plato, the body-building metaphor was adopted, elaborated upon, and transformed by various architectural thinkers. Vitruvius, Alberti, Michelangelo, and many Byzantine writers have much to say on the subject.

In the ancient Greek world, as R. Padel has shown, the Greek theatre-structure embodies notions of the inner and outer self, of male and female attributes.[78] In a similar fashion, I believe that the Greek temple – with its surrounding columns, independent yet related, standing equal yet never exactly the same, and together supporting a common goal – embodies the Greek notion of citizenship. Its extrovert character emphasizes the importance of the outer, thus public, life. The *symmetria* of the temple (in Greek *symmetria* means proportional equality, balance, and equilibrium) reflects the *isonomia* (equality in law) of its citizens. And yet *symmetria* was also the necessary condition for the health of the body. "Health is the *symmetria* of the elements of a body and beauty the *symmetria* of its parts," says Polykleitos the sculptor, whom Galen the physician quotes. Then again, since Justice is the "health of the city" according to Plato, it also depends on *symmetria*. Health, strength, beauty, and justice all depend on balance and due measure. Hence, through *symmetria* and its embodiment in the temple, the human body, the civic body, and the building seem to reflect and illuminate one another.

In the Greek world the ability to uphold both the concrete and the abstract colouring of a word is reflected in a tectonic ability to embody both the concrete and the abstract. Capturing this ambivalent connection in building would explain life through artefacts; life itself could be viewed as an artefact. Concurrently, artefacts could be perceived and enjoyed as embodiments of the conditions of life.

This notion of architecture as embodiment is out of favour in our times. We tend to talk about architecture in terms of "concepts" and "ideas" and place a disproportionate emphasis on the visual. We seem to favour the abstract, the cerebral, and the visual at the expense of the concrete, the corporeal, and the tactile. Yet, as the ancients could tell us, these two conditions need not be at odds. It is within the power of architecture to bring them together and celebrate their unity. "What I am missing most in modern buildings," says Mario Botta, "is the 'erotic dimension.'" This is the dimension that makes a building "feel" like a body, a building that demands our fullest attention as a "living being."

We may, therefore, remind ourselves from time to time that not so long ago to "carve" meant also to "endow with life," and to "build" was also understood as to "embody the forms of life."[79] After all, a Doric temple, as the ancients understood it, was a built embodiment of the rhythms of the Doric way of life.

NOTES

1 Plato *Cratylus*; 428e; 388c; 428e.

2 Ibid., 436b.

3 There are other verbs such as *teucho* (make, fabricate, construct) or *poieo* (make), but their use is much broader. *Tektaino* (earlier form: *tektainomai*) and *demo* define the building operation. See H.G. Liddell and H. Scott, *Greek-English Lexicon,* (Oxford: Oxford University Press, 1940); Anastasios Orlandos, *Lexicon Archaion Architectinikon Oron* (Athens: Library of the Greek Archaeological Society 1986); Pierre Chantraine, *Dictionnaire Etymologique de la Langue Grecque* (Paris: Edition Klincksieck 1980); Johanes Lund, *The History of Words Pertaining to Certain Crafts in the Principal Indo-European Languages*, private ed., distributed by the University of Chicago Libraries (Chicago 1953). *Lexicon of Homeric Dialect*, ed. Cunliffee, L.L.B. Blackie and Son (Glasgow and Bombay 1940); Hesychius, *Lexicon*, ed. K. Latte (Copenhagen: Copenhagen and Oxford 1953); *Etymologicon Magnum Lexicon*, Oxonii, E Typographeo Academico, M.DCCC.XLIII.

4 See Chantraine, *Dictionnaire; tekton: "charpentier, constructeur de bateaux."* Liddell and Scott: *tekton:* worker in wood, carpenter, joiner.

5 Chantraine, *Dictionnaire Etym.*, 1100. The Indo-Eoropean *$*tek^s$* is transformed into *$*tek^T$* in Greek; *$*tek$* is a simplification; see Benveniste, "Le probleme du Indo-Europeen," *BSL* 38 (1937): 140–1; See also Lund, *The History of Words Pertaining to Craft*, 5.

6 The verb *pelekao* (working with a *pelekys*) was used in both stone and wood work; see *peleako, pelekema, pelekisis, pelekites*, etc. Orlandos, *Lexicon*, 202; for Greek tools on wood, see Orlandos, *Ta Ylika Domes ton Arcaion Ellenon* (The materials of construction of the Ancient Greeks), 2 vols., 1: 39; for tools on stone, *Ylika*, 2: 116–21; see also Orlandos, *Lexicon*.

7 Hesychius, Souidas, Polydeukis, Apollodoros of Karystos and others; for example, Hesch: *tekton: pas technites* (every artisan); Souidas: *tekton laoxoos ke o ton xylon eidemon* (the stone carver and the wood expert).

8 There are a few exceptions such as *tekton keraxoos* (tecton working in horn, Homer *Iliad*, D, 110); *tekton halkou* (tekton working in bronze, CIG III add. 4158). For a detailed discussion of references to *tekton* and its various notions presented in ancient texts, see Orlandos, *Ylika*, 2: 36–8. Also Lund, *The History of Words Pertaining to Crafts*, 4–8.

9 IG II 2² (1) 1672 $_{185}$.

10 Orlandos, *Ylika*, 1: 36.

11 Polydeukis, On.1,12.7,117. Also Orlandos *Lexicon*, 247.

12 For the Hellenistic view of *tekton* see Orlandos, *Ylika*, 1: 37.

13 Plato, *Politicus (Statesman)*, tr. by H.N. Fowler (London: Loeb Classical Library, Harvard University Press 1962), 282B.

14 *Techne* and *tekton* belong to the same family, sharing the root *tek-; Chantraine, *Dictionnaire*, 1112.

15 (Epidauros) IG IV 1² 102, $_{165}$. IV 1² 102$_{206}$. IG IV 1² 102$_{167, 196, 206}$ 103$_{11, 35,}$ $_{56, 58, 59}$ Theophrastos, V, 5.6 (Wimmer 1: 149). Pausanias, IX 3,7.

16 I. Philoponos 12.9 (ed. H. Rabe, Lipsiae 1889). See Orlandos, *Lexicon*: *synthesis, diairesis, tekton*.

17 In most cosmogonic accounts there is first an undifferentiated whole. At some point this divides and splits into two. The two (opposing) forces or parts created then come together and other things are brought into existence by their union. Separation and union define and describe creation.

18 There are four mathematical operations: addition, subtraction, multiplication, and division; multiplication is a form of addition (*prosthesis*), and subtraction a form of division (*diairesis*).

19 For a discussion of this aspect of mathematics, see Walter Burkert, *Lore and Science in Ancient Pythagoreanism* (Cambridge Mass.: Harvard University Press 1972).

20 *Iliad*, 5.60.

21 *Greek Musical Writings*, 1 and 2, ed. A. Barker.

22 T. Georgiades, *Greek Music, Verse and Dance* (New York: Merlin Press 1995).

23 *Tektonarchos* (Sof. fr. 159): from *tekton* and *arche* (first, principal, chief); the exact reverse of *architekton*. Orlandos, Lexicon, *tektonarchos*, 247; Chantraine, *Dictionnaire, tekton*, 1100.

24 *Tikto*: to bring into the world; mainly of mother: to bring forth, to bear; but also of father: to beget. *tekon*: father; tekousa: mother; *tekontes*: parents.

Liddell and Scott. For the etymological suggestion offered here, see E. Kofin-iotes, *Lexicon Omerou*. Older Philologists such as Georg Curtius associate the two words and their roots, **tek* and **tik*, in a common concept of "begetting," "producing." Recent etymologists such a Chantraine disagree; but see Liddell and Scott, *Greek-English Lexicon, v. tikto;* also J. Rykwert, *The Dancing Column* (MIT Press 1996), 444n.27.

25 "And I ask you, who would not prefer such fatherhood to merely human propagation, if he stopped to think of Homer, and Hesiod, and all the greatest of our poets? Who would not envy them their immortal progeny, their claim upon the admiration of posterity?" Plato, *Symposium*, 209d.

26 See n.24.

27 Aeschylus, *Agamemnon*, 1406; Euripides, *Medea*, 409.

28 Aeschylus, *Iketides* (Suppliants) 590–95.

29 Chantraine, *Dictionnaire*. 261–62; Benveniste, "Homophonies radicales en Indo-Europeen," *BSL* 15–21; Orlandos: *Lexicon*, 67; Lund, *The History of Words Pertaining to Crafts*, 8–10.

30 Chadwick and Baumbach, *The Mycenean Greek Vocabulary* (Cambridge: Cambridge University Press 1963).

31 *Lexicon of the Homeric Dialect*; see also Cantraine, *Dictionnaire*, 262, and Benveniste, "Homophonies Radicales," 18.

32 *Demo* was also used in road construction (Herodotos) or the construction of a level plot, for example, a vineyard (Homer); Benveniste, "Homophonies Radicales," 17.

33 Homer, *Iliad*, Z 315/316; *Iliad*, E, 59. For a detailed reference to all instances in which Homer uses the two words, see *Lexicon of the Homeric Dialect*.

34 Chadwick and Baubach, *The Mycenean Greek Vocabulary*; see also Chantraine and Benveniste. The meaning of "*e te do mo*" has not been deciphered because the meaning of "*ete*" is unknown; Benveniste thinks that "*ete*" may refer to a type of edifice that still needs to be identified; for a discussion, see Benveniste, "Homophonies Radicales en Indo-Europeen," *BSL* 51 (1955): 19n.1.

35 Orlandos, *Lexicon* and *Ylika*; Chantraine, *Dictionnaire*.

36 Chantraine, *Dictionnaire*, *phreno-tekton* (Ar.), 1100.

37 Chantraine, *Dictionnaire*, 261; The only exception is the Mycenean *demeontes* (part. fut.), cf. Chadwick and Baumbach. See also Liddell and Scott, *Lexicon*.

38 Chantraine, *Dictionnaire*; Benveniste, "Homophonies Radicales"; *Lexicon of Homeric Dialect*; for all technical terms that derive from *demo*, see Orlandos, *Lexicon*.

39 Snell, *The Discovery of the Mind*, (Oxford: Oxford University Press 1953); "Homer's View of Man," 1–22.

40 Chantraine, *Dictionnaire*, 261; Benveniste, "Homophonies Radicales," 18n3; also *Lexicon of Homeric Dialect*.

41 In advbl. acc. with genit., *demas*: in the build of, after the similitude of, like; (as "like" has developed fr. orig. Teutonic *liko-, body, form). *Lexicon of Homeric Dialect*.

42 In his discussion of the root *dem-, Benveniste mentions *demas* only in a footnote. He finds it abstract since, he says, it is never used for a material construction; he believes that it signifies "form" or "configuration." But can form be separated from material in Homer?

43 Hesychius, 600, 7; *Etymologicon Magnum*, 255, 36–43.

44 *Etymologicon Magnum*, 255, 36–41; 737, 36, 37, 39.

45 In Homer, *harmonia* is a means of fastening the planks of a boat; *Lexicon of Homeric Dialect*.

46 Ibid., 5. Aristarchos was the first to notice that in Homer *soma* was only the dead body; he also expressed the opinion that for Homer *demas* was the live body. Lehrs, Aristarch 86.160; 86f. Plutarch, poes. Hom. ch.124. Snell does acknowledge that the word that comes closer to denoting the human body as a whole is *demas*, but he does not find it satisfactory since, he argues, it meant the "structure or the form" and its use was limited. Snell thinks this is true only in certain cases. Yet, he concludes, "Aristarchus is right: in the vocabulary of Homer *demas* comes closest to playing the same role as the later *soma*." As I was finishing this paper I came across B. Knox's *Backing into the Future: The Classical Tradition and its Renewal* (New York: W.W. Norton 1994). There, in a short paragraph, P. Knox refers to *demas* and *phye* as the two words that describe the Homeric body in its totality (50–4).

47 Austin, "Unity in Multiplicity," in *Archery at the Dark of the Moon*, ch. 2, 81–129. Also R. Padel, *In and Out of the Mind* (Princeton: Princeton University Press 1992), 45–6. Sullivan in *Psychological Activity in Homer* (Ottawa: Carleton University Press 1988), documents attacks on Snell since the 1930s.

48 Austin, *Archery at the Dark of the Moon*, 113–14.

49 *Odyssey* 20.365–7.

50 For the impossibility of translating *phrenes* with one single word, see Padel, *In and Out of the Mind*, esp. 20–4. "*Phrenes* contain emotion, practical ideas, and knowledge." *Phrenes* are containers: "they fill with *menos* (anger)

or *thymos* (passion) … They are the holding center, folding the heart, holding the liver … You are struck, you know, understand, tremble, feel, or ponder in that responsive, compact, containing center" (21). "But sometimes *phrenes* are an active initiating force … people feel intense love and grief in *phrenes*. *Phrenes* are actively, decisively emotional and imaginative. (22).

51 *Odyssey* 10.553–4.

52 For this use of *isos* which literally means "equal," see Vlastos, "Equality and Justice in Early Greek Cosmologies," in *Classical Philology* 42 (1947).

53 *Iliad*, 16.805.

54 See *lyo* in Orlandos *Lexicon*.

55 Ibid., p.173.

56 Herodotus, 1, 186.

57 For all the technical phraseology see Orlandos *Lexicon*, 37, 38, 67, 68, 173.

58 *Demas* as a derivative of *demo* implies both structural completion and binding. In addition, *demas* (body) and *dema(s)* (a bundle or a rope) are suspiciously close even though, etymologically, the former is a derivative of *demo* and the latter of *deo* (tie). (For *dema(s)* see Hesychius, 600,6). In ancient building terminology, a *dema* was a means of connecting stone or wood members, therefore a fastening element (Orlandos, *Lexicon*, 67).

59 Austin, *Archery at the Dark of the Moon*, 113.

60 Liddell and Scott, *Lexicon*; also *Homeric Lexicon*: *phrenes* as opposed to *psyche* (the departed soul).

61 For a discussion on this aspect of the Greek language see Padel, *In and Out of the Mind*. "It might be worth" she says, "to imagine a use of language in which both the abstract and the concrete coloring of each word are part of its sense, spoken into a physical world familiar with innards whose visible markings tell humans beings things about divinity they could not otherwise see for themselves" (40). She also points out that in Homer our distinction between material and immaterial is not made (37n86).

62 *Iliad*, XXII, 255.

63 See n.24.

64 God, the *Demiourgos*, is referred to as *tektainomenos*: acting as a *Tekton* (*Timaeus*, 28C).

65 Plato, *Timaeus*, 28, 41A, 41C, etc.

66 Ibid., 29B–D. It is absolutely necessary, Plato says, that the world is the image of something and that it should be built according to a model (*paradeigma*).

67 Ibid., 39E, 47E, 67C, 69A–C, 87C, etc.

68 The following is not a complete list but just a few references: *tektaino*: 28C, 33B, 39B, 68E, 69, 70E, and others; *harmotto* or *synharmotto*, 32B, 35B, 36E, 56C, 69B, and many others; *oikodomo* or *dioikodomo*: 69E, 70, 70B, and many others.

69 Ibid., 29E.

70 Ibid., 45B and 45C.

71 Ibid., 33B.

72 Ibid., 32C.

73 Ibid., 30B.

74 Ibid., 69B–70.

75 Liddell and Scott, *Greek-English Lexicon*.

76 In *Phaedo*, Plato talks about the human body as being held in tension and in tune like a musical instrument; 86b.

77 Ibid., 69E, 70, 70B, etc.

78 R. Padel, "Making the Space Speak," in *Nothing to Do with Dionysos?* (Princeton: Princeton University Press 1990).

79 Ventris and Chadwick, *Documents in Mycenean Greek*; *qe-qi-no-me-no* (*geginomenoi*: carved, perhaps in origin "endowed with life" (576).

Juan Bautista Villalpando's Divine Model in Architectural Theory

Alberto Pérez-Gómez

6.1 The Dome of the Rock identified with the Temple of Solomon, in a medieval image of Jerusalem from the *Liber chronicarum* by Hartmann Schedel.

> All that was described in [Ezekiel's] vision became true when the Lord, expiring on the Cross, shouted (Matthew 27:51) "and the veil of the Temple tore in two halves from top to bottom."
>
> J.B. Villalpando, *El Templo de Salomón*, 270.

THE BIBLICAL DESCRIPTION of the Temple of Solomon in Jerusalem has generated many diverse architectural speculations throughout our history. According to tradition, the Temple followed the designs of God and therefore could be interpreted as the archetypal work of architecture – a work that revealed a true order beyond the whimsical tastes of man and any temporal expressions of political power. In diverse times and cultures, mythical accounts of technological making and building demonstrated mankind's keen awareness of the problems involved in transforming a given "sacred" world for the sake of survival. In the Christian tradition the Temple of Solomon in Jerusalem has been identified as "the image of production as a path to salvation" (Joseph Rykwert), in oppo-

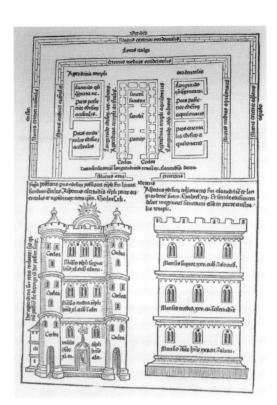

6.2 An early Christian reconstruction of the Temple of Solomon by the Franciscan Nicolas of Lyre (late twelfth century), published in 1502.

sition to the worldly city that is regarded in the Scriptures as the necessary (and potentially evil) product of Cain's toil, and more particularly to the Tower of Babel, a symbol of man's arrogant defiance of the order of Creation.

During the Middle Ages, the biblical Temple was identified with the Dome of the Rock in Jerusalem, a centralized archetype whose factual history remained unknown. Under this guise the Temple often had a direct impact on European church building. Moreover, Judeo-Christian cities from the Middle Ages to the end of the *ancien régime* were often construed as an anticipation of the Heavenly Jerusalem. In Medieval cities, the intentional physical changes were minimal but effective, achieving their objectives through their analogy with the mythical geography and topography of Jerusalem. The Renaissance city was a layered, syncretic symbol of both (Greco-Roman) cosmic order and the (Judeo-Christian) Temple. Eventually, urban extrapolations became less frequent but more literal. Castel Clementino (today Servigliano, in eastern Italy), commissioned by Pope Clement XIV in 1772 as a reaction to Enlightenment urban life, was the most literal large-scale materialization of the Temple in European urban history. Ironically, however, it was no longer a "true" architecture; the society that gave birth to it was obviously losing faith in the Temple of Jerusalem as an archetype of order and instead was considering the possibility of actually building utopia.

All traditional reconstructions of the Temple of Jerusalem are based on a handful of ancient texts, some archeological remains, and the topography of Jerusalem. The results, however, are surprisingly diverse since they depend on each author's cultural context, theological presuppositions, and personal imagination. Prior to the advent of scientific archaeology in the nineteenth century, reconstructions almost always were imagined unabashedly in the "style" of the author's preference in contemporary architecture. Thus, "original Truth" was sought through a living architectural practice. It was Maimonides who initiated the Jewish genealogy of reconstructions in the twelfth century and produced the first orthogonal version of the Temple. Juan Bautista Villalpando's late-sixteenth-century project, as I will explain, examined all available precedents, drawing particularly on the first Christian reconstruction by the Franciscan Nicolas de Lyre (*c.* 1270–1349) and on other Renaissance works such as François Vatable's interpretation of the Temple.

After the Renaissance and the Reformation, architects' passionate concern for embodying a mathematical cosmic order in their buildings led them to glean proportions and details from Ezekiel's description of the Temple of Jerusalem in the Bible. These rules, based on the divine *logos*, would constitute a solid ground for good architecture, especially if they could be aligned with the theory of classical architecture. Juan Bautista Villalpando's *In Ezechielem explanationes* ... (1596–1604) is the most important work in this tradition and became the obligatory point of departure for later speculations.[1] Thus, Villalpando's work must be understood as an architectural treatise in the traditional sense, bent on revealing the metaphysical dimension of architecture through the "Example of examples" and so disclosing how architecture may reveal a transcendental order for humanity. The questions raised by this treatise remained crucial for European architectural theory throughout the seventeenth and eighteenth centuries.

While shifting the discourse away from a divine or astrological cosmology, seventeenth- and early-eighteenth-century writers and architects started to give greater importance to a genealogy of divine buildings that

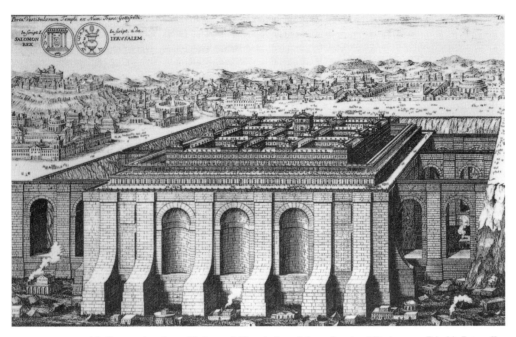

6.3 Perspective view of Solomon's Temple from Johann Bernhard Fischer von Erlach's *Entwurff einer Historichen Architectur* (1721), with the Temple surrounded by the great monuments in the genealogy of architecture. This image is based directly on Juan Bautista Villalpando's reconstruction proposed in his *In Ezechielem* ... (1596 and1604).

might legitimize the architecture of the present by linking it to that of the mythical past. These works, such as Juan Caramuel de Lobkowitz's *Architectura civil recta y oblicua, considerada y dibuxada en el Templo de Ierusalem* (1678) and Johann Bernhard Fischer von Erlach's *Entwurff einer Historischen Architectur* (1721), focused more on significant fragments (the Temple's "oblique" windows) or on the qualitative aspects of the building (such as its "Roman" magnificence) that might provide guidelines for contemporary architectural practice. The hermetic tradition, surviving after the Renaissance through the Rosicrucian movement and through eighteenth- and nineteenth-century Freemasonry, also showed great interest in the Temple. As the most important work of divine geometry, it was regarded as the origin of the Masonic tradition and the embodiment of a reconciliatory *techné*. This sacred order, stemming from a coincidence between natural philosophy (science) and revealed religion, could be "put to work" by the architect for the benefit of an enlightened mankind.

Theoretical reconstructions of the Temple were pursued not only by theologians and architects but also by scientists such as Sir Isaac Newton. Each interpretation offers a key to the broad epistemological implications of a particular author's work and often reveals important assumptions in the author's cultural context. In short, the history of the Temple constitutes a crucial chapter in the history of our architectural tradition, especially after classical culture became syncretically connected to the Judeo-Christian tradition. While the Temple currently is of interest mainly to historians, the issues that fuelled the obsession with the Temple's architecture in the early modern era (between the late sixteenth and the late eighteenth century) are still relevant: for architects in a technological world, driven by secularized dreams of eternal life in paradise, is it possible to build in a way that our actions become more than a mere solipsistic expression of a will to power?

Juan Bautista Villalpando's *In Ezekielem explanationes ...*, published in three volumes, presents a thorough literary and visual reconstruction of the Temple of Solomon. Although the first volume was signed by Jerónimo de Prado (1547–1595), the other two (by far the more interesting) are unquestionably the work of the architect and Jesuit priest Juan Bautista Villalpando (1552–1608). Villalpando had been a disciple of Juan de Herrera, the well-known architect of the Escorial, whose project was advanced by political motivations not unlike those of Villalpando's own work. King Philip II financed both the Escorial and Villalpando's project to promote economic power as symbolic power, to legitimize colonial exploitation, and to demonstrate his Solomonic wisdom. The king's new Catholic seat of government, a college-monastery-palace-sanctuary, was conceived as a new embodiment of Solomon's Temple and inaugurated a building type that was emulated in the following two centuries. Juan de Herrera and the king shared a passion for occult disciplines such as numerology, alchemy, magic, and the Lullian arts, and it was probably through Herrera that Villalpando secured the support of the king for the production and printing of his monumental work.[2] Villalpando's treatise, in fact, may be regarded as Herrera's theoretical justification. There are obvious formal connections between the plan of the Escorial and that of Villalpando's version of the Temple, as well as close parallels between the drawings prepared for both buildings. In this connection, it is important to point out that Villalpando's reconstruction

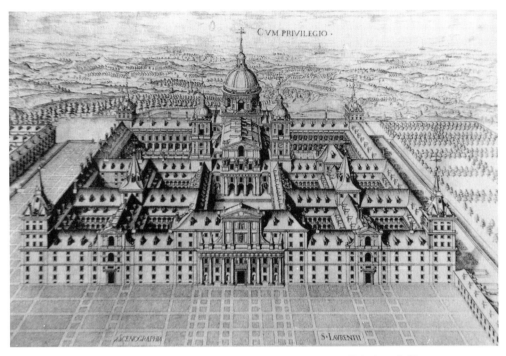

6.4 Aerial perspective of S. Lorenzo en Escorial (the "seventh project"), by Juan de Herrera .

was originally visual, the text having been completed much later. The engravings for *In Ezekielem explanationes ...* are superb by sixteenth-century standards. The thoroughness of the reconstruction, unmatched by any other imaginary or real building of that period, clearly demonstrates the status ascribed to the Temple and reflects the renewed spirituality expected of architecture following the Council of Trent and its program for the Counter-Reformation.

Villalpando was convinced that Ezekiel's Temple was a divine design that would enable mankind to deduce the rules of a perfect architecture, an architecture with the same status as the divine word revealed by God. In his preface to the reader, Villalpando presents God as an architect who, through Christ, commanded us to "take care of our house," a world created by Him for us. To Villalpando, this meant the physical as well as the spiritual. From the outset he regarded the Temple as a human product of the mystery of Incarnation and believed that it should become a model for constructing a world based on Christian values. To him, the Temple was analogous to the body of Christ,[3] a position developed through his immense research of the Scriptures, the fathers of the church,

Jewish texts, classical philosophers, and medieval theologians. The details of Ezekiel's vision, revealed through these extensive readings, were understood as a spiritual prefiguration of Christianity and as an implicit model for action. The invisible, for Villalpando, was always present behind sensuous experience; Ezekiel's vision of Heavenly Jerusalem was not a result of the Jewish prophet's will but an act of God, the father of Christ.

Villalpando's work is divided into five large sections or "Books." Book One includes a justification of Ezekiel's vision as an archetype, followed, significantly, by an extensive discussion of optics based on classical and medieval theories. In Book Two is a section devoted specifically to architecture, including the stunning graphic reconstruction of the Temple. A detailed exegesis of almost every word in Ezekiel's commentary, including a description of the parts, proportions, building tools, and implements of the Temple fill the rest of Books Two, Three, and Four. Book Five discusses the material wealth and cosmological significance of the Temple and other more speculative topics of considerable relevance for architecture.

Villalpando considered the graphic reconstruction to be crucial importance for his exegetic project. Given the hermeneutic difficulties and contradictions that are often present in biblical texts, especially with regard to measurements, he emphasizes the importance of first having the "idea" of the building (in drawing form) in order to understand the prophecy. Visualization played an important role in the Jesuit religious practices established by Ignatius Loyola, since it would be impossible to understand without first "seeing." This vision was ultimately construed as a sharing in the light of God by the godly in each one of us. Thus, Villalpando proposes his reconstruction as a perfect, coherent building that "could have been ... or perhaps was built."[4]

This vision, emphasizes Villalpando, "fixes the renovation of the temple, the city, the region, the law, and the republic."[5] Although he claims that his intention is not to teach architects, he believes that they can learn much from this true architecture.[6] Moreover, Villalpando affirms the importance of architects in a Christian society, insisting on the intellectual dimension of their practice and on the affinity between the work of architects and the work of philosophers. Quoting Plato and Vitruvius, he emphasizes that architecture is "a theory" that invokes intellectual discipline rather than craftsmanship, while the building is "a thing."[7] By radicalizing the analogy between God's mind and the architect's, and declaring that the architect must possess both wisdom and a knowledge of pragmatic science, Villalpando emphasized the "theoretical" (that is, speculative and geometric) character of architecture, to the extent of making the discipline almost autonomous from the practice of building as learnt and exercised through traditional apprenticeship.[8] The distinction here between theory and practice is indeed much sharper than in previous Renaissance writings, where the Vitruvian balance between *fabrica* (what is made through the hands' dexterity) and *raciotinatione* (the reasons for acting, on the principles of proportion) had always been taken for granted. While this assertion must be understood within Villalpando's theological framework, its epistemological structure prefigures conditions for theory in modern practice – ranging from the theoretical projects after Giovanni Battista Piranesi and Claude-Nicolas Ledoux to the instrumentalization of theories as reductive methodologies.

Vitruvius is present throughout Villalpando's vast discourse, constantly alternating with scriptural commentary. Villalpando reads this ancient Roman author closely and with reverence, seeking in *The Ten Books* the crucial points for his argument and testing its coherence with his vision of the divine origins of architecture. Yet he does not write a comprehensive tract on architecture. His topics in Book Two are carefully selected to redefine what he considers crucial for architecture, and his aims thus differ from those of previous humanistic commentaries such as Alberti's *De Re Aedificatoria*. One such crucial point for Villalpando is the nature of architectural representation, starting with the distinction between architecture and painting. Architectural drawings do not imitate; they are geometrical because they must be translated into building. Only drawing guided by "optics" can be helpful for architects. Villalpando argues that the three forms of drawing that Vitruvius calls "ideas" (plan or *ichnographia*, elevation or *orthographia*, and perspective or *scenographia*) must acknowledge optics so that the "small drawings" of the architect truly may correspond to the building.

Villalpando is the earliest writer in European architectural theory to identify architectural ideas (plans and elevations) explicitly with sections through the perspectival cone of vision. This assertion that perspective is a fundamental generative device for architecture is exceptional among late-Renaissance commentaries on the traditional Vitruvian recommendations. He emphasizes that the architect must first conceive the totality

6.5 Air view of the Temple of Solomon in its site, from Villalpando's *In Ezechielem* ...

of the building in his mind, and that this concept can be documented only with lines that are fixed "like writing," using various kinds of drawings. According to Villalpando, Christ Himself taught that man must contemplate the full consequences of his acts before starting to build. This theological argument for "planning" is also an innovation. In this context, perspective provides a whole vision of the future building.

Villalpando entered the Renaissance debate about what Vitruvius had intended in his discussion of architectural "ideas," since he seemed to include *scenographiam* side by side with the plan and the elevation, as the three types of drawings required to conceive architecture. Earlier writers such as Daniele Barbaro had argued that geometrical perspective belongs to a different species than plans and elevations because it is useful for painting and stage-set design but not for conceiving buildings. Barbaro claimed that Vitruvius probably had meant *sciographiam*, a shaded sketch that he associated with the section drawing and named *profilo*.[9] Villalpando regards this interpretation as the result of a misunderstanding. Cicero had defined *sciographiam* as a shaded sketch, and

6.6 Frontal elevation of the Holy of Holies, from Villalpando's *In Ezechielem* …

while these drawings may be useful to painters, their lack of precision makes them useless for architects. Perspective, on the other hand, presents all parts of the building through a graphic assembly of lines and angles, "even though all the lines may converge at a point." Perspective is relevant because it shows how the building's "façade and its sides appear as if presented to a single vision,"[10] as may be evident when the building is finished. Unlike painting, it uses lines and shadows, not colours or renderings of materials. Villalpando also insists that the plan and the elevation belong to "optics" because they are merely particular cases of perspective.

This signals a radical change in the history of architectural "ideas" – a change that would not become clear until a century later, in the works of another Jesuit, the painter and cook Andrea Pozzo.[11] Villalpando calls all Vitruvian ideas "perspectives" because they must maintain the same proportions (in scale) as the intended object of design, following the principle of sectioning the cone of vision. Despite his polemical position, he acknowledges that Vitruvius himself might not have agreed

ISPECTVS TESTVDINIS WERARII ET PAVIMENTI SANCTI SANCTORVM ATQVE ARCA TESTAMENTI CVM CHERVBIN

6.7 Interior perspective
of the Holy of Holies,
from *In Ezechielem ...*

with this interpretation, because Vitruvius assumed that optics has
nothing to do with drawings.[12] Villalpando, however, believes that
optics and drawing are related by means of a "practical optics," that is,
perspectiva artificialis.[13]

Nevertheless, all this is not free from ambiguity. Although Villalpando's words seem to anticipate that most seventeenth- and eighteenth-
century reconstructions of the Temple would include aerial perspectives,
he confesses that he could not draw a full perspective of the Temple
because the task was too complex. The only perspective among the
Villalpando plates is the interior of the *Sancta Sanctorum*, the Holy of
Holies, shown as a mysterious space of uncertain depth, both limited
and limitless, containing the Ark of the Covenant symmetrically flanked
by cherubim. This depiction, as I will elaborate, is consistent with
Villalpando's description of the ambivalent dimensionality of this most
sacred space. Furthermore, while perspective is useful "to observe the
regularity and distribution [of a building] and to propose it to the critical
eyes of others," it is *not* adequate to determine the proportion of the

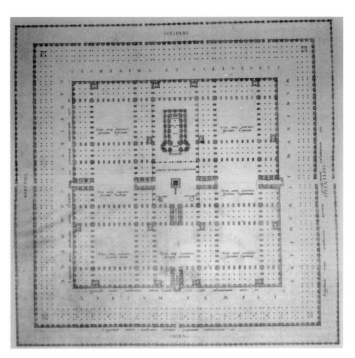

6.8 Plan of Villalpando's reconstruction of Solomon's Temple based on Ezekiel's prophecy.

whole work and its parts because "as the lines become more distant ... they concentrate on one point."[14] Indeed, in Villalpando's depiction of the Temple's site, the building is presented not in perspective but as a frontal isometric projection that barely distorts its geometry and clearly discloses the "symmetry" and regularity of the plan. Perspective, he adds, can cause misunderstandings for those who execute the building, while plan and elevation "were invented so that any craftsman may compare any part of the building to the whole." It is crucial that buildings derive their measures from a model, "in Hebrew *tchachennith*," a model from which the dimensions of all parts of the future building may be clearly taken. Therefore, it is necessary to use a "new part" of optics in architecture, that which "studies the whole through parallel lines."[15]

This fascinating argument marks the beginning of a modern confusion between orthogonal drawings – *ichnographia* and *orthographia*, traditionally understood as physical traces – and parallel projections, seen by Villalpando as a "new kind" of perspective. However, Villalpando's parallel projections do not depend on a point at infinity *in* the world. To

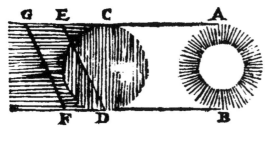

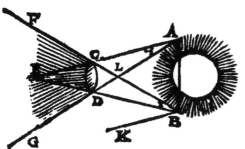

6.9 Diagrams illustrating Villalpando's speculations about perspective in relation to the projection of light and the consequences of parallel rays.

explain his "new optics" he draws at length from phenomena of light projection. He devotes many pages to comparing extromission and intromission theories, unconvinced by the simple notion that light travels in straight lines.[16] He concludes that these theories appear true only in two dimensions, because real light is "diffused everywhere around, like a corporeal sphere in three dimensions." He traces this position back to Aristotle and maintains that it is true not because light is a physical body, as some authors have mistakenly believed, but because light is received through the whole length, breadth, and depth of the medium, not on an abstract point, line, or surface. Villalpando could not conceive of vision as a mechanistic, merely passive phenomenon (as we might imagine, using Johannes Kepler's analogy of the *camera obscura*). For Villalpando, the sense of sight and the meanings it conveys in perception are simply not autonomous from the other senses. "This [however] does not impede our consideration of a pyramid from any point of the medium ..."[17] He then explains that, if an opaque body is larger than the light source, the shadows would be cast in a pyramid that increases in size; and vice versa: if the source of light is larger than the object, the shadows would reduce in size. Only if the source is the same size as the object would the lines remain parallel. Following this example of light, we can therefore imagine that parallel projections in architecture imply an eye of the same size as the object being examined (or designed).[18]

Villalpando insists that we should understand plans and elevations as sections cut through the cone of vision. Vertical sections, such as Barbaro's *profilo*, are merely a variation of elevations. The unstated model for parallel projection, however, is light from the sun, the light of God: a light that is immaterial yet present everywhere in our tactile lived space, literally making the human world possible (intelligible) and therefore infinitely close rather than infinitely distant. The identification of God, and even Christ, with the sun was a popular theme in late-Renaissance hermetic writings, which were obviously well known to Villalpando. For him, plans and elevations are analogous to perspectives because we can see like God; we can visualize the truth of the Scriptures, but infinity is an otherworldly property. The plans and elevations of the Temple of Jerusalem are given as a "model" because it appeared to Ezekiel in the light of God. Thus, Villalpando insists, we must understand Vitruvius's *ichnographia* and *orthographia* as miniaturized (scale) drawings. He argues that the Greek term for plan, "from ιχηνς (plan) and γραφια (drawing or description)," explains its nature better than the Latin *vestigium* (a trace). While he recognized the affinity between the plan (*planta* in Spanish) and the sole of the foot (*planta del pié*), he still defined the plan as "a common section of a plane parallel to the pavement," like the shadow and light projected by a "small building" (a model) onto a surface. Villalpando then acknowledged the difficulties of drawing details projecting over a plan, which in the case of the Temple were "also measured by the angel."[19] He recommends drawing only one *ichnographia* that includes plans of all levels drawn in different colours to avoid terrible and potentially dangerous mistakes.

In retrospect we can recognize the affinity between Villalpando's understanding of architectural representation and the systematic use of projections as a paradigmatic modern tool of reductive design.[20] Yet the theological motivations behind Villalpando's understanding of architectural representation are striking. The issue for him certainly was not to usurp God's place but to realize human works in God's light and vision. His depiction of the Temple, a true "visual theology," is imagined as God's own vision in the context of Jesuit practices of visualization: a projective vision involving not distorted images but rather precise plans and elevations that the architect might share as a point of departure for his own ideas. This amounted to a "divinization" of the architect, following the medieval model of the Augustinian Creator-Architect. At the same time it signalled a potentially modern intentionality; once this architect's status was accepted but secularized, it would transform the traditional nature of architectural theory and practice.

A crucial discussion that fills many pages of Book Five concerns the meaning of the Temple in the Holy Scriptures and its glorious material realization. Judeo-Christian beliefs traditionally had been divided on the importance (and even the very possibility) of building the house of God on earth – an issue of great consequence for all human constructive activities. Clearly there were distinctions between the aims of the institutional church founded by Saint Peter, embodied in the late Roman tradition, its buildings, and political hierarchies, and the church of pilgrimage represented by Saint Paul, the church of the desert, and Saint Francis, with its roots in the Jewish exodus from Egypt and the old prohibition against making graven images. Villalpando's analysis of the meaning of "temple," both in Latin and in Hebrew, implied a possible reconciliation of this dilemma through the archetype itself and through the earthly manifestation of Heavenly Jerusalem. In Latin, *templum* is related to contemplation (rather than building), to the human capacity of understanding, through vision, the order of the world. Villalpando argues that *tueri* implies both the vision required for contemplation and the physical protection from a threatening climate (*tempus-temperatura*) that makes such human understanding possible. In Hebrew, on the other hand, the word for temple (*hahecal*) was connected to several related words: walking forward or marching (*halach*), the road leading to the temple (*halic*), the sanctuary itself (*hacal*), and its entrance or threshold (*hecal*). Is it possible to recognize in this discussion a desire to present the Temple, that most holy of concrete presences, as the embodiment of its absence? The temple as pilgrimage? This may be a key to uncover both the difficulties and the ethical possibilities involved in the materialization of an ideal order. Beyond Villalpando's obvious religious and political agenda (the Catholic Counter-Reformation and its practice of persuading through the senses), this ethical question still looms large in discussions of the mysterious origins of technology.

Indeed, the whole of Book Five is devoted to praising the material glory of the Temple while also describing the invisible structure that reveals it as a syncretic model of order, as a mimesis of the cosmos. In the wake of the Renaissance it was no longer enough to prove (as Villalpando thought he had) that this architecture was in total agreement with the Scriptures. For Herrera's and Villalpando's work to be significant (that is, appropriate and ethical) it had to represent an order that effectively "stood for all," particularly in the wake of the European religious wars – an order that was *mythical* and could be accepted as primordial, rather than appearing as the result of rational or dogmatic argumentation.

Thus, Villalpando sought to align this "revealed" architecture with the cosmological order in the philosophical and occult speculations of that time, particularly the astrological order.[21] He maintains that sacred architecture constitutes the true origin of all architecture, and that the profane architecture of which Vitruvius spoke is merely a copy or shadow of the sacred. According to Villalpando, no one had extracted the rules of architecture from the Holy Scriptures, although it is likely that Vitruvius (and the Romans) may have learned all about architecture from the Temple of Jerusalem. Although he is focusing on only this one building, he argues that some norms surely can be extracted from it because it is "the only site consecrated to God." He then emphasizes that his norms coincide with those of Vitruvius, just as the Vitruvian concepts of measurement and proportion relate to the concept of order in Hebrew: *tachnith* (to measure) derives from *thacan* (to place in order), and *thacan* is always according to number, weight, and measure.[22] Solomon himself applied the "symmetry" of the Temple in his wise deeds and used it for other building projects such as his own palace, the famous hall of justice that according to Villalpanlo, provided the rules for Roman (and eventually Christian) basilicas.[23]

In a similar vein, Villalpando discusses the tools and units of measurement cited in Ezekiel's prophecy, metaphorically building the church with the "live stones" which are the faithful.[24] He reconciles the apparently incongruous measurements with the use of the "cord" (for foundations and thickness of walls) and the "cane" (for all external measurements). His greatest concern is the precise length in cubits of the cane, and he concludes that this unit (six cubits plus one-quarter cubit or four fingers) was invented by God to measure the Temple and therefore is the module of the building, in the sense of Vitruvius, assuring the perfect coherence among all the parts and the whole. Villalpando then examines two opposed connotations of the "cord" or line (snap-line, ruler, plumb-line,

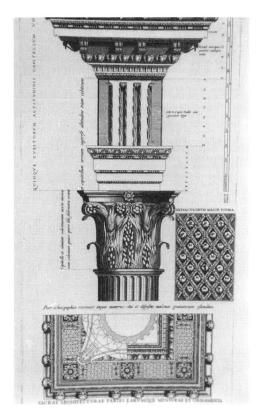

6.10 The primal order of Solomon's Temple, from Villalpando's *In Ezechielem* …

and so on) in the Bible, revealing both the constructive and the destructive potential of the geometry of architecture and its instruments. The Hebrew word is *cau*, and the Lord states that His house shall be built on it after He had extended the "cord" upon Jerusalem. Also, when the Lord punishes, Villalpando adds, He extends His "line" (of justice and right judgment) in order to destroy.

In Book Five the details of the Temple's architecture are described in a narrative that argues for the origin of the classical orders of columns (the Doric, Ionic, and Corinthian) in the Temple itself, all derived from one primal architectural order.[25] Villalpando claimed that the description of triglyphs in Vitruvius's treatise should have referred to Solomon's Temple rather than to the architecture of the Greeks, because only in the Temple were they proportioned correctly. For Villalpando, the incorporation of triglyphs in this primordial order is truly important, and it is tempting to speculate that this emphasis on "tri-glyphs" and their mysterious origin may be due to their potential symbolic prefiguration of the Holy Trinity. Regardless, Vitruvius indeed had considered the triglyph as a problematic detail in classical architecture, and Villalpando speculates that this lack of understanding led Vitruvius to disregard Solomon's Temple as the origin of his own norms. Similarly, Villalpando argues that the Corinthian order originated in the capitals of Solomon's Temple, exchanging acanthus for palm leaves in the classical fable of the Corinthian virgin.[26] Villalpando's narrative of origins was evidently a convenient argument for the Counter-Reformation, with its deep-seated suspicion of pagan classical themes.

According to Villalpando, God Himself made the drawings for the first Temple and gave them to David, who in turn passed the design down to Solomon. These drawings are sacred, just like God's handwriting imprinted upon Moses's Tablets of the Law.[27] Villalpando explains that while Hiram was the Master Builder, Christ, the son of God, was the true architect, because Christ is the foundation and cornerstone of the Temple, responsible through his Incarnation for accomplishing its truth.[28] Proportions are all-important because they relate the Temple to the Tabernacle, to the world, to the human body, and to Christ's church. The Temple's divine cubic architecture establishes analogies among musical and Pythagorean harmonies, astrology, Biblical symbolism and numerology, the theory of the Aristotelian elements, and the bodily humours. Through its cosmic links, this building could act as a powerful talisman, making concrete man's God-given powers as a magician. Harmony, however, could be perceived only through the senses, through reason enlightened by Divine Wisdom, both "praying with humility and tears," and by means of a Solomonic Divine Wisdom that Villalpando explicitly identifies with Vitruvius's theory (that is, "the ability to explain by reason the perfection of things realized"). Of course, this wisdom is analogical, never instrumental. The Tabernacle is identified as the "type" that God imitated in designing the Temple. In fact, argues Villalpando, God drew the Tabernacle first. Throughout his treatise he has been describing the Temple's body, but it is now time to describe its invisible "soul": the Tabernacle *as* world, and the universe *as* man; the Temple *as* the Heavens and God's throne, and the Heavens *as* the Tabernacle.[29]

Villalpando regarded the Tabernacle in the desert as a "preliminary sketch" for the Temple. The verb *ahal* in Hebrew, meaning "to camp, to set a tent," is related to *ohel*, the Tabernacle and also the gateway to the Temple, a lintel or curtain.[30] The disposition of the camp for Israel's

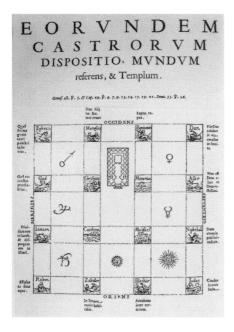

6.11 The twelve tribes of Israel camped around the Tabernacle, and the same astrological order embodied in the plan of the Temple of Solomon, from Villalpando's *In Ezechielem* ...

twelve tribes around the Tabernacle was like a primitive schema for the Temple's courtyards. Villalpando pays special attention to the banners of the tribes, especially those at the corners, and describes their emblems and corresponding precious stones. Like the edifice of the world itself,[31] this constituted a perfect plan that was related to the four elements, the four humours of the body responsible for health and passion, the celestial orbits of the visible planets, "Christ the true Sun and the seven lamps of His grace,"[32] and the twelve signs of the zodiac. In the design of the Temple, Solomon followed the same scheme, doubling the original dimensions and using more permanent materials to build "outside this frame, outside this circle ... fortifications for each tribe." The height of the Temple, according to Villalpando, is the diameter of the celestial orbit. The Temple literally "squares" the circle and "demonstrates" how these two primordial geometric figures are reconciled. From this act alone, "it is clear that this is the House of the Lord, containing it all and yet having its contents not limited by anything."[33] Not surprisingly, Villalpando had declared that the cubic Holy of Holies (whose internal space is depicted in the only perspective drawing in the treatise, and which measured 20×20×20 cubits, a most appropriate number to represent the Heavens, according to Saint Ambrose) had no windows, although he had drawn them in plan to show architects that their exclusion was due not to structural necessity but to the sacredness of the space.[34] Villalpando identifies this cube with "the New City that St. John Evangelist saw descend from Heaven, whose length, width and height are the same."[35]

Thus, Villalpando thoroughly incorporated Vitruvian theory, its interest in proportions and astrobiological framework, syncretically reconciling it with minute biblical exegesis. This led him to an understanding of the classical style of the Temple as "type" (a prefiguration in the Biblical sense), repeated in ancient classical architecture and its five orders, and all synthesized in view of the ultimate task of man: to build an architecture *as* the mystical body of Christ. Indeed, the Temple comprises not only the first Israelite encampment but also the Catholic Church. Villalpando relates numerology to program: "The Temple was realized by taking into account the structure, customs, and obligations of man." Numbers are also read as "anticipations" of Christian attributes. Solomon's Temple, argues Villalpando, is already the real church, founded upon holy laws by the same God, though it was only later that "He took on the appearance of man." Villalpando then relates God's human appearance (as Christ) to the importance of human proportions and their correspondence in architecture. After discussing the Christian significance of the Temple's module (the cane), Villalpando reiterates his argument: "Christ the Lord is represented by means of the Temple's whole edifice ... God's will decided that the building is Christ's body to be contemplated by all."[36]

The significance of this assertive, almost literal identification cannot be overemphasized. Christian tradition was responsible for legitimizing the manifestation of the ideal *as* real, through its incarnation of God in human life, death, and bodily resurrection. This amounted to a "Platonic" inversion of the truth of reality as given in human experience, a truth that Plato himself never could have imagined but that became the fundamental assumption underlying the new science of Galileo (with its roots in the Jesuit Roman College) and our technological world. Villalpando discusses the important biblical episode in which Christ rises against the Temple, and concludes that what He wanted to show was precisely that His body *was* the Temple. Although the Temple was made by man, it offers the body of Christ "spontaneously ... in all its parts and proportions." A prefiguration of Christ may be recognized in its parts, such as "the stone discarded by the builders which became the keystone (*piedra angular*)." Referring to a biblical passage, he interprets this "angular stone" as a *unique* and *triangular* tympanum that crowned and joined the two side walls of the Holy of Holies. We may recall here that, just as the squaring of the circle was a popular problem in alchemy, signifying the reconciliation of opposites, the term "angular stone" was often used as a synonym for the philosopher's stone. Furthermore, the image of Christ on the cross can be imagined as the plan of the Temple, His head corresponding to the Holy of Holies and His hands and feet to the gateways, and the cruel nails of love that perforate His extremities providing access to the Father for all the faithful.

Having "demonstrated" the continuity and essential oneness of the Jewish Temple and the Catholic Church, Villalpando devotes almost a hundred pages at the end of his treatise to the immense resources and wealth of the Temple. Comparing the Temple to the other "great marvels" of the ancient world, he demonstrates its unquestionable superiority in size, luxury, and magnificence. This glory, he insists, was due mainly to Christ's presence, which enabled the Temple to surpass its previous physical and temporal fame.

THE SEQUEL

The Jesuit reconstruction of the Temple had obvious political implications. At stake was the possibility of a Christian architecture in a "modern" world with a living classical tradition. It is not surprising that Villalpando's enterprise had to overcome various difficulties, including theological objections and serious financial limitations. Villalpando had arrived in Rome in 1590 and Jerónimo Prado was appointed in 1592 to collaborate with him. Prado's contribution to the project, which is in many ways a dissenting text, has been recently located in the Houghton Library of Harvard University.[37] One can only speculate whether Prado's appointment was motivated by the enormity of the task or by alarm from the religious hierarchy concerning some of Villalpando's conclusions. The two men previously had collaborated on a preliminary interpretation of Ezekiel's text, but in Rome they had serious disagreements. Prado wanted to censor some of the more speculative sections and wished to change the designs that had been approved already by Philip II. The two men could never agree on the definition of their particular writing assignments. Prado died in 1595, having signed only the first volume of the *Commentaries*, which is of little interest beyond strictly theological matters. Thus, Villalpando was set free to write his treatise and add his speculative appendices, which appeared as the second and third volumes of the collaborative project.

Prado's manuscript, prepared for the King of Spain around 1593–94, enables us to compare his ideas with those of Villalpando. The two Jesuits assumed a fundamental identity between the temple described by Ezekiel and the Temple of Solomon. Perhaps more important for architecture, both believed in connections between the Temple and the Vitruvian classical tradition. Prado, however, certainly would have avoided the mythical and magical themes, and possibly the literal identification of the Temple with its powerful manifestation in the Escorial.

Following Jerónimo Prado's careful exegetic practice, Benito Arias Montano was perhaps the most significant contemporary opponent of Villalpando's reconstruction. Also an exegete by profession, Montano questioned Villalpando's cosmobiological framework, insisting instead on a more careful consideration of other biblical buildings such as Noah's Ark and the Tabernacle of Moses, which he saw as archetypes in a genealogy culminating in the Temple.[38] Although Montano's own reconstruction is hardly archaeological and draws heavily from Spanish Mannerist architecture, his more "historical" attitude is indeed different from Villalpando's, and it became the dominant framework for seventeenth-century writers who were interested in this problem. Avoiding Ezekiel's description precisely because it was merely a prophecy, he tried to grasp the reality of the first Temple, acknowledging that it had suffered alterations and speculating that Herod's temple probably had been more luxurious than the original structure by Solomon. Particularly poignant is Montano's drawing of the plan of Noah's Ark (the first building in the sacred genealogy) in the form of a coffin containing the dead body of Christ, from which sacred proportions could be generated. This is radically different from Villalpando's Vitruvian man and his syncretic, Renaissance vision. Like Hans Holbein's painting showing Christ entombed as a decaying cadaver prior to resurrection, Montano seems to emphasize God's mortality. The authority based exclusively on the physical proportions of a mortal Christ is of a different order than the syncretic harmony and numerology which, though manifested by Christ, were still assumed by Villalpando to have been dictated by the

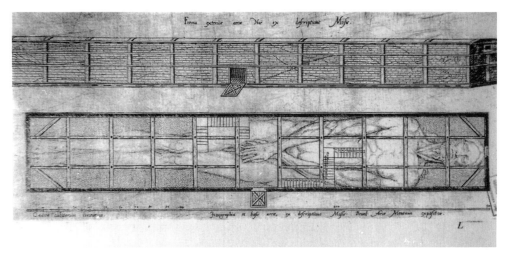

6.12 Plan and elevation of Noah's Ark by Benito Arias Montano (1571–72).

remote, disembodied eternal Creator. Montano's Temple is not a perfect geometry, and this profoundly disturbed Villalpando. The lateral walls of the courtyard around the Holy of Holies converge slightly, suggesting a Baroque awareness of disjunction between "presence" and "appearance" and a desire to make the Temple appear more vast than its "true" dimensions. This modern disjunction was alien to Villalpando's concept of Divine architecture.[39]

Juan Caramuel de Lobkowitz (1606–82), the most distinguished Spanish successor to Villalpando in the field of architectural theory, also engaged in a polemic with him regarding the Temple. Caramuel was a polymath and prolific writer whose *Arquitectura Civil Recta y Oblicua*, "drawn from the Temple of Jerusalem ... [and promoting] its ultimate perfection in the Temple and Palace of the Escorial" (1678), was the only explicitly architectural treatise to include the Temple as a model. Temple reconstructions usually were autonomous or were contained within theological writings. Caramuel's openness to invention and his questioning of Vitruvius's authority were legitimized by a genealogical understanding of architecture originating with the Temple. Adopting some of Montano's critical premises, he used Jacob Jude Leon's reconstruction as a point of departure, arguing for the greater legitimacy of a rabbinical version. Leon's "Jewish" reconstruction, an asymmetrical variation on Villalpando's, is perhaps no more than a convenient metaphor for

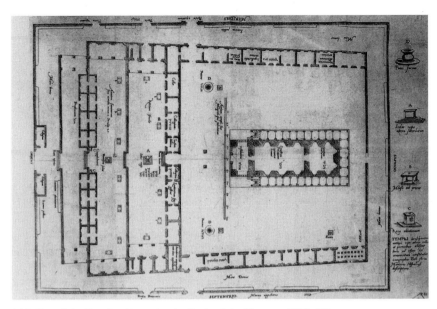

6.13 Plan of the Temple of Jerusalem by Benito Arias Montano (1571–72).

Caramuel's argumentation in favour of oblique architecture. Indeed, although Caramuel bases his whole argument about oblique architecture on its origin in the Temple (Ezekiel twice mentions the Temple's "oblique" windows), his complex genealogy of the problem never discusses the building as a whole. On the other hand, Caramuel takes great care to describe the "true" history of the Jewish temple, differentiating between the first Temple of Solomon and later reconstructions, and placing these monuments in the context of the great architectural marvels of the ancient and the modern world. This is indeed the first architectural treatise in which the "history of architecture" plays such a significant role. The dispersion of Babel, represented by the multiplicity of artefacts (and languages) in our tradition, was recognized as a fundamental problem in the seventeenth century, especially after the Reformation. A resolution to the dilemma (the reconstitution of a universal language) nevertheless was considered possible; it was to be achieved by relying on a genealogical enterprise with an allegorical dimension rather than on a belief in cosmological unity that is directly accessible. According to Caramuel, if "oblique" architecture was arguably superior to "straight" (Vitruvian) architecture, this was because God had created the world obliquely (the mountains, the orbits of the planets, and so on). Caramuel finds evidence of this obliquity in the details of the Temple and its "mythistory." Like Descartes and Perrault, he rejects the absolute value

LAMINA·A·

TEMPLI HIEROSOLYMITANI ACCVRATA DESCRIPTIO

6.14 View of the Temple of Solomon, from Juan Caramuel de Lobkowitz *Arquitectura Civil ...* (1678)

of authority and even recognizes that the architecture of the Temple, "from a different time and place," cannot be applied directly to the present. Yet his confidence in the theological guarantee of purpose, and in the possible recovery of a cabalistic mathematical discipline, allows him to present his argument as the truth of architecture and a sure guide to practice.[40]

Claude Perrault's reconstruction (1678), based on Maimonides, is the first to reproduce a historical Jewish "style" in its elevations, rather than simply relying on contemporary design practices. This attitude may have been motivated by Perrault's dislike of Villalpando's reconstruction and also by the French architect's Jansenist leanings, which are closer to Protestantism than to Catholicism. Despite these connections, Perrault never rejected his Catholic background. A much larger issue is involved in his proposal. This first archeological attempt to reconstruct the Temple is deliberately *independent* of theological preferences, in line with Perrault's proto-positivistic understanding of science and architecture. Perrault indeed was the first architectural writer to question the inveterate proportional relationship between macrocosmos and microcosmos,

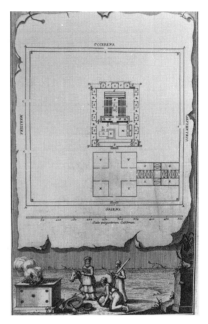

6.15 Plan, section, and elevation of the Temple of Solomon by Claude Perrault, based on Maimonides's medieval reconstruction (from *De Culto Divino*, 1678).

and to regard theory as a book of recipes whose sole purpose was an efficient practice.[41]

Isaac Newton's reconstruction of the Temple, driven by mystic and religious speculations, also aims to show a coherence between the Old and New Testaments. Newton, however, disagrees with Villalpando and ignores Vitruvius. He believes that the tradition of the Temple is exclusively Judeo-Christian. Nevertheless, his reconstruction assumes a cosmological order that would not have displeased Villalpando. This "conservative" aspect of Newton's epistemology is consistent with the metaphysics and theology that implicitly underlie his natural philosophy. Newton's obsession with singular and self-evident explanations is especially evident in his physics. His postulation of the absolute space of universal gravitation and its identification with God probably derived from Jewish medieval sources. The unity of historical traditions, together with the unity of rational Nature, was crucial for Newton and for eighteenth-century art and architectural theory. It also plays an important role in the historical legitimation of Freemasonry, whose affinity with Newton's deism has often been pointed out. The survival of the

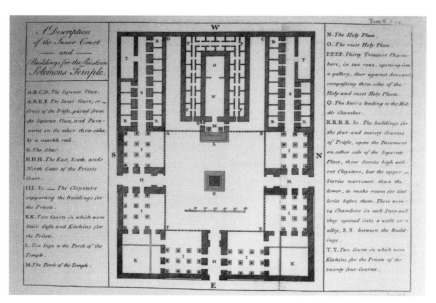

6.16 Plan of Sir Isaac Newton's reconstruction of the Temple of Solomon, published posthumously in 1728.

Temple archetype in masonic initiation rituals is well documented, as is the masonic association of many eighteenth- and nineteenth-century European architects.

Today we know more about the archeological reality of biblical buildings, their topographical location, possible formal features, and so on. Since the nineteenth century, attempts have been made to "reconstruct" the Temple using "scientific," archaeological methods.[42] Nevertheless, even the so-called Temple or Wailing Wall in modern Jerusalem is not a factual fragment of the ancient building. It is a political construction, a symbolic ruin that serves to "found" the modern state of Israel and ironically reminds us of the Diaspora. From our historic vantage point, we can distinguish among the first Temple (by Solomon), the legitimizing role of the Tabernacle of Moses, the particularities of Ezekiel's vision, the less important second Temple (after the Babylonian exile), and Herod's modification of the Temple – all within the social and political reality of ancient Judea and Israel – yet our "reconstructions" not only remain conjectural and politically biased but are fundamentally lacking in imagination.

As mortals, we remain pilgrims in the desert who belong to the earth rather than own the world. How should we build in order to dwell?

Reconstructing the temple is always a founding project, one that should concern every architect. Even though contemporary culture is not homogeneous and operates outside the linear genealogy of the Judeo-Christian tradition, the fundamental questions that we must address as human beings remain forever present. Architects today seldom have the courrage to engage these issues through programs that may acknowledge the same questions translated into contemporary concerns. In this light, Villalpando's carefully crafted reconstruction of the Temple appears not merely as an arrogant and "imaginary deception" intended to demonstrate the absolute Catholic truth amidst the polemical context of the Counter-Reformation. The current premise that architecture is merely an act of political "clarification" for a social "reality" begs the question of what role is played by the personal imagination of the architect – a role that has been so crucial in traditional works yet one that our political wisdom often characterizes as fraudulent. Is not this imaginative faculty the very vehicle by which an ethical dimension might occupy an intersubjective (political) space in architectural practice? A deterministic premise would negate the importance of this dimension, which is where I believe the specificity of architecture is located. In other words, for a historicist reading, the distinction between the Temple of Jerusalem (as the archetype of a *techné* of reconciliation) and the Tower of Babel (as a *techné* of arrogance and domination) is a mere delusion; both have the *same* status as architecture as long as they embody the "real" order of society. Despite, or rather because of, the abominations that have issued from technology during our century, a reality made possible in the first instance by the theological assumptions of modern Christianity, cultivating our ability to perceive such differences is paramount. While redemption, as promised by the vision of the Temple, is an unfashionable word, perhaps an impossibility, an architecture practised in view of this difference, one that does not simply correspond to a dogmatic distinction between absolute "good" and "evil," is perhaps our only alternative if we want to operate *through* technology rather than be led into a nostalgic impasse under the pretense of "popular taste" or "political correctness." While we should question the modernist obsession to actualize utopia at "the end of progress," we must nevertheless embrace a utopic vector as the construing of "possible realities," the vector of the imagination that may allow our culture (and its architecture) to survive the present epoch of nihilism.

NOTES

1 Juan Bautista Villalpando, *In Ezechielem explanationes et apparatus urbi ac templi hierosolymitani* (Rome, 1596 and 1604). I have used the first unabridged Spanish translation of José Luis Oliver Domingo published under the title *Dios, arquitecto. J. B. Villalpando y el Templo de Salomón*. This is a three-volume set, including forty-eight facsimile illustrations, of which twenty fold out. Volume One, *El Templo de Salomón según Juan Bautista Villalpando*, contains the vast text by Villalpando, which is the primary source for this article, and the graphic reconstruction of Solomon's Temple. Volume Two includes Jerónimo de Prado's unpublished manuscript, *Compendio de la segunda parte de los comentarios del profeta Ezekiel* (c. 1593). A collection of essays entitled *Dios Arquitecto*, edited by Juan Antonio Ramírez, includes articles by himself, André Corboz, René Taylor, Antonio Martínez Ripoll, and Robert Jan van Pelt, and is included as a separate volume (Madrid: Ediciones Siruela 1991).

2 The relationship of Villalpando's reconstruction to the Escorial is described extensively by René Taylor in his essay "Architecture and Magic," in the Festschrift collection *Essays in Honour of Rudolph Wittkower* (London: Phaidon 1973).

3 Villalpando, *In Ezechielem* ..., 12. This point is discussed extensively in the "Fourth Debate" of Book Five, 468.

4 Ibid., 38.

5 Ibid., 50.

6 Ibid., 54.

7 Ibid., 56. Villalpando says that the building is "*algo fáctico.*"

8 Ibid., 58.

9 While Barbaro still tried to differentiate between optics (*perspectiva naturalis*) and geometrical perspective (*perspectiva artificialis*), discussing their potential consequences for architecture, Villalpando assumed "optics" to be a synonym of geometrical perspective. See Alberto Pérez-Gómez and Louise Pelletier, *Architectural Representation and the Perspective Hinge* (Cambridge, Mass.: MIT Press 1997).

10 *In Ezechielem...*, 76.

11 In his *Perspectiva Pictorum et Architectorum* (Rome, 1693–98) Pozzo established the homology between perspective and painting. See A. Pérez-Gómez and L. Pelletier, "Architectural Representation in the Age of Simulation," in *Perspecta* 27 (1994): 20–39.

12 Indeed, in Vitruvius's *Ten Books* optics concerns the correction of proportions in buildings and issues of light and orientation drawn from the heavenly bodies.

13 Villalpando, *In Ezechielem ...*, 75.

14 Ibid., 77. Emphasis added.

15 Ibid.

16 Ibid., 62.

17 Ibid.

18 Ibid., 77.

19 Ibid., 80.

20 This could happen only after perspective theory and philosophy could assume that infinity exists *in* the world, while human action, in the form of modern technology, came to be in a position to "corroborate" this assumption. These transformations, which took place between the mid seventeenth and the early nineteenth century, are examined in A. Pérez-Gómez and L. Pelletier, *Architectural Representation and the Perspective Hinge*.

21 The symbolism of Villalpando's Temple is described in detail by René Taylor in his article "Juan Bautista Villalpando y Jerónimo Prado: De la Arquitectura Práctica a la Reconstrucción Mística," in Juan Antonio Ramírez, ed., *Dios, Arquitecto*, 153ff.

22 Villalpando, *In Ezechielem ...*, 351.

23 Ibid., 361

24 Ibid., 101.

25 Ibid., 348.

26 Ibid., 382.

27 This theological priority of the graphic sign is also prophetic of things to come, from technology to literary deconstruction.

28 *In Ezechielem ...*, 389–90.

29 Ibid., 392–3.

30 Ibid., 204–5.

31 Ibid., 393–5.

32 Ibid., 397–8.

33 This geometrical/alchemical problem has been a concern of artists, philosophers, and architects since its first rational formulation following the inception of Euclidean geometry. Not until the nineteenth century was the irrational nature of π generally accepted. The problem symbolized the desire to reconcile fundamental dualities of human experience (male/female, earth/sky, and so on) into a unity.

34 Villalpando, *In Ezechielem* ..., 248–51.

35 Ibid. 403.

36 Ibid. 401–2.

37 The Prado manuscript has been published as a second volume in the Spanish translation of the work. See note 1.

38 See Antonio Martinez Ripoll, "Del Arca al Templo. La Cadena Ejemplar de Prototipos Sagrados de B. Arias Montano," in *Dios Arquitecto*, 87–9.

39 In this sense, Montano's project may question the utopian imperative that drives our incomplete post-urban "paradise," itself a projection of the messianic expectations associated with the Heavenly Jerusalem.

40 For a more extensive discussion of Caramuel's architectural theories, see A. Pérez-Gómez and L. Pelletier, *Architectural Representation*.

41 See A. Pérez-Gómez's introduction, to Claude Perrault's *Ordonnance for the Five Kinds of Columns after the Method of the Ancients* (Santa Monica, Calif.: The Getty Center for the History of Art and the Humanities 1993). Perrault's radical "archaeological" attitude may be better grasped by comparing his reconstruction with the Protestant versions of Coccejus and Johannes Lund. Starting like Perrault from a disagreement with Villalpando and an examination of alternative Jewish sources, Coccejus and Lund propose familiar visions for Protestant spaces of worship. See *Dios, Arquitecto*, 105, 131.

42 An interesting early attempt in this direction is the work of André Perrot and Charles Chipiez, who collaborated between 1882 and 1914 in the production of a massive ten-volume *Histoire de l'art dans l'antiquité* (Paris: Hachette 1889). Although their approach was explicitly positivistic, they focused on Ezekiel's vision rather than on the first Temple and argued that the building effectively built by Solomon was not important and that its real physical configuration remains unknown.

Fragmentation, Improvisation, and Urban Quality: A Heterotopian Motif in Siegfried Kracauer

Henrik Reeh

Chora

INTRODUCTION

Towards the end of the second millennium, the issue of whether fragmentation is part of modernity is no longer in dispute. In many spheres
of human endeavour and perception, phenomena linked with fragmentation express a general diversification in social and cultural life. One
only has to think of the social division of labour which has distanced
architecture from engineering, and both of these professions from urban
studies in the social sciences as well as in the humanities. Furthermore,
fragmentation has had profound spatial consequences, since privately
owned parcels of space are used for construction rather independently
of one another. In this way, disintegration – but also a certain heterogeneity – has come to characterize modern landscapes and cityscapes.
Finally, fragmentation remains a fundamental force in the electronic
media that give our informational reality such an ephemeral shape. One
could continue to enumerate such fragmentations in everyday life, many
of which are perceived as nuisances.

Given a budding millenarianism and this fragmented state of the
modern life-world, it might not be surprising that internal crises involving theoretical concepts and human values may be traced back to some
sort of fragmentation as well. Since roughly the late 1970s, critical
intellectuals have been troubled by painful doubt that the totality of
social life can be grasped by one general theory or analysis. Yet this
tendency has been present in writing on epistemological and historical-
philosophical questions for at least the past two centuries.

However catastrophic some of its appearances, the *formal* principle
of fragmentation certainly should not be considered an unambiguous
threat to human life and thinking. Fragmentation indeed may dissolve
certain forms of social, spatial, and mental coherence, but it also facili-
tates the emergence of new patterns of life that are as contradictory and
ambiguous as development in capitalist modernity. It would therefore be
false to presuppose a general contradiction between fragmentation and
quality[1] in modern life.

Instead, fragmentation needs to be understood as a formal feature with
a variety of meanings and qualities. This explains why the composite
theme of "fragmentation" can summarize an unavoidable condition of
social and cultural activity. Even when perceived as a source of incon-
venience, fragmentation is an aspect of social reality that imposes itself

7.1 Barcelona, 1993. All photographs by the author.

on anyone wishing to intervene in cultural and economic life. To put it prescriptively, fragmentation should be addressed as a challenge to cultural speculation and practice. Although the concept of "quality," for example, may seem undermined in certain respects by the crisis in the former master narratives of architecture and social theory, the fragmented world that is made responsible for this development should be described and investigated both spatially and socially before ultimately abandoning – or renewing – hope of finding a reservoir for artistic creativity and intellectual normativeness.

An approach to fragmented modernity that is experimental, literary, and also theoretical can be observed in Siegfried Kracauer's urban essays. Originally an architect with interests in anonymous architecture and in sociology, Kracauer turned to social-philosophical journalism in the early 1920s. Among his nearly 2000 articles from the inter-war period, his numerous writings on urban culture – especially when he was a cultural editor of an influential German newspaper, the *Frankfurter Zeitung* – reveal a surprisingly coherent attempt to come to grips with the evasive social-cultural universe of the modern city. Kracauer's experiments with diverse genres such as the novel, the newspaper essay, and the cultural-historical monograph represent progressive elaborations of a major intellectual project involving modern urbanity. The central element of Kracauer's analytic work is his attempt to transform objectified *space* into mental and social *place* by means of literary, sociological, and philosophical interpretations. It is remarkable that Kracauer's inter-war writing on cities never views urban architecture as an ensemble of beautiful forms. Instead, it proclaims that the quality of architectural space depends on its capacity to be transformed by the ever particular and hazardous process of subjective reappropriation.

Moreover, Kracauer's shifting interpretations of the fragmented city may be considered a long chain of variations on the concept of ornament.[2] Opposed to the general repression of ornament in the Modern Movement of architecture (beginning with Adolf Loos's 1908 essay, "Ornament and Crime"), Kracauer values ornament as a common denominator for a kind of spatial experience which goes far beyond the three-dimensional paradigm prevalent in modern discourses on architecture. Because of his preoccupation with the rich world of ornament, Kracauer focuses on aspects of spatial perception and imagination that are non-utilitarian and mainly two-dimensional but also increasingly non-representable.

When we address the particular issue of architectural and urban quality in a fragmented world, a single aspect of Kracauer's urban essays seems to make them immediately relevant to the description and valuation of social spaces. One of his essays from the mid 1920s provides a social-spatial analysis of fragmentation. This text pushes the conceptual and textual experiment so far that it promotes fragmentation as a source and a main criterion of urban quality. The principle of fragmentation is no longer considered a menace to quality but the very foundation of it. So Kracauer detects the particular circumstances under which a certain kind of fragmentation can establish the ground of *urban quality*. In the conclusion of his text, Kracauer explicitly integrates fragmentation into the normative basis for evaluating cities. In this way fragmentation is present in the only positive definition of city quality to be found in Kracauer's entire writing on modern urban culture.

WRITING FRAGMENTED URBAN SPACE

The text in which Kracauer establishes a link between fragmentation and urban quality is brief. Less than three pages is required to translate a specific experience from the late summer of 1926 into a social-aesthetic essay. On a journey in southern France, Kracauer was accompanied by the philosopher of urban modernity, Walter Benjamin, whose articles he promoted for publication in the *Frankfurter Zeitung*. Kracauer went for long walks with his friend through the labyrinths of Marseilles and other Mediterranean cities. Both wrote substantial articles on various aspects of Mediterranean urban culture, and these articles contain the seeds of a certain approach to modern urbanity, full of hope and utopian imagination.

This optimistic vision prevails in Kracauer's essay "Stehbars im Süden"[3] – in English, "Stand-up Bars in the South." Among the best textual elaborations of urban fragmentation in southern European cities, this text locates its subject matter in the typical street bars found all around the Mediterranean.

Before we examine the particular forms of fragmentation and their mutual relationships in Kracauer's rather condensed text, it should be noted that even today stand-up bars are central features of urban life in southern Europe. These bars differ from the cafés for students and younger people that have spread all over the Western world during the last few decades. In a city such as Barcelona, for instance, many traditional bars are nothing but extensions of the sidewalk, physically as well as socially. As soon as the weather permits, the façade between indoors and outdoors is removed, enticing people of all ages and social classes to stop their course through the city for a minute and join each other at the counter for a cup of coffee or a drink. The stand-up bar in the south is far more than an arbitrary segment of three-dimensional urban architecture. It is a distinct cultural place whose constellation of interior and exterior life, young and old clients, visitors and residents, men and women, rich and poor could hardly be reinvented in northern Europe or America.

Better than any photographic record, Kracauer's written account of this semi-public place reflects the role of the stand-up bar as a mobile and subtle expression of urban life. Based on his own travel experiences, Kracauer's analysis of the Mediterranean city tends to omit traditional sociological considerations of power and politics.[4] Instead, he focuses on the body's immediate perception of city space. At this concrete level of experience, the presence of the sun[5] is a definite force of fragmentation, since it "burns holes in the tissue of the cities."[6] The intense light of the sun is compared to "invisible, spread fingers that separate what belongs together."[7] This is why reality in the Mediterranean is viewed as "stripes of dream images,"[8] which themselves are "lückenhaft,"[9] that is, full of holes, fragmented. If political issues were apparently left out of consideration in Kracauer's text, they return when Kracauer points out fragmented perception of urban space as a virtual source of utopian dream images.

A similar procedure is active in the social-aesthetic material space of the stand-up bar as it is perceived and transcribed by the traveling "fragmentist."[10] Visual and mental fragmentation are no longer ascribed to matters of climate but to concrete space. Yet this material space is but the starting point of a complex interpretive chain in which every link represents a new and separate sort of fragmentation.

Kracauer's descriptive interpretation of the bar room reveals three main types of fragmentation that may be termed architectural fragmentation, representational fragmentation, and social-semiotic fragmentation. In Kracauer's presentation of both fragmenting and fragmented space in the Mediterranean city, all three sorts of fragmentation contribute to his final valuation of the stand-up bar as a particular place of normative urban quality.

7.2 Barcelona, 1993.

7.3 Barcelona, 1993.

The first sort of fragmentation involves three-dimensional architectural space. Describing the bar room as the scene of a gigantic "sale of architectural styles,"[11] Kracauer stresses its heterogeneity of styles, materials and periods, and mentions how Baroque and Gothic elements fight traces of the Renaissance. Fragmentation of space does not even stop at the front door. The bar room continues into the street (and vice versa). A diversity of signs outside the bar makes concrete the relation between indoors and outdoors, between bar place and city space. And a permanent scaffolding seems to keep all the styles together and maintain the somewhat deteriorated building in an upright position.

This type of fragmentation is the only one that vaguely recalls the conscious use of stylistic collages in postmodern architecture. Yet the diverse components in Kracauer's urban bar never come together in a coherent architectural form. This complexity of styles is unintentional. It illustrates a general Mediterranean tendency to mix colours and forms in unorthodox and ornamental ways. It also shows how the spatial envelope of human life may be affected by the ambiguities of historical time; materials and forms are inscribed in a twin time-space relation that makes individual segments of space circulate as colourful parts of a long-term metamorphosis.[12]

A second kind of fragmentation concerns the visual representation of the architectural space. Kracauer observes how mirrors, reinforced by electric illumination, amplify the size of the room and turn it into a "public treasure hall."[13] His main interest, however, is how these mirrors fragment the visual and functional autonomy of the architectural elements: "The mirrors, which make an effort to multiply every poor electric bulb, expand the bar into a public treasure hall. It is overflooded by reflections in which the objects are mixed and quartered. Their independent reality proves illusory, although the mirrors do not let anything more real through."[14]

Thanks to mirror multiplication and decomposition of visual appearances, the objects and constructive elements of the bar room lose their individuality and gain access to a more sublimated level of reality. Thus the initial fragments of space are affected by a visual fragmentation, through which they enter a new (but equally illusory) universe of mirrors. As a consequence of its material and visual fragmentation in Kracauer's description, reality suddenly has become an issue of interpretation.

This interpretation of spatial reality is developed further in Kracauer's account of a third fragmentation, engendered via human, social-semiotic practice. Regardless of their intended uses, bottles of all colours, matchboxes in huge piles, and diverse cigarette packages compose impressive mosaics in the eyes of drinking and conversing visitors. Their visual and semiotic unity depends mainly on the human gaze. These objects in the bar room receive meaning only through use or contemplation.

The visitor's disinterested and therefore aesthetic contemplation, however, still acknowledges the social character of the place. In fact, the relationship between visual entities is highly temporary. Other clients will arrive, move chairs and tables around, and change not only the organization of space but also the significance of the objects, taken individually or as parts of a composition. Integrated with this third social-semiotic level, the initial forms of spatial and representational fragmentation prove to be stages in a discontinuous yet multifaceted interpretation process.

Kracauer's triple fragmentation deconstructs existing entities and reconstitutes new forms of meaning and visibility. The absence of durability pointed out by Kracauer certainly may signify a social lack. Nevertheless, the serial and anonymous relationships between individuals at the counter also guarantee a certain suspension of social differences. This explains why, in the end, Kracauer regards fragmentations resulting from both varying interpretations and mobile social relations as favourable to changes in everyday life.

HETEROTOPIA, IMPROVISATION, AND URBAN QUALITY

Kracauer's description of a stand-up bar deliberately seems to conceal the basic theoretical organization of its argument. In fact, the various kinds of fragmentation are hardly indicated in the textual montage, the inner order of which remains implicit. Nor can his description be translated easily back into an image that follows the measures and proportions of profane, three-dimensional reality.

Kracauer's essay leads one to imagine a traditional café but rather something like the peculiar junk shop (or art gallery) that Ben – a French artist with links to Fluxus and Neo-Dadaism – constructed around 1960 in a side street in Nice,[15] exactly where Kracauer's stand-up bar had been situated.[16] At any rate, Kracauer's descriptive metamorphosis of urban

7.4 Paris, 1988.

space transcends the traditional concept of space as either material or represented. His essay on urban bars instead points towards a new spatial order. Like Benjamin's,[17] Kracauer's urban space is devoted to social and cultural experiencing.

Although Kracauer's reader may perceive his street-bar as a literary construction, the term "description" – and not construction – has been maintained throughout the present analysis. This is due to the underlying hypothesis that Kracauer was exploring, in 1926, a type of spatial description that Michel Foucault was to render in programmatic form some forty years later.

In a 1967 conference manuscript entitled "Des espaces autres,"[18] and translated into English as "Of Other Spaces," Foucault outlines what he calls "heterotopology."[19] Although he imagines "a sort of systematic description"[20] of particular and heterogeneous places in everyday life, it would be imprecise to expect this descriptive practice to be traditionally scientific. Anticipating the kind of spaces to which he devotes his analysis, Foucault stresses that such a description should "take as its object the study, analysis, description, and 'reading' (as some like to say nowadays) of these different spaces, of these other places. As a sort of simultaneously mythic and real contestation of the space in which we live, this description could be called heterotopology."[21] While spatial analysis may be scientific, it may also aim to give an imaginatively powerful and critical reading of those empirical social spaces for which Foucault invented the term "heterotopia."

As opposed to idealist and abstract utopias, Foucault's heterotopias are concrete spaces which nevertheless express a critique of reality. Foucault portrays them as "real places – places that do exist and that are formed in the very founding of society – which are something like counter-sites, a kind of effectively enacted utopia in which the real sites, all the other real sites that can be found within the culture, are simultaneously represented, contested, and inverted."[22] The spatial heterogeneity of heterotopias is due to the fact that they are capable of resisting and defying the very social-cultural system they depend on and somehow express. To demonstrate this critical dimension in heterotopias – the condensing and distorting mirrors of society – is the task of the intellectual, as he or she is implied by Foucault's heterotopology.

Siegfried Kracauer never termed his urban analyses "heterotopologies." Nor did he consider his spatial motifs as heterotopias. But in many

7.5 Paris, 1993.

cases Kracauer's urban writings do meet the standards of Foucault's program for a description of heterotopias.

Kracauer's emphasis on spatial and social heterogeneity indicates a possible link to Foucault's heterotopology. First of all, his description of a bar in Nice explores a site that, like Foucault's heterotopias, is a condensed expression of urban space in general since it unites spatial and social-temporal elements of various origins. Kracauer's way of transforming social-spatial description into a nearly magical montage of disparate observations and interpretations also corresponds to Foucault's methodological and literary prescriptions. A quick reader[23] of "Des espaces autres" might consider "streets," "cafés,"[24] and thereby the city excluded from the field of heterotopology as it is delimited by Michel Foucault. Yet Kracauer's essay "Stand-Up Bars in the South" points to many of those characteristics that Foucault mentions when stating his particular interest for sites "that have the curious property of being in relation with all the other sites, but in such a way as to suspect, neutralize, or invert the set of relations that they happen to designate, mirror, or reflect."[25]

The most striking affinity between the two authors, however, is illustrated in Kracauer's conclusive remarks wherein spatial fragmentation in southern stand-up bars receives its fourth and irrevocably utopian interpretation. Kracauer is close to Foucault in his choice of metaphors: for Foucault, the "ship is the heterotopia par excellence"[26]; and Kracauer describes the Mediterranean[27] stand-up bars as "tiny harbours from which one can depart."[28] The departure he has in mind is of *social-cultural imagination,* stimulated by the encounter with fragmentary space and practices. In this way the individual's contemplation of a stand-up bar (in which he himself is a guest) somehow is supposed to become the point of departure for a critique of dominant social standards.

The question may still be asked how such a critique is made possible. Kracauer provides a concrete yet allegorical answer by noting that, when bar mirrors reflect social and architectural reality, this reflection becomes virtually critical, owing to its visual fragmentation of space. According to Kracauer, this spatial inversion of social-cultural criteria, a fundamental characteristic of heterotopias, is in turn prolonged and given concrete meaning by the bar visitor himself. Being like a boat in the harbour of the stand-up bar, the guest "loses sense of the measures of life that lie behind him. It falls apart for him into nothing but separate parts, *out of*

7.6 Paris, 1993.

which he may improvise the fragments of another life."[29] In this way, the elements engendered in the perceptive mind by the deconstruction of social-spatial reality may become a departure for a new everyday life.

This final step in Kracauer's description accomplishes the theoretical development which has been under way since his initial comments on the fragmenting sun of the Mediterranean. After having shown the role of fragmentation in a composite urban bar space, in distorting mirrors and in ephemeral human practices, Kracauer sums up its possible significance for social-spatial imagination. Rather than postulating a necessary and automatic translation of spatial fragmentation into social-cultural critique, Kracauer pays continuous attention to those products of a fragmented reality that may be reinscribed in new and unexpected practical constellations. Thus fragmentation is approved of insofar as it contributes to the constitution of new social-cultural possibilities – to the detriment of an unsatisfactory and repressive immobility.

Although Kracauer seems to withdraw from excessively abstract formulations on life in general, he cannot help addressing the normative and highly complex question of urban quality. In this perspective, fragmentation is interpreted as a crucial source of urban quality via the specific concept of improvisation. Fragmentation is implicitly present in a decisive formulation of urban quality at the very end of Kracauer's essay: "The value of cities is determined by the number of places in them which have been left to improvisation."[30] Departing from the particular space of southern bar life, Kracauer's words seem to apply to any city, whether in the Mediterranean or, even more important, in homely northern Europe.

From Kracauer's viewpoint in a stand-up bar in the south, fragmentation is a decisive source of urban quality. Without any apparent ambiguity, this last sentence suggests that the value of a city depends on a particular kind of fragmentation that generates improvisation. Issues of social power play no explicit role in this definition of urban quality; fragmentary improvisation is promoted as the sole test of urban space. In other words, it is through improvisation that fragmentation ensures the critical dimension of urban heterotopia.

In some of Kracauer's other essays, fragmented life is viewed as a serious threat to traditional forms of social fantasy (and to ideals of material welfare and social justice), but his text on stand-up bars in the south resolutely affirms the possible value of fragmentation itself.

Theoretically conscious of the social inertia[31] which may neutralize and appropriate the liberating forces of cultural fantasy, Kracauer carries his experiment on fragmenting perception of fragmented *space* to the point where fragmentation informs a decisive definition of urban quality.

Kracauer's experiment continues to suggest[32] to the present reader of "Stand-Up Bars in the South" that a multidimensional approach to fragmentation and spatial perception is required. Without forgetting the social framing of culture, it may therefore be fruitful to promote and develop heterotopological observation in the analysis of architecture, city, and society.

NOTES

1 The present essay is an extended version of a presentation given at the international conference "Architectural Quality in a Fragmented World," at the School of Architecture, Aarhus, Denmark, 8–10 May 1993.

2 Henrik Reeh, *Storbyens Ornamenter – Siegfried Kracauer og den moderne bykultur* (Odense: Odense University Press 1991). The book contains a 6000-word summary in English, "The Ornaments of the City: Siegfried Kracauer and Modern Urban Culture" (259–75).

3 Siegfried Kracauer, "Stehbars im Süden," in *Straßen in Berlin und anderswo* (Frankfurt: Suhrkamp Verlag 1964), 67–9. The text was initially published as a newspaper article in the *Frankfurter Zeitung*, 8 October 1926. Reprinted in Siegfried Kracauer, *Schriften* 5.1 (Frankfurt am Main: Suhrkamp Verlag 1990), 383–5.

4 The absence of an explicit social theory distinguishes Kracauer's analysis from a recent study of rhythm in Mediterranean cities by Henri Lefebvre and Catherine Régulier. Their "Essai de rythmanalyse des villes méditerranéennes" finds its starting point in a conflictual relation between the cities and the states of the Mediterranean (as opposed to cities of the north). This power relation is elevated into a social framework for understanding the particularity of rhythm (a concrete relation between time and space) in these cities: "[E]n Méditerranée la puissance politico-étatique gère l'espace, domine les territoires, contrôle ... les relations extérieures sans arriver à empêcher les citadins-citoyens de disposer de leur temps et par conséquent des activités qui la rythment. Cette analyse permet de comprendre qu'en Méditerranée, berceau de la Cité-Etat, l'Etat, qu'il soit intérieur ou extérieur à la cité, est toujours resté brutal et impuissant – violent mais faible –

unificateur mais toujours ébranlé, menacé." Henri Lefebvre et Catherine Régulier, "Essai de rythmanalyse des villes méditerranéennes," in Henri Lefebvre, *Eléments de rythmanalyse* (Paris: Editions Syllepse 1992), 102–3.

5 Henri Lefebvre and Catherine Régulier also mention the importance of the sun in Mediterranean cities: "Quant aux villes méditerran

6 éennes, elles bordent une mer (presque) sans marées; alors le temps cyclique du soleil y prend une importance prépondérante." (Ibid., 101.) The particular intensity of the sun, however, seems less significant to these authors than to Siegfried Kracauer, a man of the north.

7 "Stehbars im Süden," 68.

8 Ibid.

9 Ibid.

10 Ibid.

11 Anne Cauquelin, *Court traité du fragment* (Paris: Aubier 1986).

12 "Stehbars im Süden," 67.

13 Two remarks in Kracauer's initial description of the stand-up bar show the degree to which circulation and metamorphosis of materials in time and space play a role in his perception of the Mediterranean city. The circulation of spatial elements within the history of the city is indicated by a comment about a scaffolding that sustains the front doorway: "The scaffolding probably always stands, if not at this place, then at another; there is no lack of things which were to be torn down." ("Stehbars im Süden," 67). Fragile and perishable constructions, like scaffoldings, thus form a decisive part of the city and its architecture. But material fragmentation and metamorphosis seem to govern more than architectural space. Kracauer exemplifies his vision of ongoing metamorphosis in a description of the enormous coffee machine in the shop window: "In the shop window rises the red mega-temple of a coffee machine which reseparates the drink into its ingredients. What is swallowed as a hot brew is later dissolved into the coffee grains' black molecules." (Ibid.) The coffee machine embodies Kracauer's particular ecology of urban space and images. Devoid of harmony, this ecology is devoted to the mosaic-like culture of Mediterranean cities – places for a colourful and chaotic recycling of forms and materials.

14 Ibid.

15 Ibid., 67–8.

16 Ben's work is now reconstructed and exhibited at the Centre Georges Pompidou in Paris. When exhibited at the Musée National d'Art Moderne, Ben's

fabulous shop – an example of art after Duchamp – is elevated into a work of art. Yet it defies the distinction between art and everyday life.

17 "Stehbars im Süden," 68.

18 See Henrik Reeh, "Le labyrinthe du texte urbain: Walter Benjamin et le Paris du XIXe siècle," in G.T.I de l'Ecole Normale Supérieure de St. Cloud, *Miroirs de la ville – Perceptions et projections* (Paris: Didier Erudition 1985), 73–84.

19 Michel Foucault, "Of Other Spaces," in *Diacritics* 16, no. 1 (1986). A French book-version of this text (originally a lecture given at the Cercle d'études architecturales, in Paris, on 14 March 1967, published for the first time in *Architecture, Mouvement, Continuité*, no. 5 (October 1984): 46–9) is now available in Michel Foucault, *Dits et écrits*, vol. 4, 1980–88 (Paris: Gallimard 1994), 752–62.

20 "Of Other Spaces," 24.

21 Ibid.

22 Ibid.

23 Ibid.

24 A simplistic vision of heterotopias as distinct from city space is proposed by Sylviane Agacinsky in her *Volumes: Philosophies et politiques de l'architecture* (Paris: Galilée 1992), 107, when she associates non-place and heterotopia: "Le paradoxe de chef-lieu de cette humanité abstraite, universelle – et peut-être pas simplement bourgeoise – c'est qu'il est aussi un non-lieu, un nulle part, un peu ce que Michel Foucault, *sans y inclure la ville,* appelait une "hétérotopie," c'est-à-dire un lieu qui concentre ou représente tous les lieux" (emphasis added). The ambiguity of diversified urban space – private/public, affirmative/negative – developed by authors such as Kracauer and Benjamin suggests that city space is not only comprised by, but crucial to, Foucault's concept of heterotopia. See Henrik Reeh, *Den urbane dimension – tretten variationer over den moderne bykultur* (Odense: Odense University Press 1997), part II, chapters 4–9. The book contains a 4000–word summary in English: "The Urban Dimension: Thirteen Variations on Modern Urban Culture."

25 "Of Other Spaces," 24–5.

26 Ibid., 24.These places may also comprise arcades (as investigated by Walter Benjamin). See Henrik Reeh, *Den urbane dimension,* chapter 8.

27 "Of Other Spaces," 27. Foucault's fascination with the ship derives from the mixture of open and closed autonomy when a boat is sailing on the sea. In his literary and yet philosophical conclusion, he says: "If we think, after all, that the boat is a floating piece of space, a place without a place, that exists

by itself, that is closed in on itself and at the same time is given over to the infinity of the sea and that, from port to port, from tack to tack, from brothel to brothel, it goes as far as the colonies in search of the most precious treasure they conceal in their gardens, you will understand why the boat has not only been for our civilization, from the sixteenth century until the present, the great instrument of economic development ... but has been simultaneously the greatest reserve of the imagination. The ship is the heterotopia par excellence. In civilizations without boats, dreams dry up, espionage takes the place of adventure, and the police take the place of pirates." "Of Other Spaces," 27.

28 The link between city and sea is established in most literature on Mediterranean cities. In his masterwork *La Méditerranée et le monde méditerranéen à l'époque de Philippe II*, Fernand Braudel emphasizes the socio-economic importance of city life for the conquest of the sea (and vice versa): "Mais les villages maritimes, cellules de base, ne suffisent pas à créer une région vivante de la mer. Il y faut l'appoint irremplaçable d'une grande ville, fournisseuse de capitaux; une ville avec ses boutiques et ses marchands, ses affréteurs, ses assureurs et les multiples formes d'aide qu'offre un milieu urbain ... Quel rendez-vous de l'aventure! ... Faits divers quotidiens. Les circonstances aidant, ils s'additionnent et des changements se marquent à grande échelle." Fernand Braudel, *La Méditerranée et le monde méditerranéen à l'époque de Philippe II* (Paris: Armand Colin 1966), tome I, 133–4.

Henri Lefebvre and Catherine Régulier subscribe to the same hypothesis in the following sentences that join sun, sea, and city in the determination of urban rhythm: "Sans prétendre en tirer une théorie complète et à titre d'hypothèse nous attribuons beaucoup d'importance à ces relations entre les villes et surtout les ports avec l'espace et le temps (cosmique) par la médiation de la mer. S'il est vrai que les villes méditerranéennes sont des villes solaires, on peut s'y attendre à une vie urbaine plus intense que dans les villes lunaires mais aussi plus riche en contraste à l'intérieur même de la ville." Henri Lefebvre et Catherine Régulier, "Essai de rythmanalyse des villes méditerranéennes," 102. This expectation is largely confirmed by Kracauer's "Stand-up Bars in the South."

29 "Stehbars im Süden," 68.

30 Ibid. Emphasis added.

31 "Der Wert der Städte bestimmt sich nach der Zahl der Orten, die in ihnen der Improvisation eingeräumt sind." Ibid.

32 See Henrik Reeh, *The Urban Challenge in Siegfried Kracauer's Essay "Das Ornament der Masse,"* Working Paper # 19 (Odense: Humanities Research Center 1993).

33 Walter Benjamin praised "Stehbars im Süden" as "a definitive deciphering of this never-ending melodious text" that is the Mediterranean stand-up-bar and promised Kracauer to keep the article "more as a prospect for future travels than as a travel souvenir" of the walks he and Kracauer had taken together. Translated from Walter Benjamin, *Briefe an Siegfried Kracauer* (Marbach am Neckar: Deutsches Literaturarchiv 1987), 33. Benjamin's letter was written on 5 November 1926, upon his receiving Kracauer's articles on urban experiences in southern France.

Vitruvius, Nietzsche, and the Architecture of the Body

Mark Rozahegy

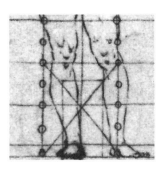

Chora

THIS TEXTUAL RUMINATION will compare two different stories concerning the beginnings of society and social existence. The first is drawn from the earliest surviving architectural treatise in the Western tradition, *The Ten Books of Architecture* by the Roman architect Vitruvius; the second is taken from *On the Genealogy of Morals* by the German philosopher Friedrich Nietzsche, a text that is both temporally and theoretically much closer to us. The purpose of this unlikely juxtaposition of *The Ten Books of Architecture* and *On the Genealogy of Morals* is to consider the relationship between philosophy and architecture, a relationship that I feel has everything to do with the body. The paper itself is divided into two sections. The first section focuses on the role of architecture in the Vitruvian account of the origins of human society as a movement from the cave towards the erection of permanent dwellings. In the second section, I develop a more precise understanding of the function of architecture in the development of human social existence by interpreting the Vitruvian myth from the perspective of Nietzschean genealogy. When viewed from this perspective, the relationship between architecture and civilization that Vitruvius develops in *The Ten Books of Architecture* leads to the possibility of understanding the role of architecture in the "reduction of the beast of prey 'man' to a tame and civilized animal, a *domestic animal*," in terms of the body.[1] In other words, I shall argue that understanding Vitruvius's account of the origins of society according to Nietzsche's argument that architecture makes "men to a certain degree necessary, uniform, like among like, regular, and consequently calculable"[2] actually opens a way for considering the possibility that the buildings we inhabit are actively involved in the formation of our bodies. As a result, instead of conceptualizing the body as containing the generating principle of architecture, I shall argue that architecture actually participates in structuring the bodies that inhabit its spaces.

In an article entitled "The City in Pieces," Victor Burgin brings together disparate historical examples of "representations of body and city"[3] from various architectural treatises and from the writings of different philosophers in order to demonstrate how contemporary theorists such as Walter Benjamin and Jean-François Lyotard attempt to overcome the humanism inherent in much of Western thought. In the present paper, I wish to reserve judgment concerning the validity of Burgin's argument;

8.1 Drawing from
Francesco di Giorgio
Martini, *Trattati di
Architettura Ingegneria e
Arte Militare* (volume
terzo), 1482.

instead, I would like to take issue with his humanist interpretation of
The Ten Books of Architecture. In his article, Burgin focuses on the third
book of the treatise, in which Vitruvius discusses the design and construction of temples. From his reading of this section of the treatise,
Burgin concludes that the central purpose of the treatise is to suggest
that all buildings should "display the same harmonious relation of parts
to whole as ... found in the human form."[4] As a result, Burgin argues
that, for Vitruvius, "the body is not simply that which is to be contained
by a building; the body *contains* the very generating principle of the
building."[5] According to this interpretation, Vitruvius presents the
human body as the blueprint for all buildings; well-constructed buildings
are to be built according to the harmonious relations between part and
whole that characterize the human body. For Burgin, the progression in

8.2 The Discovery of Fire. Woodcut from *Vitruvius*, Como, 1521, fol.31,v.

Vitruvius's treatise is obvious: as the generating principle, the human form precedes the form of the building that houses and contains it. The human body is, consequently, the organizing principle behind the built environment. But is this the last word on Vitruvius? Does his text simply suggest that the human body be conceived as the organizing principle for well-constructed buildings, or is there another way to understand the relationship between body and architecture in Vitruvius?

In the first chapter of Book II in *The Ten Books of Architecture*, Vitruvius relates a myth that recounts the beginnings of human society. According to the myth, human beings – who were originally "born like the wild beast, in woods, caves, and groves, and lived on savage fare"[6] – were first brought together into a community by the comfort that they found in the heat given off by a fire that had been ignited by the rubbing together of branches during a violent storm. Although terrified at first, the "inhabitants of the place ... drew near, and observing that they were

8.3 The Discovery of Fire.
Woodcut from *Vitruvius*,
Nürnbert, 1548, fol.61.

comfortable standing before the warm fire, they put on logs and, while
thus keeping it alive, brought up other people to it, showing them by
signs how much comfort they got from it."[7] As a result of this gathering
together, a common language was formed and they began to construct
shelters for themselves: "Therefore it was the discovery of fire that
originally gave rise to the coming together of men, to the deliberate
assembly, and to social intercourse. And so, as they kept coming together
in great numbers into one place, finding themselves naturally gifted
beyond the other animals in not being obliged to walk with faces to the
ground, but upright and gazing upon the splendour of the starry firmament, and also in being able to do with ease whatever they chose with
their hands and fingers, they began in that first assembly to construct
shelters."[8] Moreover, the myth contends that it was through the development of language and the construction of shelters that human beings
were eventually able to escape from their barbaric beginnings and

8.4 Erection of Primitive Buildings. Woodcut from *Vitruvius*, Como, 1521, fol.32.

achieve cultural refinement: "[T]hey next gradually advanced from the construction of buildings to the other arts and sciences, and so passed from a rude and barbarous mode of life to civilization and refinement."[9]

Hence, for Vitruvius, both language and architecture were at the root of civilization. For the purposes of this paper, however, we shall focus our attention on the role of architecture in the institution of society and social existence and on the fact that his mythic narrative places the architecture of the house, of the shelter, at the origins of the institution of social order. As Erwin Panofsky argues in *Studies in Iconology*, the progression of humankind's development in the Vitruvian myth of beginnings is unmistakeable. Following the event of the spontaneous forest fire, the remaining imagined events occur in a rational order, from the development of language to "the erection of permanent dwellings, the establishment of family life, the domestication of animals, the development of arts and crafts … and the institution of social order in general."[10] According to Panofsky, the Vitruvian myth "imagines the rise of humanity as an entirely natural process, exclusively due to the innate gifts of the human race, whose civilization began with the discovery of fire, all ensuing developments being accounted for in a perfectly logical way."[11] In other words, the Vitruvian myth draws an interesting distinction between human beings before and after their encounter with fire. Initially, human beings were closer to nature; we were born like animals and lived in caves. However, with the appearance of fire, and the development of language and architecture, we began to become civilized and were finally able to separate ourselves from the animals.

What is especially intriguing about the logic of the Vitruvian story is the fact that the rise of human beings towards civilization required their movement out of *caves* and into *constructed shelters*. More specifically, the myth highlights the idea that human beings had to become architects in order to develop a social form of existence in the world. But why was architecture so instrumental in the realization of human social existence? What role did architecture play in the conversion of human beings from animals into civilized social subjects? Throughout *The Ten Books of Architecture*, Vitruvius is quite explicit about the relationship between architecture and the civilized social subject, specifically between architecture and issues of intellectual propriety. For instance, in the same chapter in which Vitruvius recounts the myth of the origins of civilization, he also appears to defend the construction of his treatise, a move that suggests a possible correlation between housing and order. After discussing the movement of humanity away from barbarism and towards civilization through architecture, and after promising to talk about "the origins of the building art" in the remainder of Book II, Vitruvius appears to defend the arrangement of the first two books which discuss the qualities that an architect should possess, the proper building of a town, and the material that should be used for construction. According to Vitruvius, the first chapter of a text on architecture should discuss the function of architecture, "the branches of learning and studies of which it consists … its departments, and … of what it consists,"[12] while the second should treat "the origins of building art, how it was fostered, and how it made progress, step by step, until it reached its present perfection."[13] But why wait until the second book? Why not open the text itself with an explanation of the arrangement of the books? Perhaps because by leaving this discussion for the second book, which discusses proper building techniques (including how to choose the proper materials for building as well as how to construct walls), Vitruvius is suggesting an implicit connection between good construction and good writing, between orderly construction and orderly writing. Hence, the economy of construction is similar to the economy of writing in which everything is "in its proper order and place;"[14] textual economy is somehow equivalent to architectural economy. However, the ordering of the books – in which the education of the architect precedes the section on building techniques – does suggest that the mind of the architect must be properly trained before the architect can begin to build properly. In other words, good building follows from the ordering of the intellect. For Vitruvius, good architecture, in which everything is in its proper place, is therefore a natural outcome of an educated and reasonable mind.

In the introduction to Book VI, Vitruvius continues to make suggestions concerning the relationship between architecture and the civilized social subject in his account of the story of a Socratic philosopher named Aristippus who, after being shipwrecked on the shores of the Rhodians, teaches his companions that knowledge is a person's most valuable possession. After washing ashore and discovering traces of geometric figures drawn on the ground (a clue which suggested to Aristippus that they were close to civilization), "he made for the city of Rhodes, and went straight to the gymnasium. There he fell to discussing philosophical subjects, and presents were bestowed upon him … When his companions wished to return to their country, and asked him what message he wished them to carry home, he bade them say thus: that children ought to be provided with property and resources of a kind that could swim with them even out of a shipwreck."[15] In other words, the property and resources that one gains through learning are what Vitruvius calls "the true supports of life;"[16] those defences constructed through learning provide one with the stability and steadiness necessary to move through life with assurance. Moreover, the proper arrangement of the mind, the putting of everything in its proper place within the mind through education, is something that, unlike material fortune and property, "never fails, but *abides* steadily on to the very end of life."[17] At this point, the connection between building and learning becomes more explicit: education is itself a question of good housing, of the proper construction of the mind as a house in which knowledge resides. From the organization of the chapter, one can draw a correlation between the economical

8.5 Erection of Primitive Buildings. Woodcut from *Vitruvius*, Paris, 1547, fol.16.

arrangement of the mind and the physical arrangement of the domestic space of the house. But is the treatise suggesting that the rational arrangement of intellectual possessions is a model for the house, as the space in which one's material possessions are arranged in the proper (most economical) order? In this chapter, does the proper order of the house simply mirror the order of the mind, or is there another way to understand the relationship between the house and the intellect, between the ordering of space and the ordering of the mind?

The myth recounted by Vitruvius in Book II suggests a connection between the ordering of the mind and the ordering of domestic space, specifically when he explains how the education of human beings followed from their building experiences: "And since they were of an imitative and teachable nature, they would daily point to each other the results of their building ... and thus, with their natural gifts sharpened by emulation, their standards improved daily."[18] According to the myth, since human beings had to live in constructed shelters before they could become educated, the organization of the mind was dependent upon our ability to organize space and construct dwellings. But, by demonstrating that Vitruvius predicates the order of the mind on the proper, economical arrangement of the domestic dwelling, I have in no way contradicted Victor Burgin's assertion that the human body contains the generating principle for architecture; instead, I have merely extended his argument and demonstrated that the human body, as the template for all building, is also the generating principle for the organization of the mind. However, one must remember that in the Vitruvian myth the temple was not the first structure to be built by the humans gathered around the fire. According to the myth, the first things they constructed were shelters for themselves; consequently, architecture for Vitruvius begins with the domestic house and not with the temple. But then one is left to wonder about the organizing principle behind this constructed shelter. If the body for Vitruvius contained the organizing principle for the temple, must we simply assume that the body was also the principle behind the constructed shelter? This assumption would contradict the fact that the human beings gathered around the mythical fire had no set design for their shelters but instead simply improved their building standards by emulating one another's constructions. Furthermore, at no point does Vitruvius even suggest that these "first" architects modelled their buildings on the structure of their bodies; in fact, they seemed to learn how to build properly through their gift of emulation[19] and through a process of trial and error. As a result, I am left to wonder about the origin of the human body that, later in Vitruvius's text, comes to contain the organizing principle for temple construction. Where did that body originate? How was it produced? How did human beings acquire such an orderly and harmonized body that became the model for temple construction in Vitruvius and, by the time of the Renaissance, the organizational standard for the built environment?

What I shall argue in the remainder of this essay is that the relationship in *The Ten Books of Architecture* between the ordering of domestic space and the organization of one's intellectual space does provide a possible avenue for exploring the origins of the ordered human body. However,

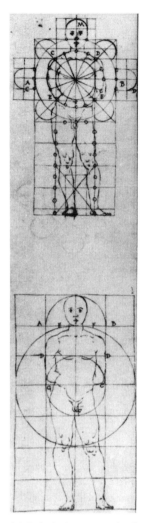

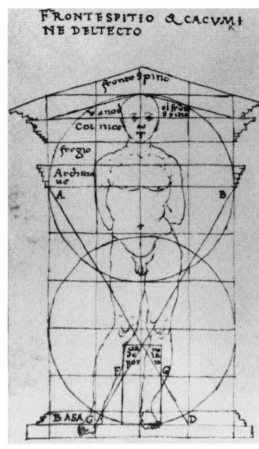

8.7 Right: Proportioning scheme of the façade of a temple with a longitudinal plan; from Francesco di Giorgio Martini, *Trattati di Architettura Ingegneria e Arte Militare* (volume terzo), 1482.

8.6 Left: Anthropomorphic Proportioning in the design of a temple with a longitudinal plan; from Francesco di Giorgio Martini, *Trattati di Architettura Ingegneria e Arte Militare* (volume terzo), 1482.

at this point, I shall turn my attention away from Vitruvius and toward *On the Genealogy of Morals* by Friedrich Nietzsche. What I have in mind is to interpret the Vitruvian myth in light of Nietzsche's belief that states of consciousness are the product of bodily states, that the education of the mind is first and foremost an education of the body. Since architecture in Vitruvius functions as the organizing principle of the mind, and since the mind, for Nietzsche, is organized by the body, I shall argue that the Vitruvian myth of the origins of social existence is the myth of the origins of the becoming flesh of the social individual through architecture, which, instead of simply being a product of the body, is presented in this essay as one of those practices that Nietzsche refers to as "the means to ... the *sovereign individual* ... in short, [to] the man who has the *right to make promises* – and in him a proud consciousness, quivering in every muscle, of *what* has at length been achieved and become flesh in him."[20] In other words, since the development of the social individual, an individual with the right to make promises, requires the initial embodiment of that individual, the social individual for Nietzsche is first made flesh before that mode of existence can rise to consciousness. One implication of this connection between the writings of an ancient architect and a modern philosopher is that architecture can be understood as a material channel through which what has been achieved historically – such as humanity's separation from the animals and the development of the ability to construct its own shelters – has become embodied within the body of the individual, within its flesh, and has subsequently risen to the level of consciousness. Or, to put it another way, this connection enables architecture to be understood as a material practice through which the embodiment in the individual of such historically determined distinctions as those between inside/outside and nature/culture is realized, distinctions that then work to structure an individual's mode of consciousness. What is at issue here is the primacy of the body in the constitution of the subject. Consequently, in the next section, I shall employ Nietzschean genealogy to argue that the civilized, social individual of Western history is not a psychological achievement but, in fact, the becoming flesh, the becoming embodied, of a new form of being in the world. By suggesting that social existence is the result of the becoming flesh of the individual with the right to make promises, Nietzsche represents a possible way of thinking about the role of architecture in the emergence of the conception of the body that underwrites the emergence of the human being as a social subject in the context of the Vitruvian myth. As a consequence of this position, the body is no longer an ahistorical, permanent thing but an historical object situated in the world and influenced by external forces that impinge upon it. In fact, the historicization of the body is, to my mind, the most important aspect of the genealogical methodology that Nietzsche develops in *On the Genealogy of Morals*. Instead of consciousness being a substance separated from the world, Nietzsche requires that consciousness be understood in relation to the involvement of our bodies in the world.

Before looking at Nietzsche's work directly, I should like to investigate the potential for Nietzschean genealogy to move from the concept of the body as the source of culture – as Victor Burgin argues when he states that the body contains the generating principle of architecture – towards an understanding of architecture as a cultural source of the body as it is articulated in the work of French philosopher Michel Foucault. According to Foucault, one of the ground-breaking consequences of Nietzschean genealogy is its disavowal of the liberal notion of the autonomous, transcendental subject that acts in the world. As he explained in a 1977 interview published as "Truth and Power," genealogy is a methodology that enables one to "dispense with the constituent subject, to get rid of the subject itself, that is to say, to arrive at an analysis which can account for the constitution of the subject within a historical framework."[21] Instead of working from the assumption of the subject as producer, genealogy reverses the terms of historical investigation and raises questions concerning how the historical subject was produced by seeking what Foucault, in an article entitled "Nietzsche, Genealogy, History," refers to as "the subtle, singular, and subindividual marks that might possibly intersect in [the subject] to form a network that is difficult to unravel."[22] There is no doubt about the distance between the liberal, constituent self and Foucault's unique concept of the subject as an entangled intersection of various markings and tracings, a concept that enables Foucault to "turn from the concrete, subjective world of the individual – and the preconditions for such a world – to a broader historical and political analysis of such preconditions."[23] Following Nietzsche, Foucault actually deepens the concept of the subject by searching for the preconditions for the inner subjective world of the self outside of the subject and within history. Instead of simply starting with a presupposition concerning the a priori existence of the inner world of consciousness, genealogy attempts to uncover the historical conditions that lead to the production of the constituent self. Therefore, genealogy does not dispute the actuality of "the concrete, subjective world of the individual"; instead, it searches for the foundations of that world, for the conditions that make that individual possible. But how does history effect the subject? Through what channels is consciousness produced? Where are the historical conditions of the self rooted if not in consciousness?

Basically, genealogy is based on the proposition that consciousness is rooted in the body. In "Nietzsche, Genealogy, History," Foucault develops an intriguing interpretation of the process of genealogy according to the two objectives of descent and emergence. More specifically, he argues that by investigating the *descent*, or legacy, of the body "[genealogy] cultivate[s] the details and accidents that accompany every beginning; it will be scrupulously attentive to their petty malice; it will await their *emergence*, once unmasked, as the face of the other."[24] As a search for origins, genealogy does not search for original identities through an "attempt to capture the exact essence of things, their purest possibilities, and their carefully protected identities, because this search assumes the existence of immobile forms that precede the external world of accident and succession."[25] Instead, the genealogist finds behind the world "not a timeless and essential secret, but the secret that [worldly things] have no essence or that their essence was fabricated in a piecemeal fashion from alien forms."[26] In other words, genealogy is a radical form of historicism; instead of positing autonomous actors behind the events of history or the immobility and ahistoricity of ideas and values, genealogy rejects all forms of essentialism and seeks the origin of things in the context of the external world of random events and chance. Instead of referring to the unbroken continuity that demonstrates the orderly and progressive evolution of the subject, genealogy "permits the dissociation of the self, its recognition and displacement as an empty synthesis, in liberating a profusion of lost events."[27] Moreover, genealogy does not seek the origins of the modern autonomous subject in some ahistorical, transcendental notion of consciousness but in the vicissitudes of history. Like Nietzsche before him, Foucault seeks the conditions under which the body of the social self was constituted.

In fact, throughout *On The Genealogy of Morals*, Nietzsche explores the physiological constitution of various intellectual traditions and moral value systems. For example, in the third section of the text, Nietzsche investigates the physiological order upon which science and scientific knowledge depend, and he discovers that the scientific temperament, like the ascetic ideal, is founded upon "a certain *impoverishment of life* ... [wherein] the affects have grown cool, the tempo of life slowed down."[28]

But what is at the root of this impoverishment of life? Nietzsche presents both the scientific condition and the ascetic ideal as symptoms of the slowing down of the human metabolism, a process that can be traced back to the beginnings of human society. It is here that the relationship between Vitruvius and Nietzsche really becomes fascinating. Like Vitruvius, Nietzsche's investigations into the origins of human civilization – and the beginnings of such modes of being as the scientific condition and the ascetic ideal – focus upon a highly complex set of processes that made possible our emergence as social subjects: the process of internalization that led to the development of the soul; the process that led to the development of memory and, as a result, the right to make promises; and the process that precipitated the splitting of cause from effect, which ultimately led to the development of the idea of "being." What makes Nietzsche especially interesting for architectural theory is his proposal that the shift towards social existence was made possible through our physical confinement behind *constructed walls*,[29] and that the constituent subject at the heart of social order was the outcome of a physiological change in human beings brought about through architecture.

In the second essay of the text, Nietzsche explicitly argues for the relationship between architecture and the development of the social subject when he recounts the process of internalization that led to the development of a soul within human beings. Nietzsche traces the origins of the social individual back to the moment when we turned our instincts inwards and acquired a soul: "[T]his is what I call the *internalization* of man: thus it was that man first developed what was later called his 'soul.' The entire inner world, originally as thin as if it were stretched between two membranes, expanded and extended itself, acquiring depth, breadth, and height."[30] What is particularly interesting is Nietzsche's statement that the soul is the result of inhibiting the discharge of instincts towards the exterior. He speculates about the relationship between the internalization of man and "the most fundamental change [man] ever experienced – that change which occurred when he found himself finally *enclosed* within the walls of society and the walls of peace."[31] Once again the relationship between the intellect and the body is brought to the fore; an intellectual condition is interpreted by Nietzsche as the result of a fundamental change in the physical surroundings of the human being. For the first time in history, human beings had become enclosed within walls wherein "one dwells protected, cared for, in peace and truthfulness, without fear of certain injuries and hostile acts."[32] In other words, the literal confinement of the body behind walls fundamentally changed the physiological order of the human body such that the body was forced to turn its instincts inwards, producing within the individual what comes to be known as the soul.

Therefore, according to Nietzsche, the literal enclosure of human beings within the walls of society leads to the production of an expanded and extended interior space within human beings that is one of the conditions for the realization of the social individual. Instead of simply existing as the thin space between two membranes, a physiological trait that caused the Nietzschean noble to forget quickly any injury that was done to them, the inner world of the social individual exists as a true middle space in which things can be stored and accumulated. In fact, by contrasting the noble individual, who is "incapable of taking one's enemies, one's accidents, even one's misdeeds seriously for very long,"[33] to the social subject, whose gestures are invested with seriousness, Nietzsche is drawing attention to the differences in the relationships that each has with themselves and with others. Although these differences are psychological, the aim of Nietzschean genealogy is to understand their emergence as being physiological in origin. To accomplish this, one must investigate the bodily economy, the metabolism, of both the noble individual and the constituent social subject.

In the case of the social individual, Nietzsche argues that the organization of the body interrupts the process of forgetting – which Nietzsche equates to a form of digestion – by restricting the possible exits from the body and thereby requiring that all experiences be absorbed into consciousness and stored there for future use. But, for Nietzsche, active forgetting is absolutely necessary for psychic health: "Forgetting ... is responsible for the fact that what we experience and absorb enters our consciousness as little while we are digesting it (one might call the process 'inpsychation') ... To close the doors and windows of consciousness for a time; to remain undisturbed by the noise and struggle of our underworld of utility organs working with and against one another; a little quietness, a little *tabula rasa* of the consciousness, to make room for new things, above all for the nobler functions and functionaries, for regulation, foresight, premeditation."[34] Since the deactivation of active forgetting is a necessary precondition for the breeding of a calculable and regular human animal with the right to make promises, then one can infer that active forgetting causes the radical subversion of self-identity; in other words, active forgetting would not allow the individual to establish a stable sense of self and would not allow the individual to have a secure and fixed relationship with themselves or with others. However, when active forgetting has been restricted or interrupted, that person "may be compared (and more than merely compared) with a dyspeptic – he [who] cannot 'have done' with anything,"[35] especially with himself. The interruption of active forgetting allows for the construction of a stable self-identity and, as a result, enables "[man to] become *calculable, regular, necessary*, even in his own image of himself."[36] The concepts of calculability and regularity are the foundation upon which the sovereign social individual, the animal that has the right to make promises, is erected. In fact, because of the future action implied in promising, the person making the promise must be able to remember the promise and fulfil it at some future date irrespective of the events or circumstances that erupt in the interim: "The task of breeding an animal with the right to make promises evidently embraces and presupposes as a preparatory task that one first *makes* men to a certain degree necessary, uniform, like among like, regular, and consequently calculable."[37] Therefore, the way to make people regular and uniform is through the imposition of a will not to rid oneself of one's experiences; what is required is that the activity of forgetting be actively bred out of the human animal.

Concerning the suppression of forgetting, however, the question still remains as to the relationship between the mind and the body. How is the mind induced to remember? What sort of changes in the physiological economy of the individual blocks the process of forgetting and brings the subject under the full influence of the demand for responsibility? What sort of body economy breeds an animal that is unable to forget? Nietzsche provides an answer when he talks about forgetting as a closing of consciousness to "the noise and struggles of our underworld of utility organs working with and against one another."[38] It is here that the body economy makes itself felt at the level of consciousness; unless consciousness has the power of active forgetting, it cannot escape from the noise and struggles of the body. In the larger argument concerning self-identity, active forgetting allows consciousness to be closed off from the influences of the body and, as a result, the individual is unable to attain any level of self-consistency. However, if the process of active forgetting is abolished, then the mind is unable to close itself off from the influence of the body economy and, as a result, the individual becomes calculable and regular. In other words, identity for Nietzsche is written into the body; identity is therefore a body economy that orders the intellect through the organization of various relationships in the body.

What is most significant about the body economy of the sovereign individual with the right to make promises is the expanded and extended space of its inner world. We have already seen how, through the blocking of external discharge, society has been able to breed an animal that is calculable and regular by inducing changes in the physiological economy of the human body. Consequently, since the human animal develops an inner world through the retention of energy meant for discharge and is able, as a result, to make promises, the breeding of the social human being is a matter of physiological economics. In order to produce a calculable and regular individual one must inscribe a body economy upon that individual which, in an attempt to hold them accountable, induces remembrance. As Nietzsche explains, the problem that society faces, because of social requirements such as civility and orderliness, is that of creating a human animal with a memory: "How can one impress something upon this partly obtuse, partly flighty mind, attuned only to the passing moment, in such a way that it will stay there?"[39] Hence, in terms of breeding an animal with the right to make promises, it was simply a matter of mnemotechnics. And, as Nietzsche recounts, the methods used for breeding such a memory into the human animal were anything but gentle: "[P]erhaps indeed there is nothing more fearful and uncanny in the whole prehistory of man than his *mnemotechnics*. 'If something is to stay in the memory it must be burned in: only that which never ceases to *hurt* stays in the memory.'"[40]

Apart from the relationship between memory and punishment that Nietzsche develops throughout *On The Genealogy of Morals*, what is important to realize about mnemotechnics is its connection to the body: memory, for Nietzsche, is not about impressing something on the mind but is, instead, all about burning something into the body. Consequently, the body becomes the carrier of memory; for our purposes, it would be more precise to state that memory is the result of the inscription on the body, through such cultural practices as architecture, technology, and corporeal punishment, of a specific order that regulates the circulation of energy through the body. In terms of architecture, if one accepts the idea that a building is an assemblage of parts organized according to some central theme,[41] then the suggestion that architecture organizes the economy of our bodies seems reasonable. As well, one can begin to understand the importance of the concept of a physiological body economy to the argument developed in this essay. Because buildings – as assemblages of various parts that are situated in determinate relationships with one another and as the concrete expression of certain cultural distinctions – can be considered as concretized economies, these economies become inscribed upon the bodies of their inhabitants.

Lastly, a rather startling conclusion concerning architecture and its relation to ontology can also be drawn from Nietzsche's investigation of memory, of the breeding process through which an animal with the right to make promises is produced. Immediately after his discussion of the development of the faculty of memory, Nietzsche tries to explain the consequences of such a development upon the individual: "[The ability to make promises] involves no mere passive inability to rid oneself of an impression, no mere indigestion through a once-pledged word with which one cannot 'have done,' but an active *desire* not to rid oneself, a desire for continuance of something desired once, a real *memory of the will*: so that between the original 'I will,' 'I shall do this' and the actual discharge of the will, its *act*, a world of strange new things, circumstances, even acts of will may be interposed."[42] This splitting of the will through the development of memory into the moment of promising and the moment of discharge introduces an interesting opposition into the life of the individual. Before the development of memory, there was no such doubling of the act, there was no separation between cause and effect. According to Nietzsche, this separation "which conceives and misconceives all effects as conditioned by something that causes effects, by a 'subject'" was introduced only as a precaution to protect the weak against any expression of strength by the strong. What the process of internalization and the development of memory introduced was "a neutral substratum *behind* ... men ... [that placed] *being* behind doing, effecting, becoming."[43] What these developments lead to is the positing of a doer, some form of being, behind the deed. As Nietzsche explains, "the popular mind in fact doubles the deed; when it sees the lightning flash, it is the deed of a deed: it posits the same event first as cause and then a second time as its effect."[44] Consequently, our development of both a soul and the faculty of memory – processes that to some degree were facilitated by architectural practices – seem to have introduced the category of being behind doing; in other words, through these processes, humanity became ontological.

In conclusion, I want to suggest that what Nietzsche is alluding to throughout his genealogical investigation into the origins of society is the process of our "ontologization." According to Nietzsche, the development of the constituent social subject through the process of domestication is made possible through the development of an ontological interpretation of human existence. In order to breed an animal with a soul and with the right to make promises, one must first introduce the idea of being behind doing, of a "doer" behind the deed. The subject as a social individual requires the introduction of a substratum of being behind doing, which means that any attempt to make human beings regular and calculable requires that they be understood ontologically, according to the category of being. What Nietzsche comes to understand in *On The Genealogy of Morals* is that this substratum is a necessary fiction that must be developed if one is to breed such an animal as social man. As he explains about the ontological substratum, "'the doer' is merely a fiction added to the deed."[45] This raises interesting questions about the relationship between ontology and architecture. If, as Nietzsche suggests throughout his text, architecture was essential in the development of the social subject, then what is its role in our "ontologization"? How is architecture involved in the production of the substratum of "being" as a fundamental category in our understanding of ourselves and our place in the world? Is the outcome of Nietzschean genealogy that architecture is implicated in the development of this ontological layering of existence? If so, then his thinking presents a rather odd understanding of the relationship between material, worldly practices and the ontological foundation of our existence (what Martin Heidegger refers to as the relationship between the ontic and the ontological). That may be fruitful to pursue in future projects concerning the question of architecture.

NOTES

1 Friedrich Nietzsche, *On the Genealogy of Morals/Ecce Homo*, trans. Walter Kaufmann (New York: Vintage Books 1968), 42. Unless otherwise indicated, italics in quotations are found in the original material.

2 Ibid., 59.

3 Victor Burgin, "The City in Pieces," *Prosthetic Territories: Politics and Hypertechnologies*, ed. Gabriel Brahm, Jr and Mark Driscoll (San Francisco: Westview Press 1995), 6.

4 Ibid.

5 Ibid.

6 Marcus V. Pollio Vitruvius, *The Ten Books of Architecture*, trans. M.H. Morgan (New York: Dover 1960), 38.

7 Ibid.

8 Ibid.

9 Ibid., 40.

10 Erwin Panofsky, *Studies in Iconology: Humanistic Themes in the Art of the Renaissance* (New York: Harper and Row 1939), 41.

11 Ibid.

12 *Ten Books*, 41.

13 Ibid.

14 Ibid.

15 Ibid., 167.

16 Ibid.

17 Ibid., 168; emphasis mine.

18 Ibid., 39.

19 The importance of emulation in Vitruvius could be related, through the notion of mimesis, to the mimetic faculty that Walter Benjamin posits as a fundamental human ability. See Walter Benjamin, "On the Mimetic Faculty," *Reflections*, trans. Edmund Jephcott (New York: Schocken Books 1978), 333–6.

20 *Genealogy*, 59.

21 Michel Foucault, "Truth and Power," *Power/Knowledge: Selected Interviews and Other Writings 1972–77*, ed. Colin Gordon (New York: Random House 1980), 117.

22 Michel Foucault, "Nietzsche, Genealogy, History," *Language, Counter-Memory, Practice*, ed. Donald F. Bouchard (New York: Cornell University Press 1977), 145.

23 Keith Hoeller, "Editor's Foreword," *Dream and Existence: Michel Foucault and Ludwig Binswanger*, ed. Keith Hoeller (New Jersey: Humanities Press 1993), 13.

24 "Nietzsche," 144; emphasis mine.

25 Ibid., 142.

26 Ibid.

27 Ibid., 143–4.

28 *Genealogy*, 154.

29 Ibid., 84.

30 Ibid.

31 Ibid.; emphasis mine.

32 Ibid., 71.

33 Ibid., 39.

34 Ibid., 57–8.

35 Ibid., 58.

36 Ibid.

37 Ibid., 59.

38 Ibid., 57.

39 Ibid., 60.

40 Ibid., 61.

41 Massimo Cacciari, *Architecture and Nihilism: On the Philosophy of Modern Architecture*, trans. Stephen Sartarelli (New Haven: Yale University Press 1993), 150. In his text, Cacciari characterizes architectural constructions as existing through "the dominance of one meaning, of one direction, of one organization over the combination of materials and languages that produce the work."

42 *Genealogy*, 58.

43 Ibid., 45; emphasis mine.

44 Ibid.

45 Ibid.

A Grand Piano Filled with Sand: A Transmorphic Study

Sören Thurell

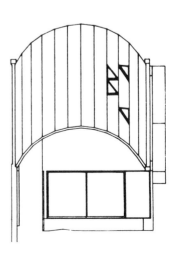

Chora

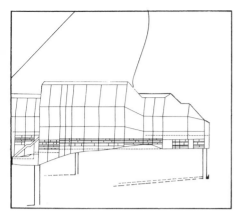

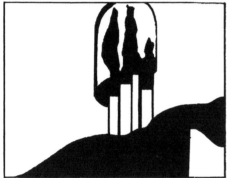

9.1 Above: The Malmi Church arranged as a three-legged piano. Transformative college by author.

9.2 Below: Sketch from *The Zone* by Reima Pietilä, arranged as a water tank. Transformative collage by author.

Polonius. *Very like a whale*
Shakespeare[1]

INTRODUCTION

If I am concerned with conveying to you the uncertainty of things, not as a sign of the failure of meaning but because of its fullness, this cannot be stated in an unequivocal manner. It is something which has to be shared, worked on together.

In this process I happen to be the speaker and I cannot know what you perceive, no matter how clear I am. I can propose a number of clues which I find relevant and hope that you can construct something out of them. I cannot prescribe what that would be and do not even want to do it.

I can suggest a scope and hope that it is used well. As far as I know, this is the way of architects.

PROPOSITION I

A Riddle Is a Riddle

It seems to me that mystery is the archetype for what is not what it seems to be. Stories are full of examples, whether they be fairy tales or myths. However, it may be helpful to start with seemingly less complicated matters, with the constructions children use to twist each other's minds.

What is black and stands on three legs in the desert?

You may already have heard this particular riddle; in any case I am sure you have met similar ones circulating in the schoolyards. The question and its answer are absurd, as they are surely meant to be. But change one of the ingredients and the constellation makes sense. A camel may be black (more or less) and stand on *four* legs in the desert, for example.

In the world of architecture, the question cannot be brushed aside so easily as a childish fantasy or as mere play; you *may* encounter a black building raised on three pillars among the dunes, perhaps a water tank designed for the cold of the night or something less purpose-laden. Certainly, you *might* very well have encountered some scarlet red thing resting its shiny slabs and struts on the grass in a park.

9.3 One of Bernard Tschumi's pavilions in Parc de la Villette, Paris. Photograph by author.

9.4 Le Corbusier's Villa Savoie, Poissy.
Photograph by author.

How can the nonsensical riddle be connected
with architecture? If it can, it would mean that
a particular aspect of life may bring something
which mostly is hidden in contact with the
realm of building. One reason why such connections may be difficult to make and also be confusing is that "riddle" has two meanings, in
English as well as in Swedish, which correspond to activities of different shallowness and
depth. The first is a quiz, a mere play on words,
the second anticipates the revelation of an
enigma.

Still, I suppose that I am enough of a postmod-
ernist to believe that the line between these two
is not a sharp one and that it may even be interesting to explore the uncertainties of the in-
between, to let bias rest for a while. It should
be added that, while the case generally seems to
be presented more seriously in architecture,
something could be discovered by making methodological analogies to riddle constructions of a
less serious kind. The serious ones have a tendency to remain enigmas and open up new
questions, but the less serious are, if not
explainable, at least more obvious (or more
clearly stated).

The true architectural riddle is a rare thing. An example might be Le Corbusier's white piano standing on its slender legs on a lawn in Poissy, west of Paris, the Villa Savoie from 1931, one of a few outstanding achievements. However, as you may remember, even this riddle may be answered in an unexpectedly absurd manner:

A grand white box filled with potatoes.

Although the answer makes actual sense, it has lost its meaning.

There exists a widespread agreement that the form in which the architectural riddle appears is essentially inscrutable, even in rather trivial cases. This goes so far that the feeling for its deeper sense has been widely lost in our own time.

In an attempt to re-establish a realm of more deeply felt references to visibility, Louis Kahn spoke of *the desire to make*, whereby he surely intended imagination at work. Even so, the real origin of the tangible usually rests in darkness or is referred to crudely.

PROPOSITION 2

A Sailing Boat Is a Moving Body Moved

Instead of being given as a set of disconnected properties to be put together again, a riddle may be presented directly to perception, undivided and conceived in its synthesized form as something that has to be understood and treated with a minimum of explanation:

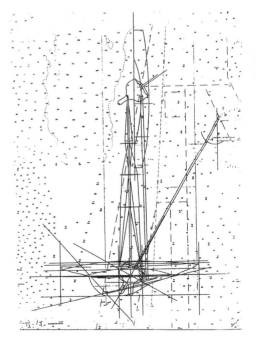

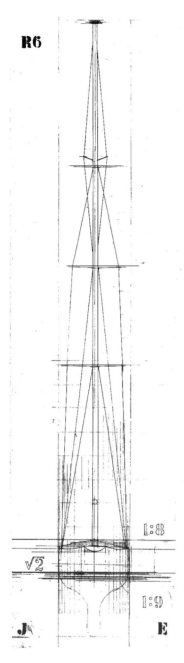

What riddle is contained in a sailing yacht?

Narratives are concerned with presenting such imaginative questions for which the answers necessarily acquire a quite personal character. The fact that exceptional architecture is particularly centred on some such quality should not be what makes it exceptional, however, since any architectural answer is bound to be personal.

Pursuing this example, architectural student Jesper Engström[2] recognized certain general principles which were used both by the designers of boats and by Giacometti in a great many of his sculptures: basic principles such as the perpendicular axis, the organization of direc-

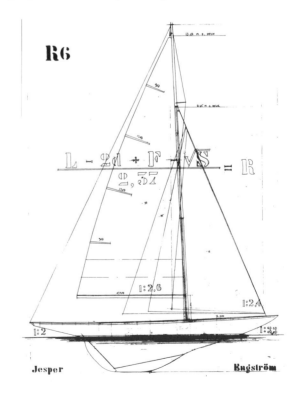

9.5 Above, right, and previous page: Drawing of an R6 sailing yacht. Transformation by Jesper Engström, 1992.

tion, and the awareness of the vast horizon. The elongated thinness of the form contrasted the concentration of counterbalanced weight.

The awareness of such valid principles originally may have promoted the riddle of the boat, not the mathematically precise design formula of this kind of racing yacht, as the student had supposed at the outset. Therefore, in the further development of its general situation, together with its particularities, this student was even able to derive a site from the curves of the hull and also a kind of spirit imagined to be present in a cider factory situated in an apple orchard. These choices may sound rather fortuituous but, then, what is coincidence really?

9.6 Above: Alberto Giacometti, *Femme debout*, sculpture, 1948. Photograph by Jesper Engström.

9.7 Left: Alberto Giacometti, *Petit buste sur socle*, sculpture, 1954. Photograph by Jesper Engström.

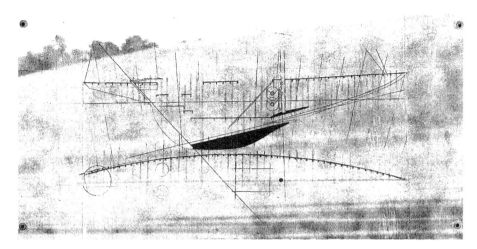

9.8 Sailing yacht transposed onto the ground. Drawing by Jesper Engström, 1992.

Through the reversal of the pleading for guilt, as it were, architectural objects can be demonstrated to be black riddles standing before our eyes. However, it is always tempting to reduce the question, as if we have an insect before our eyes.

How many legs do they have?

PROPOSITION 3

A Moving Body Is a Change in Space

What is the riddle from which Toyo Ito's pianos have emerged?

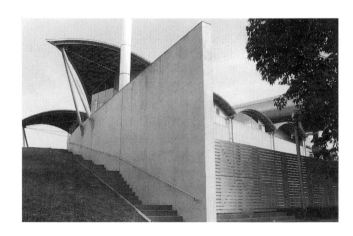

9.9 Toyo Ito, Yatsushiro Municipal Museum, 1991. Photograph by author.

Buildings such as the Silver Hut or the museum in Yatsushiro are charged with an ephemerality which Ito considers to be significant of modern life. To demonstrate this, he once opened the Silver Hut, his own house, for an invited fashion show.

Most often, such particular one-off creations remain silent enigmas, objects that do not reveal much about their sphinxical character. Ito himself provides us with some important clues, one of which is an account of his childhood experience of watching dragonflies emerge from their cocoons: "After the first split in the back of the body, head and legs emerged in a supple and continuous movement. When all the legs were out, the tail and the wings were stretched out as they stiffened. When coming in contact with the air, their milk white bodies instantly turned green, black and glowing. Their soft wings stiffened into fine panes of glass where the web of nerves appeared distinctly. In less than thirty minutes, the grotesque larvae had become shining insects that could fly. Astonished and moved I stood there, breathless, and watched the dragonflies with their shivering wings."

That his account is meant to be more than a reminder of a coincidental similarity, that it is concerned with a generative metaphor, is demonstrated in another of Ito's commentaries, in which he explicitly juxtaposes the Silver Hut with an earlier building of his design, the White U in Nakano, in the same way as they are juxtaposed in reality. The first one is a light structure of aluminum ribs, stretching out its thin panels over the space below. The second is com-

9.10 Fashion show in Toyo Ito's home, The Silver Hut; from *Shinkenchiku* (Winter 1986).

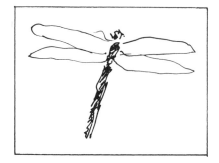

9.11 Dragonfly. Drawing by author.

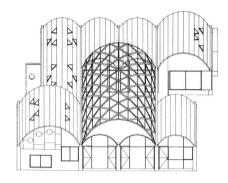

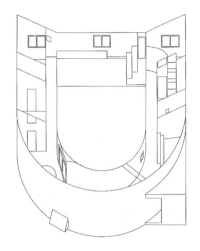

pletely turned inwards like a large curved worm facing the exterior through only a few openings. Together, the two buildings awaken most clearly an association with the newly hatched dragonfly and its cocoon lying beside it. This is pinned down by Ito himself in his statement that he could develop the Silver Hut into such a free expression because he "thought for a long time about continuity with the adjacent house."

PROPOSITION 4

A Changing Space Is a Meaning Transferred

What is common to these examples is that a riddle and its answer may be transferred, transformed, metamorphosed, and applied to different situations. It should be noted, however, that although the relation between the metaphorical point of departure and its final expression in architectural terms (the metaphor in reverse) may seem to be quite obvious in retrospect, it is nevertheless not established in any simplistic manner. It is rather like having access to a number of doors which open to a number of rooms in a more complicated way than having just one door giving onto one particular room.

Propounding one's own riddles and their possible answers seems to be the best way to acquaint oneself with this process. Some time ago, I found an opportunity to do this when working on an open-air installation where my question was:

What riddle is standing on X legs in the pedestrian mall in central Heidelberg?

Being well aware of my role as explorer, I kept a careful record of the development of the project as a self-reflection from which only glimpses can be transmitted in this context.

The town, itself a riddle composed of memories from two millennia, is dominated by a ruined castle hovering above the roof tops lined up along the river Neckar. In the palace garden, the *Hortus Palatinus*, the presence of its creator, the ingenious French architect Salomon de Caus, is still traceable.

Through a series of transformative steps, I brought the shadow of de Caus down into the heart of the city. This meant that the installation took somewhat the appearance of one of his amazing machines. At a crucial point the process was focused on the formulation of yet another riddle, through a series of associations:

What is present to us in the figure of the jester which may be relevant to this place, Kornmarkt?

Taken as a theme, the answer to this riddle was found to span from Velazquez's foolishly grinning court figure to Marcel Duchamp's more recent sardonic and enigmatic smile.

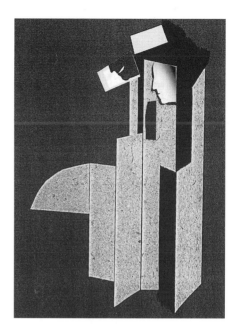

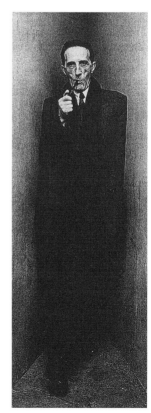

9.12 Left, top: Toyo Ito, The Silver Hut, Tokyo, 1984. Drawing by Toyo Ito.

9.13 Left, middle: Toyo Ito, The White U, Nakano, Tokyo, 1976. Drawing by Toyo Ito.

9.14 Left, bottom: Transformation of Velazquez's painting of a court jester. Drawing by author.

9.15 Right, top: Sketch for the Heidelberg Installation with reference to Marcel Duchamp's *Boite en valise*.

9.16 Right, bottom: Portrait of Marcel Duchamp by Irving Penn, 1948.

In the formulation in which it was finally expressed and brought in place, the installation became a strange provocation to passersby. One man furiously declared that it was a *pissoir*; children and women showed a quite open-minded curiosity.

It was only gradually that I became aware that the arrangement was astonishingly evocative of the castle itself. This association became strikingly evident when the installation piece was transported on the local escalator up to the palace garden and placed on a lawn adjacent to the exploded gun tower, a giant fragmented shell standing at the corner of the building complex and exposing its empty interior like the aban-

9.17a, b, above and right: Installation by Ola Granath and Sören Thurell at the Kornmarkt, Heidelberg, 1994. Photographs by Fredrik Wassermeyer.

doned cocoon of a giant dragonfly which had left during the siege of the French two hundred years ago. It is a deeply hidden enigma how this coincidence came to the surface, just as how all the minor coincidences were strewn in the way of the project.

Since this project accompanied those of nine other contributors, these coincidencies also reflected a difference in approach. I have found it to be a frequent occurrence with artists that they regard the settings of their projects as scenes which ideally should be empty or neutral, an attitude that simply reflects the gallery situation. As an architect, I naturally looked for an environmental connection, even support,

9.18a, b, above and right: the installation by Ola Granath and Sören Thurell, brought up to the Schlosspark in Heidelberg Castle. Photographs by author.

whether of a practically material or conceptually mental nature. Making this distinction, I have come to notice that there exists a considerable disagreement regarding that issue:

How self-sufficient is a riddle which is intended to be shared with others?

PROPOSITION 5

A Meaning Transferred Is a Place of Rest

Reima Pietilä's architecture is a riddle both in how it came into being and in how it can be approached. Since it was intended to be shared with others and obviously is successful in doing so, it is a rich source for study, particularly since he himself was especially concerned with formulating his own parallel riddles. This double focus may be one reason why his architecture seems so satisfying on a basic level while remaining enigmatically unsatisfactory to most professional analysis.

This is, of course, a problem of which Pietilä himself became aware, maybe even painfully so, when the shock of his first success had been absorbed by society at large. The year 1967 seems to have been a simmering, active time for him. Kaleva church and the Dipoli centre in Otaniemi were finished the year before and Pietilä threw himself into a number of competition projects with great intensity. In an article from 1967 he describes this stage:

"The 'how to say it' problem has been disturbed by an outburst of 'what to say about it.'"

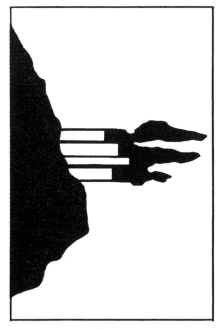

9.19 Reima Pietilä, illustration in *The Zone*, an exhibition in 1967; from *Intermediate Zones in Modern Architecture* (Helsinki 1985).

An example of this "what to say" riddle formulation is *The Zone*, a strange exhibition that he made at the same time. It consists of a number of morphological pictures in which Pietilä wanted to show the transition from theory to realization. One pertinent example is titled *The Building is a Situation*. Pietilä describes this situation as "a connection of events between the outer, unlimited content and the inner, limited content ... a morphic interval of two amorphic zones."

A characteristic project from this time was his competition entry for the Lutheran Church of Malmi in Helsinki. In "An Introspective Interview" for *A+U 9/74*, Pietilä explains: "Malmi church was to be an informal cave for formal gatherings of people ... But in its GEOMORPHIC ARCHITECTURE there is also an animal pose. Our cat Misukka was sleeping usually on the drafting board before my eyes giving a perfect idea of the 'relaxed mass.'"

Seen as an isolated object, the Tampere Main Library, designed by Pietilä in the 1980s, presents itself as a riddle, even in his own presentation:

What could the Metso-project be: a building-icon wrapped in the capercaillie physiognomy?

Recently I had the opportunity to visit this building, stylistically a paraphrase on a certain kind of architecture by Frank Lloyd Wright. Quite frankly, these overflowing pudding forms never have appealed to me when judged from presentations in books. But together with Pietilä's clue that it was designed in response to

9.20 Reima Pietilä, The Malmi Church (1967), in Helsinki, elevation drawings; from *Intermediate Zones in Modern Architecture* (Helsinki 1985).

9.21 Capercaillie. Drawing by author.

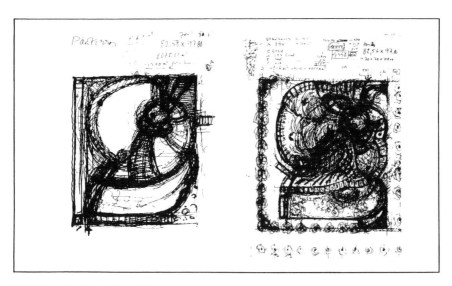

9.22 Reima Pietilä, sketches of the town library in Tampere, Finland, 1978-85; from *Intermediate Zones in Modern Architecture* (Helsinki 1985).

the Gothic church nearby, the building displays itself with the convincing clarity of contrast.

In his own comments Pietilä has pointed out that the metaphorical character of this building is based on a narrative theme. And he goes on to state what the building seems to say: "I have created my architectural space together with this place where I am."

Pietilä's consistent concern was to trace back the riddles that kept appearing to him. This is difficult to understand but simple to see, as implied by Pietilä's words in *The Zone*: "I can see already how this crowd of pictures is growing and taking on new expressions. A constant queue of pictorial connections is forming. I think I can make an adequate chain of proof – if I want to."

If this qualification of the situation of the zones seems to point to a state of duality, I wish to remind readers of Hermes Trismegistus's mystical principle that *what is inside is also outside*.

It touches on the essence of identity, again situated in the morphic interval mentioned above. In an address to Finnish architects in 1982 Pietilä said: "No elegant conceptual experimentation will guide us towards a new holistic architecture, whether it be existing or still to emerge. Those true design ideas come from the 'in-between zone'; between abstract and concrete things. There is a broad domain of creative metamorphosis in architecture still as yet unexploited by the pioneer generation or by ourselves. The future and any progress it holds is there."

PROPOSITION 6

A Place of Rest Is a Jug of Milk in a Maiden's Hands

It is a common assumption that architecture can be dealt with exclusively in terms of architecture – a view which is not held only by extremists like the *Rationalisti* but by laymen and *technici* in general. At its best, such a statement is merely a half-truth. Therefore, it is refreshing as well as instructive to consider an interpretation by architectural student Anna Webjörn[3] of Jan Vermeer's painting of a kitchen maid pouring out milk from a jug.

Of course, to a modern person it is already quite stirring to realize that such seemingly trivial motifs were painted at that time with a hidden reference to a symbolic content. It is possible, however, that something of such notions is still conveyed without the spectator being aware of it, as a riddle that gently calls for an answer, in fact a response.

9.23 Jan Vermeer, *Maidservant Pouring Milk* (Rijksmuseum, Amsterdam).

217

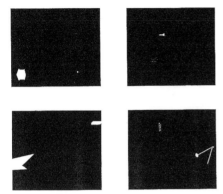

In the student's reading the references were consciously extended further and explored, inspired by observations on Marguerite Duras's fascinating way of stretching the limits of comprehension through distant associations, as she does in her short novel *Moderato cantabile*, where minor, really minor and seemingly irrelevant events in the distance take on an unexpected and mysterious meaning when brought into the focus of the main chain of events.

In Anna Webjörn's personal hermeneutics of the painting's quivering stillness, an amazing number of events start to unfold. One example is the pillar of milk strangely rising up toward an empty jug, bringing forth its own shape as a riddle to be traced and finally made resonant in space:

What is it that does what in a certain room?

The experience of seeing the riddle as such could be expressed in the form of a paradoxical quiz:

What riddle is a riddle?

To this the Steinesque answer *a riddle is a riddle is a riddle* forms a phenomenologically condensed form of syllogism. Understood in a narrow hermetic sense, the formula may obscure the fact that there is an unspoken reference involved, one that may be difficult or even impossible to define. On the other side, taken in the sense of a container for inherent possibilities, the riddle of the riddle may affirm that much more is understood of the visible than is generally realized. One reason, maybe the main one, for the lack of conception and even the misconception may lie in the way that current observation is based on assumptions and expectations, especially expectations and even, it can be said, on assumed expectations concerning the nature of inference itself.

Of course, this is one of the great philosophical riddles which has remained unsolved.

CONCLUSION

I have been told that this text is too enigmatic unless the reader is familiar with the whole context to which I am referring. It is possible that you are now ready to agree. To me, a text cannot be enigmatic in itself; only that to which it refers is enigmatic and that is unavoidable. The purpose of the text may even be to demonstrate the enigmatic glimmering which is not readily observed. How can it then but present itself as a riddle?

Together with one of the commentaries on the enigmatic, I was also presented with a text by the Estonian architect Leonhard Lapin in which a sentence tries to redress the balance between the referent and the reference:

The word is only a perfume of that action.

It is beautifully put and, to be sure, a great step forward from the semantic insistence on a one-to-one relationship. Nevertheless, I am not prepared to agree with the formulation, not at all. The word cannot be a perfume, however much perfume you put on it. To me a word is rather a key.

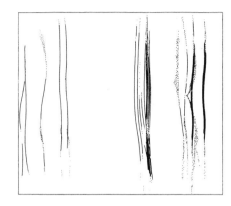

9.24a, b, c, previous page and above: Anna Webjörn, transformative sketches of the Vermeer painting, 1992.

And just as a key cannot be the door through which you enter, a key is a key only in a very loose sense as long as it does not fit. How does it fit? It may also sound beautiful to say that it is the way we see the key as key which is important. But apart from that, the key is made for a lock, never the other way around.

The word is only a key to that lock.

That is O K. Oh key!

Now, however interesting the business of constructing locks and keys, the essential thing about them is the use for which they are intended. And if the comparison with words may seem far-fetched or simplified, the matter of use makes it relevant. Doors are intended to close and to open into something beyond. With words this is less conspicuous. In architecture it has to be discovered again and again.

The perfume of that word is action would be more to my understanding.

NOTES

1 This famous passage from Hamlet (act 3, scene 2), a favourite of mine, was used in exactly this way by Roger Connah in his enigmatic book on Reima Pietilä, *Writing Architecture* (Helsinki, 1989).

2 This project on transformations in architecture which was carried out at the School of Architecture at KTH (Swedish Royal Institute of Technology), Stockholm, in 1992. For a brief presentation, see *Modus Operandi Architectural Desires* (Stockholm: KTH 1995).

3 Ibid.

Origins and Ornaments: Jean-Jacques Lequeu and the Poetics of the City in *l'Architecture Civile*

Franca Trubiano

Chora

JEAN-JACQUES LEQUEU was a most meticulous and gifted architectural draughtsman. The briefest glance at any one of the hundreds of plates given in bequest to the Bibliothèque Royale will bear witness to his great skill. During a lifetime dedicated to the representation of architecture and its historical allegories, ornamental drawings were Lequeu's principal means of expression. Many scholars have come to see, in the eyes and hands of this late-eighteenth/early-nineteenth-century *dessinateur,* the profile of the modern architectural technician. His adoption of descriptive geometry for drawing the human head and his overly exacting and analytical precision undoubtedly have contributed to this interpretation. I would contend, however, that a careful look at the words and images of Lequeu's *Architecture Civile* will reveal a somewhat different picture.

As architect, artist, author, antiquarian, historian, natural scientist, and mystic, Lequeu possessed the mind and soul of the pre-Romantic artist. Throughout his prolific drawing career, he unfailingly refused to endorse the rationalizing program of the Enlightenment. The visual and literary narratives developed in *l'Architecture Civile* were critical works of representation aimed at negating both the reductive tendency of scientific languages and the linear temporality implicit in historical positivism. In distinct opposition to prevailing practices, the drawing plates of his architectural treatise embrace an ornamental language of architecture. At the break of modernity, this artist of the pen ventured a return to the mythic origins of architecture and engaged the metaphorical languages of analogy and irony in the poetic construction of cities – albeit cities destined to remain but constructions of the mind.

DESSINATEUR

Born in 1757 to Jean-Jacques-François Lequeu, furniture and cabinet maker with interests in architecture and landscape design, Lequeu the younger inherited his father's interest in buildings and drawings. A prodigy at an early age, he began his formal drawing education at the age of nine as a student at the École Gratuite de Dessin, Peinture et Architecture de Rouën, founded by Jean-Baptiste Descamps, the celebrated court painter and member of the Académie Royale in Paris.[1] By the age of sixteen, Lequeu had already received serious recognition, his drawings having been awarded honourable mentions and prizes. In 1778, with an interest in

10.1 Jean-Jacques Lequeu, self-portrait of 1786; from Duboy, *Lequeu*.

furthering his knowledge of the art, Lequeu left his native city of Rouën. Securing financial passage to Paris by his uncle Abbé le Gentil, he was granted personal introductions to a number of architects and artists involved in the promotion of the arts.[2] His drawing skills eventually gained him admittance to the Académie d'Architecture on the sponsorship of David Le Roy and an appointment to the architectural office of Jacques-Germain Soufflot.[3] In the years that preceded the French Revolution, Lequeu had achieved success as the architect of a number of pleasure villas. By 1788, designs for four such villas had been issued from Lequeu's drawing table.[4] While no evidence exists to suggest that any of these residences were in fact built, the *Maison de plaisance appelée Temple du Silence, Cazin de Meulenaer à Grawensel*, published by Krafft and Ransonnette in their *Recueil d'architecture civile* of 1812 and described as a building of great magnitude with a large number of rooms and a remarkable decor, was believed destroyed following the Revolution.[5]

As with many architects who enjoyed professional success before the demise of the French royal court, Lequeu's fortunes changed drastically in the years that followed. However, despite the loss of his architectural career, the drawing skills that had originally introduced him to the world of architecture once again ensured his livelihood during the republican

10.2 Lequeu, elevation of the *Maison de plaisance appelée Temple du Silence*; from Duboy, *Lequeu.*

years, the Napoleonic empire, and the return of the boy king, Louis-Philippe. In his role as civil servant, Lequeu was employed from 1793 to 1815 as *dessinateur* by the École Polytechnique, the Commission des Travaux Publics, and the Ministère de l'Intérieur, for which one of his duties was executing measured and scaled drawings for the new cadastral map of the city of Paris.[6]

Yet surveys and plans were not the types of drawings that Lequeu would hand over in perpetuity to the Bibliothèque Royale; the manuscript and drawing folios in his archives are comprised of drawings of a very different nature.

———————

AVIS AUX AMATEURS ET AMIS DES ARTS[7]

Le sieur Lequeu qui à proffessé l'Architecture sous des Maîtres éclairés à Rouën … annonce un bureau où il donnera des leçons de dessin tant de la figure que d'ornement, d'architecture et des autres parties de son art.

Comme le sieur Lequeu joint a la connaissance des plans et détails du Bâtiment (dont il fait son travail habituel), le dessin de la figure à l'encre de la Chine, <u>maniere noire</u>, où coloriée &&. Persuadé que ce genre hardi pourrait interesser les personnes qu'un goût distingué pour les beaux arts anime et leur fait désirer d'avoir des regles du lavis sur le Portrait, le Paysage, la Carte et l'Architecture &&, il en donnera des leçons.

This offer of services, penned by Lequeu and addressed to all *amateurs* and friends of the arts, made known his wish to instruct in matters of fine art those with the most distinguished of tastes. Having practised architecture under the guidance of many enlightened masters, Lequeu hoped to merit the esteem and protection of the city of Rouën by offering the fruits of his knowledge to its citizens. With this object in mind, he announced the opening of a drawing studio that would instruct in the rules of drawing the figures and ornaments of architecture. Closer scrutiny of this offer of services betrays the critical distinction that Lequeu brought to this particular drawing type.

In this respect, we need recall how, throughout the scientific revolution of the seventeenth and eighteenth centuries, architectural drawing developed in parallel with the institutionalization of the applied arts and sciences. With the subsequent institutionalization of norms in the architectural profession, drawing became responsive primarily to the needs of construction.[8] As a result, the independence that the work of representation had traditionally held from the building process was now nearly eradicated. Most particularly in France, the newly defined sister discipline of civil engineering had increasingly woven its epistemological framework within the theory and practice of architecture. Jacques-François Blondel, in composing the *Architecture* section of Diderot and D'Alembert's *Encyclopédie des Lettres et Sciences*, defined the architectural draughtsman as "one who designs and amends plans, sections, and elevations of buildings according to measurements as taken or supplied" and the final drawing as "one which is approved for execution, and on which the contract is based and signed by the contractor and the client."[9] I would contend that Lequeu's definition of the *dessinateur* is not entirely in keeping with that offered by Blondel.

For Lequeu, architectural representations were not exclusively drawings of what one intends to build; they were not mere repositories of technical information. Rather, he developed the art of drawing as an alternative to the scientific making of order. Lequeu was well aware of the transformation that his art had undergone, and his drawings, in being primarily ornamental drawings of architecture, aspired to redress the accompanying loss of metaphor in the language of architecture. In Lequeu's refusal to reduce architectural drawing to an instrumental procedure serving the process of building, the role of the *dessinateur* was broadened to include activities and intentions that, while original to the

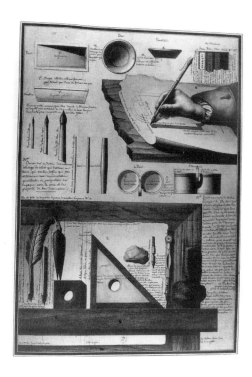

10.3 Lequeu, instruments of the *Dessinateur, l'Architecture Civile*, pl. 3; from Duboy, *Lequeu*.

art of drawing, had been long forgotten by the end of the eighteenth century.

Not surprisingly, therefore, while the drawing of plans and building details defined the basis of his work with the civil authorities, Lequeu maintained in his offer of services that his expertise also included the drawing of figures and ornaments. In observing and recording the manifold appearances of Nature, Lequeu developed a parallel art of ornamental drawing via his mastery of the human body, the garden, and, most important, architecture. For this *dessinateur*, drawing necessarily demanded the articulation of a metaphorical language of architecture. Only in this way could drawing be restored its original vocation: communicating the poetic dimension of architectural ideation.

THE ORIGINS OF DRAWING

Lequeu's lifelong devotion to drawing included not only the knowledge of geometric operations,[10] but also a profound scholarship in the history and theory of drawing. Avid antiquarian and historian, Lequeu was erudite in the mythical origins of his art and in the principles that guided its development throughout history. His 1792 treatise on human physi-

10.4 *The Corinthian Maid*, painted by Joseph Wright of Derby, 1783–84; from Stafford, *Body Criticism*.

ognomy, *Nouvelle Méthode appliquée aux principes élémentaires du dessin...*, included a lengthy dissertation on the artists, architects, philosophers, and poets believed to have been crucial in founding the first canons of the arts and sciences. More specifically, in these introductory paragraphs, Lequeu narrated an eternal history of drawing. Partly mythic, his story recounted the periodic rebirth of drawing at the hands of various artists.

Lequeu offered several versions of this founding narrative. In the first instance, he merely reiterated the claim made by many authors of antiquity that it was either an Egyptian named Philocles or a Greek named Cleanthes who was the first to trace an outline around the shadow of a man.[11] Other learned authors had claimed that it was Craton, long before Philocles or Cleanthes, who had initiated the art by recording the shadow of a beautiful woman onto a whitened table. In the final and most significant version, Lequeu delivered a lyrical interpretation of a well known classical topos cited by many authors since the Renaissance[12]: "Ainsi, croyons qu'une jeune fille qui ne voulait absolument vivre que pour son ami, désirant conserver d'une manière comparative la douce phisionomie de cet amant chérie que le salut de la patrie forçait à s'éloigner …"[13] It was believed that a young maiden, wishing to live solely for the love of her mate, desired to keep a tender physiognomy of him, for he was destined to leave, having been called to take up arms in honour of his fatherland. Out of her deep affection sprang an inflamed desire to capture the shadowed profile of his precious head. Cloaked in a floral account of young love, Lequeu's story suggested that the origin of the drawing lay in the eternal need to represent desire, beauty, and veneration.: "[A]*lors sa tête virginale levée vers le ciel nébuleux y cherche cette image précieuse; ensuite ses yeux, d'intelligence avec ses doigts, en tracèrent le profil sur le plat d'un rocher amolli d'humidité, suivant fidèlement les extrémités de l'ombre que lui offrait un csté de son visage frappé heureusement dans le moment de la lumière solaire.*"[14] While Lequeu identified his artist as "la fille de Dibutades mouleur de vases de Corinthe," an identical reference having been made by Pliny the Elder,[15] he introduced an important variation to the original tale. He insisted that this impassioned discovery was made 1388 years before Christ and 100 years before Daedalus. With this statement, Lequeu had named the maiden from Corinth as drawing's founding hero. In so doing, he had effected the first of many transgressions of accepted scholarship that would come to mark the whole of his work. In one breath, Lequeu usurped the invention of the visual arts away from Daedalus, long considered the father of the mimetic arts.[16]

His strategic revision of mythic history explicitly separated the art of drawing from those of sculpture and architecture.[17] While Lequeu went on to narrate the origins of these latter arts, the origins of drawing represented the primordial beginning of all artistic knowledge. The work of the *dessinateur,* bestowed with its own history, theory, and *techné,*[18] was deemed the most original, and thus the most divine, activity.

OF THE DRAWING OF ORNAMENT IN ARCHITECTURE

While Lequeu presented an exhaustive list of accomplishments effected by drawing's great masters,[19] he promoted the architectural drawing more particularly as the most distinguished component of the art of drawing. In a separate paragraph and under a separate title, *Du Dessin d'Ornement en Architecture*, Lequeu set forth the superiority of the ornamental drawing of architecture. Throughout history, this drawing type had portrayed the most simple rustic hut as well as the most exuberant of the gods' palatial residences. The ancients bestowed upon this great art the title of "most primitive": a pre-eminence held equally because of its antiquity and because of that which the other arts had attributed to its decoration: "Les anciens donnèrent à ce grand art le titre primitif qu'il a encore: prééminence qu'il tient autant de son antiquité, que de ce qu'il associa ensuite les autres arts à sa décoration."[20]

Most important, however, this *dessinateur* believed that drawing's honourable status was no less exalted during his own time than it had been in the past. In his own country, the ornamental drawing of architecture had achieved exceptional status by the end of the eighteenth century and Lequeu made this point in speaking of the great French artists and architects who had distinguished themselves over the last two centuries. Whether in the accomplished distribution of the plan, in decorating interior and exterior masses with elegance, in the skilful painting of finished drawings, or in having one's ideas realized with the best materials and accessories, the French had gained mastery over drawing and architecture.

This distinction, Lequeu contended, was due unequivocally to the sacred writings of their most ancient master, progenitor, and founding father, Vitruvius Pollio, who, along with other scholars, had furnished France with excellent principles with which to ornament and build: "[O]n doit l'avantage aux écrits [sacrés] de Vitruve-Pallio, notre plus ancien maître, comme aussi de quelques savans qui ont donné d'excellens principes sur cet art [de décorer et] de bâtir."[21] With this statement, Lequeu associated the great triumphs of French drawing with the written text in architecture, making explicit his belief that the *dessinateur* needed to be familiar with the theory of architecture in order to execute competently the ornamental drawing of architecture. His subsequent insertion of the word *décorer* further substantiated the role that the architectural treatise played in communicating the rules of decorum: that is, the rules of ornamentation. Lequeu once more postulated an association between architectural theory and the drawing of ornaments in honouring those who used the compass and set square to take exacting measures of both precious ornamental vestiges and extremely rare and ancient profiles. For Lequeu, those who left to posterity designs of such fragments were worthy of great esteem. In this recording of relics and remnants, drawings could safeguard ideas and inventions in a manner analogous to the written text, the architectural fragment operating as a visual character in the language of representation.

Lequeu's master, Vitruvius, corroborated the importance of the architectural treatise in communicating architectural inventions. While Lequeu listed Fussius, Varro, Septimius, and Cossustus among the venerated ancients who had written on architecture, Vitruvius had written of these same authorities in his preface to Book VII of *De Architectura;* his preface was dedicated to philosophers, artists, and architects who magnanimously left their thoughts to future generations. Vitruvius cited Fussius, Varro, and Septimius for their writings on symmetry, while Cossutus the Roman architect was cited for having designed a great temple to Jupiter with a double colonnade and a symmetrical architrave.[22] Vitruvius's long list of first records of architectural significance also included a theatre commentary by Democritus and Anaxagoras discussing the converging lines of sight of the *scaenographia,* his third drawing type. For Vitruvius, as for Lequeu, the text and drawing housed the architectural idea in perpetuity.

Most curious, however, was the actual content of this seventh book. Its themes were introduced at the very end of Book Six as including "the methods of finishing the work, so that they may be ornamental, free from defects and permanent,"[23] and in Book VII Vitruvius proceeded to describe different types of pavements, the mixing of stucco and lime, the decoration of dining rooms, the decadence of fresco painting, the uses of marble, and the different varieties of pigments. In other words, Book Seven addressed the materials, procedures, and building surfaces of the art of ornamentation. Once again, for Vitruvius as for Lequeu, the architectural ornament had been inextricably linked to the architectural text.

The importance that these two modes of representation held for architectural thought lay in their shared origins: the line. In bringing this truth to light we return to Vitruvius, who uses the term *peritus graphidos* in referring to the architect who possesses the knowledge of drawing. While *peritus* refers to one who is skilled, a closer look at the term *graphidos* signals the act of grafting, of making marks, impressions, incisions, and characters. Significantly, these activities are not exclusively the domain of drawings; they are also the defining gestures of the text. This truth was known by Lequeu, for the architect, in articulating the work of theory, participated in the original union of image and text. In adopting both the word and the image, Lequeu's nocturnal career as an architectural draughtsman participated in the making of an architectural treatise.

L'Architecture Civile was replete with both drawing ornaments and text, its orthography simultaneously engaging the *orthographie* of letters as well as the *orthographia* of the elevation drawing. These representations of architectural theory were the ornamental drawings that Lequeu claimed to be the true work of the *dessinateur*.

IN DEFENCE OF OBSCURITY

For most visual artists of the eighteenth century, drawing was considered the modus operandi par excellence. The detailed drawing and comparison of all that appeared to one's sight became the quintessential ordering device for all forms of communicable knowledge. Medicine, natural history, and the sciences in general all adopted drawing in explicating the objects and procedures of their respective disciplines. Lequeu's own exhaustive drawing opus demonstrates the extent to which he undertook his own near-encyclopedic amassment of the visual world. However, Lequeu's passionate involvement with drawing precipitated his search beyond the limits of formal and quantifiable knowledge. In his studied rendering of architecture, Lequeu gave voice to a language of metaphors.

To this end, Lequeu adopted the drawing technique of *clair-obscur*. Widely used by painters, sculptors, and delineators, it was considered a skill of only secondary importance for the architectural draughtsman. However, Lequeu made it the centre of his drawing activity[24]: "Pour premier principe de cet ouvrage, les Corps isolés et environnés d'objets composent des masses, seront éclairés d'un raïon de lumière tombent à 45 degrés sur leurs façes horizontales ou verticales."[25] This statement appears in the frontispiece of *l'Architecture Civile,* his cosmological diagram of radial design portraying both the shadow types cast by five platonic solids and the elementary geometric operations required to draw them. The centre and focal point of the drawing labelled *le Soleil, ou la Lune, ou en Flambeau, ou Enfin un Bûcher* betrays the source of all drawing to be the light ray, whether sun, moon, torch, or hearth. Not surprisingly, Lequeu had articulated once again that the principal operation around which he organized his cosmography of representation included the casting of shadows.

At first glance, our draughtsman is merely adapting to architectural representation a technique already commonplace in the visual arts, light and illumination being metaphors central to the epistemology of the Enlightenment. However, closer scrutiny of Lequeu's work will disclose the particular originality of his position. It will demonstrate why *clair-obscur*, the paradoxical union of clarity and obscurity, became the theoretical basis of his architectural treatise. While Lequeu shared the predominant world-view of the century that sought to bring to light what lay hidden in the darkness of things, his commitment to the complete denuding of knowledge would be conditional.

A literary analogue to his drawing technique of *clair-obscur* was adopted in Lequeu's game of etymologies: the study of words, their origins and changes in meaning through time. Having originated in the highly interpretive field of pictorial writing, the study of etymologies was considered far from a precise science.[26] Suspicion of etymological studies was clearly evident by the eighteenth century.[27]

Lequeu, however, had no such disdain for the open-ended, often obscure interpretation of words. Rather, he would embrace their metaphorical origins. Throughout *l'Architecture Civile*, Lequeu presented to the reader a near-maze-like unfolding of parallel imaginary worlds suggesting multiple meanings and associations across the *orthographie* of his texts.

ARCHITECTURAL ORDERS AND RITUALS OF FOUNDATION

Lequeu embraced the visual and textual language of metaphors in order to re-present the mythic origins of architecture. His intimate knowledge of antiquity's sacred and historical narratives is evident throughout *l'Architecture Civile*. With repeated references to lost civilizations and founding tales of cities long gone, Lequeu delineated an allegorical return to architectural beginnings. Endowing his drawings with rich historical anecdotes of both facts and fictions, Lequeu cultivated a critical, albeit personal, reinterpretation of architectural history.

In this regard, Lequeu drew his own exegesis of the Vitruvian orders. In the use of both traditional and newly designed ornamental characters, Lequeu redefined the role of the architectural column. Contrary to the polemic that raged in architectural theory during the eighteenth century, Lequeu's concern was not with establishing the most correct proportional system for the orders; rather, his particular interest lay in recounting the story of their origins. In the inventive portrayal of the column

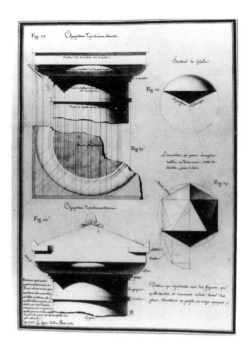

10.5 Lequeu, the Tyrrhenian order, *l'Architecture Civile*, pl. 14; from Duboy, *Lequeu*.

and its dress, Lequeu had gestured towards a history in danger of being forgotten: the principal role that the column played in rituals of foundation.

Four early drawing plates completed between 1782 and 1784 depict the different column orders: the *Tyrrhénien*, the Doric, the Ionic, and the Corinthian. The *Tyrrhénien* was a new column order introduced and developed by Lequeu. Appearing on two separate plates, the first *Tyrrhénien* column was drawn as a free-standing decorative column, topped with a pedimented headdress. In its second appearance, the column was drawn with a full entablature and labelled as an order.[28] Both of the columns were clearly named *Tyrrhénien*; however, their capital profiles were drawn interchangeably, as convex in one figure and concave in the other. In fact, while the first free-standing capital resembles the Tuscan order, the inverted profile of the second column calls upon the reader to consider this an altogether new invention.

Just as the column presents more than one capital profile, so its name *Tyrrhénien* elicits multiple myths of importance for architecture. The ancient city of Tyre, maritime capital of Phoenicia, figured prominently in mythic history as the birthplace of many illustrious minds, one of whom, "Euclid ... a philosopher of somewhat ancient date, a Greek by nationality ... born at Tyre ... published a most excellent and most useful work entitled the foundations or elements of geometry."[29] This information was not lost on Lequeu, who had drawn alongside his Tyrrhenian columns an icosahedron and a dodecahedron, both derived from the pentagon. Another illustrious character associated with Tyre was Hiram, the king of Tyre, builder and architect of the Temple of Solomon.[30] Once more, architecture had figured prominently in Tyre's history when, during the seventeenth and eighteenth centuries, the ruined city was visited by archaeologists who came in search of the origins of architecture. British pioneer explorer William Lithgow, who travelled to Tyre during the early decades of the seventeenth century, was reported to have seen the very columns taken down by Samson.[31] Finally, in naming the column *Tyrrhénien*, Lequeu also made reference to the Tyrrhenian seaboard of Italy, bound by Sicily to the south and the islands of Corsica and Sardinia to the west. This coastal region had been the birthplace of the ancient Etruscans, and its founder was believed to have been Tyrrhenus, "the eponymous hero of the whole Etruscan nation."[32]

Therefore, in having named his first column *Tyrrhénien*, Lequeu multiplied the metaphorical narratives associated with Vitruvius's original order. In expanding that order's association with ancient Tyre, he allegorically and syncretically united the narratives of Euclid, Hiram, Samson, and Tyrrhenus. With this, Lequeu had re-founded the Tuscan order. Lequeu's first column, in bringing to mind the names of heroes and founders, had tacitly inferred the role of columns in rituals of foundation.

In his design for the Doric order, this association was made more explicit. Entitled the *Colonne Milliaire, d'Ordonnance Dorique*, this column's ornamental language clearly referred to the founder's voyage. As a free-standing column, its principal means of ornamentation was the surface of its shaft, on which one could read "des inscriptions pour instruire le voyageur et du chemin et des distances."[33] Inscribed within the column flutes were instructions to aid the journeyman on the condition of the road ahead and the distances to traverse. Both the column name and Lequeu's text bespeak of the ancient Roman military practice of marking roads with boundary markers: vertical stones that indicate distances between towns, counted in miles: "Milliaire; colonne milliaire, en parlant des colonnes que les Romains plaçoient au près de leurs grands chemins, & sur les quelles la differance des lieux était marquée en comptant par milles."[34] However, in Lequeu's union of the Doric order with the word *Milliaire*, our draftsman had effected a literary

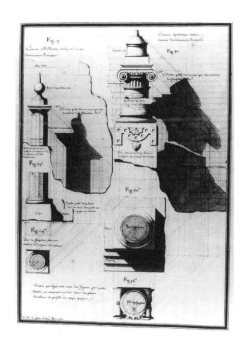

10.6 Lequeu, the Doric
and Ionic orders,
l'Architecture Civile, pl. 18;
from Duboy, *Lequeu.*

trope. In the root word *Mille*, which meant both the measure of the mile and the numerical figure of 1000, Lequeu had intended a lateral association with the term *Millénaire:* "Millénaire; on a ainsi appelé ceux qui croyoient qu'apres le jugement universel, les élus demeureroient milles ans sur la terre à jouir de toute sorte de plaisir. Ceux qui ont soutenu cette opinion n'étoient point une sorte d'hérétiques ou de schismatiques séparés de l'Eglise."[35]

The hero is central to the definition of "millenarianism." The latter pronounces the coming of an ideal society from out of the revolutionary actions of its heroes. The biblical prophecy that declared the thousand-year earthly reign of Jesus, the Christian hero, figured prominently in millenarianism. Considered primarily a heretical offshoot of Christianity, it belonged to a more occult tradition that believed in the Adamic truth of God-given revelation: Adam, in being the first hero, was believed to have been given the original sign, the original word-image.[36] It should not be entirely surprising that Lequeu may have considered millenarianism to be metaphorically, historically, and geographically appropriate to France of the late eighteenth century, a nation whose blood had been violently shed during the greatest political and intellectual revolution ever.

Moreover, Lequeu would have been familiar with the traditional narrative of the founding of the Doric order as given by Vitruvius. Dorus, son of Hellen, and the ancient Greek ruler and warrior who reigned as king over the Peloponnese, built himself a temple in the style that would take his name.[37] With "the proportions of a man's body, its strength and grace," the Doric order was the mimetic reflection of the virile male, of the hero.[38] Lequeu saw in Dorus the leader of a nation of soldiers and conquerors, one of the original founding heroes of the Doric order. Therefore, in naming the Doric order *Colonne Milliaire,* Lequeu once again expanded the column's metaphorical dimensions, binding together heroic and military founding narratives from the worlds of ancient Greece and revolutionary France.

Lequeu's design for the Ionic order, the *Colonne Historique,* was even more explicit about its relationship to the hero's journey. As with the Doric column, the shaft of this free-standing column was inscribed with text. Labelled "historial du heros," the column communicated the hero's his-stories: his journeys, hardships, and trials. However, the apogee of Lequeu's probe into the origins of columns was his desire to demonstrate more specifically how the founding of columns was synonymous with the founding of cities – ancient rituals that governed not only the physical boundaries of the city but also its laws and religious practices. Nowhere was this brought to light more clearly than in the inventive ornamental details designed for his final and most decorated order: the Corinthian.

THE CITY OF CORINTH AND THE ORNAMENTS OF SACRIFICE.

Rituals that defined the limits of a city necessarily involved the hero's narrative. "City founding, and the fathering of tribes, as well as the invention of skills and trades, are among the 'typical' characteristics of heroes … they have the strongest connection with all matters concerning death, the hunt, games, divination, healing, and mystery cults."[39] Via prayers and rites, the hero called the gods into the city, offered them as protectorates, and founded the city. Following the hero's death, maintaining the city's protectorates involved ritually re-founding the city's edge. To this end, sacrifices and festivals in the name of the hero were officiated annually at the site of his tomb.[40]

Lequeu's fourth free standing column, the *Monument funèraire, d'ordonnance corinthienne, Erigé prés le mur de la Ville./.,* was a funereal monument of the Corinthian order in homage to this ancient cult

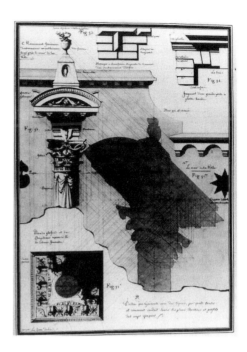

10.7 Lequeu, the Corinthian
order, *l'Architecture Civile*, pl. 19;
from Duboy, *Lequeu*.

of the dead. Both column capital and shaft abound in allegorical gestures
to the world of past souls. Ornamental urns, skulls, serpents, garlands,
festoons, torches, draperies, and guttae all attest to Lequeu's knowledge
of correlations between the founding of cities, funereal rites, and the
practice of sacrifice: "They set stones vertically in solid earth ... they
decorated them with unguents, garland and clothing ... they sprinkled
them with blood and laid fruit and frankincense, beans and vines on
them ... and when the [god's] meal had been consumed by the fire they
laid the smoking remains on the stones."[41] On the site of such practices,
temples were consecrated and cities born. Just as the bloody rite yearly
re-founded the city anew, so the column that marked the event was a
symbol of the city's continued prosperity. Lequeu's own ornamental
design for the Corinthian column made it a marker analogous to this
vertical stone stele. Erected near the city wall, it represented the sacrificial order of ancient myth.

But why would Lequeu specifically choose the Corinthian column to
reveal the role that sacrifice played in the founding narratives of architecture? A closer look at details, once again directed towards the column
shaft, discloses yet another interpretation of the origins of the Corinthian
column. In contrast to the Doric and Ionic orders, this shaft was not
inscribed with text; rather, its surface was draped by sumptuously hung

10.8 Lequeu, *Sanctuaire des Voix Célestes, l'Architecture Civile*, pl. 52, fig. 140; from Duboy, *Lequeu*.

textiles. While the allegorical role of fabric in the sacrificial ritual has already been noted, Lequeu's particular representation of pleats and folds suggests a far different allegory of sacrifice.

To comb the depths of this visual trope, we need refer to the orthographic figures that are drawn on either side of the column shaft. Located on the city wall are the *Pique, Trefle,* and *Etoile* – all figures of French playing cards. The *Pique* in particular offers an entry into Lequeu's etymological game. As drawn, the *Pique* represents the spade, the spear-like military weapon of ancient Rome, whose profile terminated in a sharp and threatening point.[42] With only a slight variation in its spelling, however, *Piqué* refers to the art and craft of textiles – more specifically, to the couturier detail in which the needle pierces both the front and the back of the fabric pieces as they are being conjoined.[43] The *Piqué* was only one of the many references that Lequeu made, both in drawing and in text, to the art of vestments.[44] Throughout *l'Architecture Civile*, ornamental fabric details abound. In his design for the *Théâtre Royale* on Plate 45, reams of ornamental fabric are used to face theatre boxes, while in Fig. 118 the *Piqué* detail articulates the base of the column statue dedicated to the goddess Cythère.

Once more, a careful look at the drapery of the Corinthian column discloses its own use of the *Piqué* detail. In fact, this particular detail was repeated in Lequeu's design for the *Sanctuaire des voix Célestes* on

Plate 52. Dedicated to the Eternal God, this sanctuary was designed as a raised, throne-like platform covered by a large, circular textile canopy. Gathered in the form of a rounded knot, the fabric detail at the scale of the room was analogous to the *Piqué* detail of Lequeu's Corinthian column.

To what end would Lequeu's game of textiles and text be directed? In two sentences, Lequeu insinuates an answer: the *Pique, Trefle,* and *Etoile* were described as "Pique et Trefles éclairent des garderobes" and "Ouverture à Etoile de la Vüe de Servitude."[45] The three figures clearly represented apertures in the city wall, openings through which the observer became enlightened as to the nature of the city that lay within. Most illuminating, however, would be his adoption of the term *garderobe*. With this one gesture, Lequeu defined his city as the city of wardrobes, bedrooms, and toiletries. This curious metaphor was nevertheless deliberately chosen, for, in looking through the *Etoile*, Lequeu's observer was offered a view toward *servitude* – yet another facet of the sacrificial metaphor.

Throughout the eighteenth century, the geography of social behaviour defined the private chambers, in which bodily rituals of clothing, denuding, and cleansing took place, as quintessential environments for the expression of natural character. This occurred at a time when the epistemology of *caractère* was still understood as partly constructed and partly innate. Natural character was the given in an individual's psyche and it acted as the counterweight to one's cultural character, which was governed by taste and custom.[46] Although these two modes of expression were concurrent, natural and cultural character were developed on different sites and within different settings. It was in the public realm that the individual was made, while one's nature was realized in the private realm.[47]

The city street defined a veritable stage of human representations; in appointed and designated public actions and in the open forum of exchange, gestures of appearance institutionalized cultural modes of behaviour. Whether one was a pauper or a prince, one's garments and stature spoke across the widening silence of increasingly hostile cities. Orchestrated appearances, in full costume and disguise, presented to the city one's social standing and rank. Visibility in the eye of the city confirmed being.[48] However, the city's "other" was the space of the *garderobe* where, in the privacy of intimate associations, one's natural

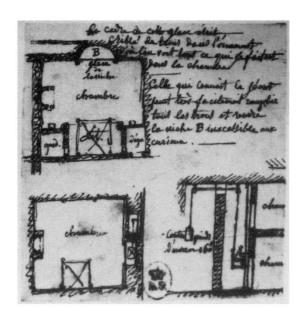

10.9 Lequeu, Bedroom peephole for the house of enchantments; from Duboy, *Lequeu*.

character was expressed. Natural character originated in the inner disposition of the soul and was independent of physical appearance, financial standing, professional affiliation, or spiritual belief. Steeped in the language of sympathies and passions, it was defined as a "sensitivity to the needs of others, no matter what the differences in social circumstances."[49] Transcendent and quasi-divine, it could not be altered or reversed either by human thought or by social convention. In the representation of the internal and hidden component of *caractère*, exploring one's natural character amounted to a discourse with the soul. Therefore, in illuminating the space of the *garderobe*, the orthographic figures of Lequeu's Corinthian column illuminated a city of the soul.

Equally critical to the development of his narrative was the eighteenth-century belief that the space of the *garderobe* corresponded to a particular gender: the female. While a similar correspondence between the male psyche and the female body had given rise to some of the earliest allegorical tales of antiquity, Lequeu delivered his own eighteenth-century interpretation in marrying the founding narrative of the Corinthian order to the rituals of prostitution. In presenting the three apertures as visual orifices in the city wall, Lequeu had metaphorically designed the city as an analogue to the *camera obscura,* the peephole device used by the *dessinateur* in capturing and isolating the subject of his interest. Lequeu was fascinated with this contrivance throughout his drawing career; his archives contain a design, in plan and section, for a bedroom

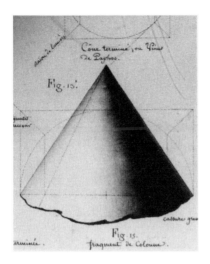

10.10 Lequeu, Geometric solids, *Cone terminé on Vénus de Paphos, l'Architecture Civile*, pl. 8; from Duboy, *Lequeu*.

10.11 Black meteorite stone from Aphrodite's temple in Paphos; from Hersey, *The Lost Meaning of Classical Architecture*.

peephole at the scale of a building. A niche, carved out of a bedroom wall and operated with a series of pulleys, was occupiable by a curious onlooker. Once inside, one could secretly gaze into the bedroom without being noticed: "Le cadre de cette glace était criblé de trous dans l'ornement d'où l'on voit tout ce qui se faisait dans la chambre. Celle qui connait le secret peut très facilement remplir tous les trous et rendre la niche B inacessible aux curieux."[50] Should the inhabitant of the bedroom discover the secret of the *trous,* she could easily close the aperture and render the view inaccessible to the voyeur. Lequeu developed the device and incorporated it into the facade of his *Casin d'enchantement* on Plate 38, a design for an observation tower for one of his many pleasure palaces. These games of surveillance, typical of Paris in the late eighteenth century,[51] had a female protagonist: the prostitute.

While he articulated his own architectural interpretation of the temple of sacred marriages with this reference to bedrooms and peepholes, Lequeu was well aware of the ancient history of prostitution. On Plate 8, he drew a solid body in the form of a conical stone and labelled it "Cone terminé; ou Vénus de Paphos." The Roman goddess of love and beauty had been substituted for Aphrodite, her Greek counterpart, but Lequeu employed a sophisticated rationale in manipulating this reference from antiquity. Having named the ancient city of Paphos, Lequeu alluded to its temple dedicated to Aphrodite, "one of the oldest, richest, and most famous of all ancient Greek holy places."[52] Originally surrounded by a sacred grove, its object of veneration was a black meteorite stone worshipped in the name of the goddess. The origin of this sacred stone lay in the mythic account of Saturn's quarrel with his father Uranus. In anger against his father, Saturn severed the paternal penis and tossed it into the sea. The member, having hit the foaming waters, turned into Aphrodite. Her worshippers thus carried bowls of sea salt and phalli to the temple in memory of the aquatic metamorphosis.[53] Lequeu's abstracted conical figure undoubtedly made reference to this black meteorite. The city of Paphos was the ancient centre of sacred prostitution; priestesses ritually incarnated the goddess Aphrodite, their bodies serving as conduits in the religious union between man and god.[54] Curiously, the city of Corinth was second only to Paphos in its involvement with prostitution, with its own temple dedicated to Aphrodite being the site of sacred marriages. Textual inscriptions bear witness to the temple having housed nearly a thousand prostitutes during the Persian Wars.[55]

Therefore, devising a link between the founding narrative of the Corinthian column and the female body was not an entirely new invention by Lequeu. In the word Corinth, the root *Kore* discloses the etymological correspondence to the virgin girl. As the personification of Persephone and queen of the underworld, *Kore* represented the domain of darkness and shadows. Akin to *Scotia*, it made reference to the near tangible vapour through which departed souls were said to travel. And finally, in relation to the ornamental lines of the column, it identified the molding whose profile cast horizontal shadows.[56]

Such an association was confirmed by Vitruvius when writing of the origin of the Corinthian order. He recounted that the basis of its invention lay in the tale of the young maiden from Corinth who died a premature death, just prior to her own marriage. "After her funeral, the goblets which delighted her when living, were put together in a basket by her nurse, carried to the monument and placed on top."[57] From this funereal offering sprang the acanthus plant lining the sides of the basket – the acanthus that Callimachus would transform into stone and sculpt into the order's principal ornament.

With his own design for the *Monument funèraire*, Lequeu once again addressed the role of the virgin in the founding narratives of architecture. While Corinth had already figured prominently in Lequeu's origins of

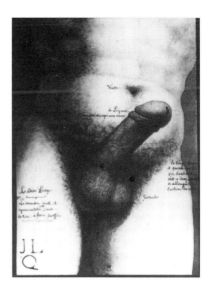

10.12 Greek funereal urn from fourth century B.C.E.; from Hersey, *The Lost Meaning of Classical Architecture*.

10.13 Lequeu, Le Dieu Priape, *Figures Lascives*; from Duboy, *Lequeu*.

drawing, the young maiden who first drew the shadowed trace of the human profile was also said to have originated from this city.[58] For Vitruvius as for Lequeu, the death of the virgin was central in the founding of the Corinthian column. Like the ancients before him, Lequeu exhorted that a particular route to knowledge lay in the servitude of women. As the conduit that insured the initiate passage to the underworld and access to the sacred domains of the soul, the female body was key to the hero's journey.

In a final observation on Lequeu's games of orthography, we may return to the original point of entry: the *Piqué*. In order to confirm the spear-like figure's association with the Corinthian column, we must recall that the acanthus ornament was the thorny bush that sealed off the maiden's basket. In a tropological reading of this plant's prickly character, Lequeu effected a gender reversal with his own *Piqué* detail. While he suggested the piercing action of the needle in his development of the textile joint and in the military weapon of ancient Rome, Lequeu would extend this interpretation in one final analogical reference – this time, to the erect male member, as it appeared in his series *Figures Lascives*.

THE PRE-EMINENCE OF METAPHORICAL LANGUAGE

Lequeu's free-standing columns, *isolées et décorées*, were first and foremost the rhetorical characters of an ornamental language. Throughout the remaining monuments, temples, and cenotaphs that Lequeu drew in the plates of *l'Architecture Civile*, the *dessinateur* had remained committed to developing a critical language of metaphors. In his games of orthography and in his use of *clair-obscur,* Lequeu had thus enacted a critical reinterpretation of mimesis – the very tradition that he himself had otherwise adopted.

Investigating the bookends of *l'Architecture Civile* will point to this truth. In a subtle but strategic absence of text, Lequeu undertook an ironical explication of the changing status of language. Plate 3, immediately following the frontispiece, was composed of two vertical columns, their headings titled "les règles de la Science des Ombres naturelles et du lavis dans le genre fini" and "Réflexions Préliminaires." Plate 78, the very last plate of the treatise, was simply labelled "Sommaire alphabètique des Termes usités dans cet ouvrage." While it would appear that Lequeu was intending to pen rules in the science of natural shadows, introductory comments, and an alphabetic summary of the different terms that he used throughout his treatise, this was not to be the case. On Plates 3 and 78 Lequeu remained silent. In a work of nearly one hundred drawings, every plate was completed except for these two. Had he simply forgotten or run out of time?

Neither. Lequeu's refusal to complete the descriptive and explanatory texts points to his overall critique of scientific languages. He would neither didactically write out the rules of drawing nor define the meaning of terms that he had used, in sharp contrast to the manner in which his first treatise had been composed some twenty years earlier. Whereas the *Nouvelle Méthode* was divided into plates that contained either text or drawings exclusively, and whereas the narratives were separated from the step-by-step geometrical instructions, in *l'Architecture Civile* such divisions were obliterated. The word and the figure coexisted on the surface of the plate. Boundaries between text and image and between historical account and procedural directions were eliminated. With the unrelenting presence of titles, anecdotes, marginal notes, and material descriptions, none of the drawings was devoid of text. In conjoining the word and the image, Lequeu had invented a new language of architectural representation.

10.14 Lequeu, *L'Etable à Vache* and the *Parc des Plaisirs, l'Architecture Civile*, pl. 74, figs. 174 & 175; from Duboy, *Lequeu*.

More important, in having brought both word and image onto the same surface, Lequeu had signalled the demise of symbolic correspondences on the eve of modernity. Repeatedly, his highly literal ornamental drawings raised pointed questions about the status of the mimetic arts. One such instance was *L'Etable à Vache tournée au midi* – the design for a barn in the form of a cow.[59] What more appropriate way to represent the barn than by giving the building an exact figuration of its internal function – the profile of what it protects? In an adjacent drawing, such a correspondence between surface and program was once more suggested. In this example, the arched entrance gate to the *Parc des plaisirs, de la Chasse du Prince*[60] was ornamented with the heads of stags, hogs, and dogs, and at first glance it declared to all the gateway to the hunt.

Yet it would be incorrect to interpret these literal representations as signs of Lequeu's adherence to the dictates of an *Architecture Parlante*, wherein the ornament expressed the inner workings of the building. It would be equally erroneous to suggest that Lequeu's portrayal of the building's function was that of a proto-postmodernist, employing the

ornament in an empty gesture of signification. Lequeu's intentions for
the imitative arts were somewhat more obscure. His cowshed clearly was
not a mere shelter for bovines.

Once again, we turn to Lequeu's etymological game. In the original term
l'Etable Lequeu alluded to yet another spelling of the word: "Retable ...
Ornement d'Architecture contre lequel est appuyé l'autel, & qui enferme
ordinairement un tableau."[61] The *orthographie* of *Retable* directed the
reader to a world beyond what appeared immediately to the eye. As ornamental frame for the display of the altar and its paintings, the *Retable* was
drawn throughout *l'Architecture Civile* in dozens of representations of
places of worship. As such, with this trope, no sooner had he named the
drawing than he had subverted its meaning: his *L'Etable [à] Vache* was
both a sacred altar and a soiled cowshed. As with his presentation of the
orders of architecture, drawing and text simultaneously enlighten and
obscure the meaning of his architectural representation.

The critical question that this example highlights, therefore, is to what
extent the analogical model of the universe could still be operative during
the nineteenth century. Throughout his interpretation of the founding
narratives, Lequeu would forge correspondences among different scales
of being, different arts and sciences, and different modes of thought. The
ritual of drawing *l'Architecture Civile* was enacted as an activity analogous to the founding of cities. However, Lequeu's discourse was also
clearly attentive to the crisis in ontology precipitated and exacerbated
by the death of the king. His demise was accompanied by the demise of
discourse grounded solely in analogical associations. For the modern
psyche, self-conscious of the rift between appearance and being, could
exist once again only in coupling analogical thought with its modern
double, its own critique. For Lequeu, this necessarily involved the introduction of irony in the act of re-presentation.[62]

To this end, Lequeu had embraced the language of metaphor, for only
in courting the nuances of rhetorical languages could he begin to artic-
ulate his fascination with the hidden, the discordant, the obscure, and
the paradoxical. Only irony could bridge the gap in Lequeu's orthographic representations and therefore point to the study of what tran-
scended the eye – of what language and architecture could no longer
reconcile. Lequeu's ornamental language, in delineating a language of
irony through obfuscation, forbade direct closure between the word and
the image.

HIS – STORIES

The city Lequeu portrayed throughout *l'Architecture Civile* was not the Paris envisioned by either the Nouvelle Convention or Napoleon. Both redesigned the new French empire by adopting a ceremonial language of empty gestures, devoid of any true symbolic content, but still modelled on the illustrious history of antiquity. While Lequeu was fascinated with these same narratives, he did not use his drawings and texts to develop a formal language of political and social order at the service of the post-revolutionary state. He did not participate in the episteme of neoclassical France; that is, he would not participate in a discourse with History.[63]

Although obsessed with founding narratives, he would not portray History. Rather, in re-presenting his tales in the form of syncretic allegories, Lequeu denied the linear temporality implicit in History. Moreover, his return to a transhistorical past sought to negate the onslaught of historicism and the accompanying rationalist push towards progress. In this, Lequeu rejected the future-oriented trajectory of the Enlightenment which denied the possibility of an authentic return to the crucial lessons of our ancestors. Oscillating between *orthographie* and *orthographia*, Lequeu's figures and etymologies struggled to reconcile the world of the ancients with that of the moderns. And yet Lequeu was fully aware of standing at the threshold of modernity. With its self-conscious relationship to time, Being in modernity was unlike that of traditional cultures that remained immersed in their past and did not question the meaning of yesterday's acts in light of tomorrow's actions.[64]

Lequeu's philosophical intentions and allegorical inventions amounted to the making of a non-history – a return to an immemorial pre-time, to a primordial time before time.[65] Throughout the *Nouvelle Méthode* and *l'Architecture Civile*, tales of cosmic beginnings were detailed; Lequeu had attributed to supernatural beings the creation of the arts and sciences, for the world was given its knowledge in the actions of gods.[66] Repeatedly, he revisited the origins of things, thus sustaining a belief in an eternal present. Lequeu's adoption of the hero's narrative was an attempt to recognize the eschatology of original myths, for he believed that the route to de-structuring sequential time lay in a return to the spirit of Adam.[67]

In Lequeu's language of pre-Romanticism, his narratives operate as a critique of History.[68] The unfolding of his language of dreams, symbols,

10.15 Lequeu, self-portrait; from Duboy, *Lequeu*.

and metaphors gave voice to his poetic visions. In the adoption of analogy, he forged an operative relationship with the natural world. In his adoption of irony, he set to transgress the social order.[69]

Lequeu's *Architecture Civile* is a rhetorical city of the mind. In this self-conscious work of fiction, Lequeu designed his allegorical return to a meaningful practice of architecture in negating the hegemony of modernity and its historically determined reading of the past. The late-twentieth-century architect might do well to recognize a creative avenue to poetic making in Lequeu's paradoxical union of analogy and irony. In the design of Lequeu's city of ornaments, the craft of drawing embraced, with both desire and fear, the often terrifying gap between ourselves and the other.

NOTES

1 Descamps remained central to the advancement of Lequeu's career. He was instrumental in securing Lequeu a teaching position, as *adjointe associé*, at the Académie Royale de Rouën in 1786.

2 Lequeu was entrusted by Descamps to deliver a personal letter of salutations to Cochin, Chevalier de l'Ordre du Roi, *secretaire historigraphe of* l'Acade-mie Royale de Peinture. Years later, in his *Nouvelle Méthode*, Lequeu named Cochin one of the greatest French artists of his time. It appears that he also

met Houël and Le Barbier, both originally from Lequeu's native city and both eventually named members of the Académie Royale de Peinture. Houël's influence is noted in the presence of forty-four of his original drawing works among the hundreds of drawings found in Lequeu's apartment at the time of his death. Werner Szambien, "L'Inventare après décès de Jean-Jacques Lequeu," *Revue de L'Art* 90 (1990): 104–107. Le Barbier's early life paralleled that of Lequeu's more closely. He also received great acclaim at the age of seventeen from the Académie de Dessin de Rouën, went on to travel in Switzerland and Rome, and exhibited his drawings at the 1814 Salon. *Crosscurrents, French and Italian Neoclassical Drawings and Prints* (Washington, D.C.: Smithsonian Institution Press 1978), 73.

3 Philippe Duboy, *Lequeu, An Architectural Enigma* (Cambridge, Mass.: MIT Press 1987), 353.

4 They included: the circular *Temple de la Nature* for Mᴿ. Q...ˣˣˣ; *Avocat du Grand Conseil;* the *Temple du Silence,* designed for one of France's most notorious characters, Mᴿ. S...ˣˣˣ; *Fermier Général,* the royal tax collector who administered the king's agricultural resources and estates; and the majestic temple front residence built for le Comte de Bouville, a wealthy freemason from Boulogne sur Seine. Lequeu, MS (Ha 80 à 80c rés Folio 3, Plate 3).

5 Krafft et Ransonnette, *Recueil d'architecture civile* (Paris: Scherff 1812), 14.

6 Lequeu, MS *Architecture Civile,* Folio 1. Letter, *Au Nom de la Convention Nationale – Commission d'Employé,* Letter, *Ministère de l'Intérieure,* Letter, *École Impériale.*

7 Lequeu, MS *Architecture Civile,* Folio 1. N.B. Throughout this article Lequeu's orthography will appear in the manner in which he penned it. The translations that follow in the notes are my own. Where translations are not provided in the notes, they are incorporated in the main body of the text.

(Trans.) "NOTICE TO AMATEURS AND FRIENDS OF THE ARTS: Sir Lequeu, having practised architecture under the guidance of Rouen's enlightened masters ... announces a studio wherein he will give drawing lessons on the figure as on the ornament, on architecture and on the other parts of its art. Sir Lequeu joins to his knowledge of building plans and details (which he executes during his regular work) the drawing of the figure using China ink, black line or coloured &&. Convinced that this bold genre could be of interest to persons who have a distinguished taste for the animated Fine arts, and creating in them a desire to possess the rules of washes for portraits, landscapes, maps and architecture, he will give lessons."

8 While the drawing of plans and elevations was known in antiquity to form part of the architect's education, these drawings did not dictate either the material reality of the building or the process of construction. Alberto Pérez-Gómez, "Architecture as Drawing," *Journal of Architectural Education,* vol. 36 no. 2 (winter 1982): 2.

9 Duboy, *Lequeu,* 21.

10 As pointed out by Jean-François Bedard in "The Measure of Expression: Physiognomy and Character in Lequeu's *Nouvelle Méthode,*" *Chora, Intervals in the Philosophy of Architecture,* vol. 1 (1994): 36–56, and by Duboy in *Lequeu,* 15, Lequeu's treatise on physiognomy was produced using the *physionorègle*: a facial grid used by draughtsmen and later adapted to all aspects of representation, including military architecture and civil engineering.

11 Pliny the Elder's interpretation of the origins of painting in the *Naturalis Historiae* was nearly identical to that written by Lequeu. Pliny wrote that the Egyptians claimed to have invented painting 6000 years before the Greeks: "Line-drawing was invented by the Egyptian Philocles or by the Corinthian Cleanthes." Pliny declared that, while agreement did not exist as to the specific place of origin, "all agree that it began with tracing an outline round a man's shadow." Pliny, *Naturalis Historiae* vol. IX, Libri XXIII–XXXV (Loeb Classical Library 1938), 261.

12 Joseph Rykwert, *The First Moderns, The Architects of the Eighteenth Century* (Cambridge, Mass.: MIT Press 1983), 368, 405.

13 Lequeu, MS *Nouvelle Méthode,* Plate 1.

14 Ibid., Plate 2. (Trans.): "at which time her virginal head raised towards the nebulous sky searched for this precious image; then, her eyes, with the intelligence of her fingers, traced the profile upon the flat of a rock softened by moistness, faithfully following the extremeties of the shadow as offered by the side of his face, happily struck during the moment of the solar light."

15 Ibid. In Book XXV of *Naturalis Historiae,* the invention of the profile drawing was ascribed to the daughter of Dibutabes, in a manner almost identical to Lequeu's.

16 Alberto Pérez-Gómez, "The Myth of Daedalus", *AA Files* no. 10 (autumn 1985), 50.

17 The understanding that architectural drawing could itself constitute a separate art with its own intentions, procedures, and *techné* originated in the Renaissance, when the architect used the drawing as a means of symbolic expression. The drawing was not the precise projection of the material

building but rather a projection of the ideal building. Pérez-Gómez, "Architecture as Drawing," 2.

18 My use of the Greek term *techné* refers to Hans-Georg Gadamer's definition in his essay "Poetry and Mimesis," *The Relevance of the Beautiful,* trans. N. Walter (Cambridge: Cambridge University Press 1986), 118. For Gadamer, *techné* designates both the manual production of the artisan and the poetic content of the text. The status of a work of *techné* is not derived from the use of the object; rather, its purpose is simply to exist. Furthermore, as noted by Marco Frascari, *techné* is an element of rhetoric. "The essence of *techné* is by no means technological. *Techné* belongs to the notion of *poesis*, which reveals or discloses *aletheia*, the truth, and goes hand in hand with *episteme* or *scientia*. In common language, the derivative words (technical, technique, technology) have lost the original meaning and are understood to be only of an instrumental value." Marco Frascari, *Monsters of Architecture* (Maryland: Rowman and Littlefield, 1991), 117.

19 Throughout the *Nouvelle Méthode*, Lequeu surveyed the development of drawing throughout the ages. The Tyrrhenians and Etruscans were great cultivators of the art. Republican Rome believed it to be an important part of the education of its most noble heroes. The year 1013 saw the rebirth of drawing from out of the ashes of ancient Rome and the year 1270 witnessed the crayoning of the first gothic traces by Cimabue. With Raphael of Urbino, the drawing was fully restored to its most elevated position, eclipsing both predecessors and contemporaries, while Michelangelo, Leonardo, Rubens, Titian, and the like were mentioned for having left behind prodigious drawing studies.

20 Lequeu, MS *Nouvelle Méthode,* Plate 5.

21 Ibid. His list of important treatise writers included Brunelleschi, Barbaro, Philander, Scamozzi, Palladio, Vignole, Alberti, De l'Orme, Serlio, Chambray, Boffrand, Du Cerceau, Perrault, Laugier, Daviler, and Le Camus de Mezier.

22 Vitruvius, *De Architectura*, trans. F. Granger, Loeb Classical Library, vol. 2, Book VII (Cambridge, Mass.: Harvard University Press 1983), 75–7.

23 Ibid., 59.

24 Jacques-François Blondel, in describing why the architectural draughtsman ought to possess the skill of *clair-obscur*, noted that most architects considered life drawing and ornamental design of less importance than their usual activities. Much was required "to overcome their distaste for such protracted studies." For Blondel, however, it was important that the architectural

draughtsman possess such knowledge even if only to endow better the curves of a plan with good taste, to successfully draw out a winding staircase, or "to vary the forms of a room or profile." As quoted by Duboy, *Lequeu*, 21.

25 Lequeu, MS *Architecture Civile,* Plate 2. (trans.): "The first principle of this work being that, isolated Bodies and those surrounded by objects in composing masses, will be lit by a ray of light falling upon their horizontal and vertical faces at 45 degrees."

26 Michel Foucault, *The Order of Things* (New York: Pantheon 1973), 111.

27 *Le Grand Vocabulaire François,* Tome Dixième (Paris: Par Une Société de Gens de Lettres 1762), 65: "Étymologie ... l'origine d'un mot est en général un fait à deviner, un fait ignoré, auquel on ne peut arriver que par des conjectures ... il est quelques étymologies d'une utilité evidente, par la clarté qu'elles répandent sur certains objets, il en est une infinité d'autres qu'on peut regarder comme indifférentes ou inutiles, & même comme nuisibles, si l'on considère que c'est au culte superstitieux qu'on leur a rendu, que nous devons rapporter la plupart des vices de notre orthographe." (Trans.): "The origin of a word is in general something to be guessed, something not known, to which we come to only by conjecture ... there are some etymologies which are clearly of use, given the clarity which they shed unto certain objects, there are an infinite number of others which we could consider of no relation or useless, and even as bothersome, if we remember that they've been related to a superstitious cult, to which we should correlate the greater part of all the vices of our orthography."

28 Lequeu, MS *Architecture Civile,* Plate 14, Fig. 35, Fig. 35'; Plate 16, Fig. 42.

29 The original source, Casiri, *Bibliotheca Arabico-Hispana Escurialensis,* 339, was mentioned in *Euclid, The Thirteen Books of the Elements* (New York: Dover Publications 1956), vol. 1:4.

30 James Stevens Curl, *The Art and Architecture of Freemasonry, an introductory study* (London: B. T. Batsford 1991), 239.

31 Rykwert, *The First Moderns,* 273.

32 Joseph Rykwert, *The Idea of a Town* (Cambridge, Mass.: MIT Press 1988), 157.

33 Lequeu, MS *Architecture Civile,* Plate 18.

34 *Le Grand Vocabulaire François,* Tome Dix-Huitième (Paris 1771), 100. (trans.) "Milliary; milliary column, in speaking of the columns that the Romans placed alongside their vast roads, and upon which the difference between places was indicated, measured in miles; in thousands."

35 Ibid., 96.

36 George Steiner, *After Babel* (Oxford: Oxford University Press 1992), 60.

37 Vitruvius, *De Architectura*, 205.

38 Ibid., 207.

39 Rykwert, *The Idea of a Town*, 24–5.

40 Fustel de Coulanges, *The Ancient City* (Garden City, N.Y.: Doubleday Anchor Books 1956), 142.

41 George Hersey, *The Lost Meaning of Classical Architecture* (Cambridge, Mass.: MIT Press 1988), 42. Originally quoted from the *Hyginus Gromaticus*.

42 *Le Grand Vocabulaire François*, Tome Vingt-Deuxième (Paris 1772), 195. "Pique; Sorte d'arme à longbois, dont le bout est garni d'un fer plat & pointer. Les piques qu'on voit dans les monumens fait du temps des Empereurs Romains." (Trans.): "Pike; a kind of long wooden stick, in which the end is trimmed with a metal tip, flat and pointed. The spades which we see in monuments were made during the times of the Roman Emperors."

43 Ibid., 196. "Piquer; est encore un terme fort usité dans les Manufactures est les Communautes des Arts & Métiers & signifie faire avec du fil ou de la soie sur les étoffes." (Trans.): "Stitch; is also a term often used in manufacturing and in the communities of the arts and crafts and means making with thread or silk on fabrics."

44 In a rarely cited manuscript that Lequeu also submitted to the Bibliothèque Royale, the draughtsman set out to instruct the young women of Paris on the art of washing textiles. Titled *Lettre sur le beau savonnage*, the book-sized manuscript gave detailed instructions on the washing and ironing of linen and included a series of explanatory drawings.

45 Lequeu, MS *Architecture Civile*, Plate 19.

46 Richard Sennett, *The Fall of Public Man* (New York: Knopf 1974), 91.

47 Ibid., 18.

48 Georges Gusdorf, *Naissance de la Conscience Romantique au Siècle des Lumières* (Paris: Payot 1976), 369.

49 Sennett, *Fall of Public Man*, 91.

50 Duboy, Lequeu, 59. (Trans.): "The frame of this mirror was riddled with holes in the ornament, from which we see all that takes place within the bedroom. She who knows the secret can very easily fill up all the holes and make the niche, B, inaccesible to the curious."

51 During the eighteenth century several enlightened authors believed in the institutionalization of prostitution. Ledoux himself offered his Oikema as the House of Pleasure in his city of Chaux. Restif de la Bretonne published a *Projet de Reglement* and presented it to the city of Paris in his bid to

sanitize and regularize prostitution. In his own description of one such house of enchantment, the "peephole" and "*cabinet obscur*" are central to the successful *deroulement* of the activities. Restif de la Bretonne, *Le Pornographe, ou Idées d'un Honnête Homme* (Londres: Ches Jean Nouse 1770).

52 Hersey, *Lost Meaning of Architecture*, 47.

53 Ibid., 49.

54 Ibid., 52.

55 Ibid., 66.

56 Ibid., 21.

57 Vitruvius, *De Architectura*, 209.

58 Lequeu, MS *Nouvelle Méthode*, Plate 10, Note 11.

59 Lequeu, MS *Architecture Civile*, Plate 74, Fig. 174.

60 Ibid., Fig. 175.

61 *Le Grand Vocabulaire François*, Tome Vingt-Cinquième (Paris 1773), 45. (Trans.): "Retable; architectural ornament against which the altar is placed, and which usually encloses a painting."

62 Octavio Paz, *The Children of the Mire* (Cambridge, Mass.: Harvard University Press 1974), 74.

63 My use of this term "History" refers to the nineteenth-century science of historiography in which Western societies set out to define the one grand linear narrative of human development, to the exclusion of the multiplicity of meanings inherent in different peoples and civilizations.

64 Paz, *Children of the Mire*, 8.

65 Mircea Eliade, *Myth and Reality* (New York: Harper and Row, 1963), 75.

66 Ibid., 5.

67 Ibid., 64.

68 My use of the term pre-Romanticism is based on that furnished by Octavio Paz in *Children of the Mire*.

69 Eliade, *Myth and Reality*, 33.

Architecture and
the Vegetal Soul

David Winterton

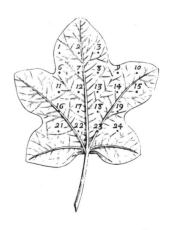

Chora

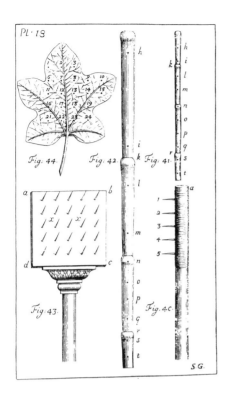

11.1 Stephen Hales, *Enlightenment botanical experiments on 'soulless,' mechanical plantlife*; from *Vegetable Staticks*, Plate 18 (reprinted in London: MacDonald 1969 [originally published in 1727]).

de rerum natura,
quae graece physiologia dicitur,
philosophia explicat ...

Vitruvius, *De Architectura*, Book I, chapter I, vii.

TO STRIVE TO UNDERSTAND the significance of the physical world is to enter into the discourse of natural philosophy. This discourse holds a privileged yet variegated position in the flux of Western thought, and studying the various meanings that natural philosophy has attributed to the world throughout the epochs reveals how humankind has placed itself in its self-defined cosmos. Such study also reveals, however, that the human subject has always been an integral part of that cosmos and that this integration has rooted culture to *place*. But we moderns know well the unease that comes with trying to comprehend our place in a universe that has been, since the Renaissance resurrection of Platonic ideals, an abstract, mathematical construction wherein the human subject is considered separately. The scientific revolution that evolved during the Renaissance allowed the epistemologically inclusive musings of natural philosophy to be superseded by something more akin to what we know as science. In other words, the modern way of explaining the world relies less on contemplation and more on a detached human gaze.

This simple shift in gaze from a living, shared world to a dead, usable one has taken us from a rapport with a living nature to a modern "environment" that is mediated, transformed, and dominated by instruments. These instruments are transformed from the stuff of nature into capital, which replicates the production until, one must assume, there is no more stuff of nature to be transformed. Superseding one technological feat by another in an already mediated planet may expose the faith in modern progress as myth. Postmodern art and theory emerged from such tedium, further exposing the myth of progress and resisting the claims to truth of late-twentieth-century capitalism. Contemporary natural philosophy that "remembers" nature and presents us with a felt, immediate world can help us to understand our place in a paradoxically placeless world and root us again to the earth.

Descartes, the intellectual forebear of the modern condition, construed *physis* (traditionally a "living" and unique nature) as the sublunar, imperfect, and lifeless component of a metaphysical, perfect universe. This Platonic concept has been entrenched in Western philosophy, even though we may feel it to be contrary to our perceptions. Architecture, at least since the Renaissance reinterpretation of Vitruvius, has always striven to reflect the purity of that abstract, metaphysical space, except for a few brief rebellious interludes variously labeled as Mannerist, Expressionistic, or Romantic. Architectural theory has rarely tried to come to terms with the so-called "imperfection" and "animism" of nature, except insofar as those terms are used disparagingly. Modern architectural thought has generally coincided with the scientific paradigm of mastery over nature.[1]

Perhaps in the face of the modern desecration of the environment and the ecological peril that has ensued since industrialization, nature must again be recuperated as the radical base for speculation in Western culture – not "Nature" as mere observable fact, to be later assuaged into some use, but as the fleshy, foliate, earthy, and olfactory extension of our selves that surrounds and is unconsciously and already inhabiting our bodies and imaginations – nature that can be recuperated as something meaningful in and of itself.

The scientific paradigm has insistently conceived of nature as Other, an alterity that our consciousnesses must overlay with significance. We perceive the world, however, not only through arbitrary signs and conventions, but also through writing and alphabetization[2] and a detached, scientific gaze. What brought me to the following study of seven mysterious Enlightenment letters was an interest in the way that these arbitrary signs, semantic constructions, and perceptual filters of the concept "Nature" mediate our direct experience of the world, and how such mediation affects architectural production. This kind of investigation, of course, raises the difficulty of representing our intuitions about nature if our intellects are trained to disregard them.

Architecture, for us "natural aliens,"[3] replaces nature as a ground for meaning in the world, and not merely in a simplistic "cave-becomes-house" replacement. Because we have seriously delimited the meaning we can take from nature (it is mere necessity, mere resource), we must supply meaning for ourselves from a world of our own building. What meaning has been ascribed, then, to late-twentieth-century North American architecture if it is increasingly buffeted by the dictates of late-capitalist marketing analyses, or is reified as harmless, mute boxes that result from building codes conceived for a *very* safe, *very* clean futurist utopia? In order to dwell on the earth with some kind of meaning – meaning that transcends technological progress or the disembodied sterility of cyberlandscapes – we must first reconcile the body with the organic world. To do so we must begin by recuperating the profundity of architecture.

THE *LETTRES SUR L'ARCHITECTURE*

The scientific revolution turned nature into instrument. Concomitant with that was the rending of mind from body, of physical from phenomenal truth, thereby inducing a paradoxical dualism. A Romantic rebellion ensued, one that insisted on holding up the truth of subjectivity and felt experience to the ever-inspecting lamps of science. One cultural document of that intellectual era, the *Lettres sur l'Architecture des anciens et celle des modernes dans lesquelles on se trouve développé le génie symbolique qui présida aux Monumens de l'Antiquité*, by Jean-Louis Viel de St-Maux, published in 1787, is an example of this rebellion applied to architectural thought. The proto-Romantic *Lettres* illuminate an attempt in the late Enlightenment to conceive architecture not as purely rational science but as experience: sensitive to site, willing to recuperate the scientifically derived systems of Nature as a relay for symbolic monuments. The *Lettres sur l'Architecture* reveal some instructive cultural presumptions about nature and architecture.

Recent scholarship has treated the *Lettres sur l'Architecture* as a significant cultural document of late-eighteenth-century architectural thought, "one of the keys to revolutionary architecture."[4] Viel de St-Maux was clearly influenced by Enlightenment French thought. The immediate matrix of the *Lettres* is Paris of the 1780s, but the larger ambit of Saint-Maux's speculations are the tomes of natural history and the vicariously experienced travel reports of European *voyageurs* and antiquarians.[5] The *Lettres* were penned at a time when the possibility for place-bound monuments was fast eroding; when metaphors could no longer be employed with impunity to explain the observed facts of nature; when allegory was a suspect way of making sense of history's fragments; and when symbol was not needed to unveil the order in nature. Credulity in the sacredness of places was evaporating into the newly discovered chemical ingredients of air, and Viel de St-Maux perceived the gravity of the loss.

The *Lettres* are reactionary, a result of at least a century of tweaking the rules of scientific method. When the new metaphysics of seventeenth-century Cartesian rationality finally destroyed the "fleshy" cosmos, revealing that the world worked according to mathematical rules, *Nature* was invented. "Nature" (with a capital N) is that system, then, whereby everything non-human, but nevertheless subject to human-derived laws, is defined as Nature. In its rationalist manifestation, Nature is actually beyond common experience; it is, rather, a metaphysical and scientific truth that is introduced as the real nature. In place of a world literally resonating with human analogy and symbolic meaning, seventeenth-century scientists considered nature to be viewable and studiable by a detached observer. This is our predominant intellectual heritage. It contrasts with the medieval vision of a physical world comprised of empathetic signs and with the animate, soul-filled world of Epicurus and the Greek atomists. It even contrasts with the ways we actually live in the world.

As Alfred North Whitehead explains, "the new basis for thought was the report upon facts, directly observed, *directly employed.*"[6] One early personality that employed this new basis in thought (one that we can pair with Descartes to illuminate the implementation of his method) was the French military engineer Sebastien le Prestre de Vauban (1633–

1707), Louis XIV's master of siege craft during the French attacks on the Low Countries in 1667. Among many other natural historians, engineers, and physicians, Vauban absorbed the new way of imaging the world that forever changed our way of relating to nature. We can pinpoint Vauban as the engineer who introduced the modern "space of war" or "sight machine" on the landscape.[7] He understood territory as cartographic and logistical, not as "place" with its own contained, experienced horizon. For him, the land was mapped out with the tools of science, not with those of myth and perception. Settlements were no longer the delimited, wholly placebound cities of the Middle Ages and the Renaissance, enclosed by walls that invoked divine geometrical order and lodged each city within the cosmos. Now they were nodes in a logistical network, part of a cartographic network henceforth called the nation state, a territory extended through space, needing to be defended at strategic points on its frontier. Vauban's rationalized territory was projected onto the New World. Here, then, is the beginning of the settlement of the landscape by nihilism.

Since Descartes's infectious rationality banished the human intellect from the sensible, living world and hurried it along the path to homogeneous, mechanistic space, and since Vauban encouraged the development of the nation-state as territory, it became necessary by the Enlightenment to distinguish – indeed to proclaim – Nature as a distinct force, as object, separate from man, the subject. The multifaceted idea of *Nature* – that which is separate from the intellect and civilization – was so vast, so immanent, that it could cure illness and decadent societies; it supplied the theories of gravity, electricity, and morality with their credibility; it inspired language, religion, and the monuments of architecture; it offered an explanation of a material soul *and* was the privileged site of the burgeoning scientific disciplines. In the panicky years before the French Revolution, the mode of conceiving Nature teetered over the pit of instrumentality but had not yet fallen in. In Viel de St-Maux's time, the last half of the eighteenth century, a tenacious faith had grown up around Nature, as sign, as moral model; *as truth itself*. St-Maux and literate France awaited the revelation of a great unity in Nature that would explain all and correct a faulty society. The radical philosophical and existential change of the Revolution, however, saw that faith turn into a convenient model for controlling an objectified and instrumentalized Nature.

In the absence of the cosmological guarantor of God, Viel de St-Maux's contemporaries (such as the agricultural economists who called themselves the Physiocrats) "discovered" *Nature*, the nature that was revealed by science, exploration, and philosophy as Truth. Turning to Nature for truth led to a search for origins, for all things began in Nature, and in this quest the eighteenth century abounded in theories; the radical origins of language, society, religion, architecture, and morality were unearthed in Rousseau's primordial forest. For St-Maux, however, these epiphenomena came to fruition only in Cain's fields of grain. The beginning of farming was concomitant with the beginning of society, for better or worse. Furthermore, this concept of Nature was not only a casual assumption in the mid-eighteenth century, but also a driving intellectual force. By honing Nature's potential in the practice of agriculture the Physiocrats and natural historians could justify seeing only utility in natural phenomena and thereafter apply that utility in the interests of relieving human need.

As briefly outlined above, the eighteenth-century European mind cast a new web of order and materialist rationality onto the more alchemical Renaissance construction of Nature. It is to such minds that Viel de St-Maux addressed his letters. Ironically, his intuition about reinvesting culture with meaning through the use of allegory, poetry, and agrarian religion relied on the projects of the amateurs of science and natural history to continue razing what was left of the traditional cosmology. If St-Maux's intent in the *Lettres* was to resist the dangers of an overweening rationality in architecture, then the method of the *Lettres* relies on the discoveries of rational science and the new-found wonder of the natural world those discoveries excited. The *Lettres* inquire if it would it be possible to transcend reason *through* science. Ultimately, they ask if this new nature of science were approached with wonder, with the eye of the child or the agrarian and not the eye of the scientist, could the conceptual constraints that had sundered nature from humanity – thus defining it as conquerable – be resisted? This is a question worth posing now as much as then, and if it was indeed the underlying doxa of St-Maux's research, as I believe, it could cast his importance in a different light. Beyond these speculations, it is clear that the narratives and presumptions of the burgeoning disciplines of science most certainly informed his own. The ideas expressed in the *Lettres*, even though informed by science, explicitly *refute* the reduction of architecture to

11.2 Left: Bernard
Montfaucon, *Botanical
sepulchre*; from *L'antiquité
expliquée par les images*, vol.
III, Plate 19, Book II chapter
XVI (Paris 1718–24).

11.3 Opposite: Laurie
Walker, *Untitled*, 1989.
Laurel leaf, beeswax, iron-
oxide pigment; pages from
Pliny's *Natural History*. The
work was created as a pair
of endsheets for the *Eye of
Nature* exhibition catalogue
(Banff, Alta.: Walter Philips
Gallery 1991). Courtesy of
the Walter Philips Gallery,
Banff, Alberta. Photo by
Denis Farley.

function – that is, to science – by haughtily asserting that architecture
originated in the religion of agrarian culture, a culture imagined as
empathetically sutured to the physical world.

The *Lettres* are the first treatise in architectural theory to eke out a
position that would reveal the origins of what we can call the architectural impulse – the impulse to mark the world with a human explanation
of the cosmos. This impulse is tied intimately to the secrets and cycles
of the living world and is integral to an intuition that the invisible power
of *physis*[8] – nature's power – reflects absolutely cultural order. This
position on architectural origins is animated with the new speculations
of Enlightenment natural history, especially those of the celebrated
Comte de Buffon, and is convinced of a radical symbolism to be found
at architecture's beginnings.

For Viel de St-Maux, the "symbols and types relative to the causes of
nature," that is, the vegetal carvings and animal remains encrusted on

LXXVI. Among the different kinds of brambles is one called rhamnos by the Greeks, paler, more bushy, throwing out branches with straight thorns, not hooked like those of other brambles, and with larger leaves. The other kind of it is wild, darker and inclining to red, bearing a sort of pod. A decoction of the root of this in water makes a drug called lycium. *Lycium, etc.* The seed of it brings away the after-birth. The other, the paler kind, is more astringent, cooling, and more suitable for the treatment of gath⸢er⸣ings and wounds. The leaves of either kind, raw ⸢or boiled⸣, are made up into an ointment with oil.

LXXVII. A superior lyci⸢um may⸣ be made from the thorn which is also c⸢alled the⸣ boxthorn, the characteristics of whi⸢ch are descr⸣ibed [b] among Indian trees, for Indian ⸢lycium is consi⸣dered by far the best. The pounde⸢d branches and⸣ roots, which are of extreme bitterne⸢ss, are boile⸣d in water in a copper vessel for three ⸢days; the⸣ woody pieces are then taken away and the ⸢liquid boiled⸣ again until it is of the consistency of honey. ⸢It is ad⸣ulterated with bitter juices, even with lees of ⸢olive⸣ oil and with ox gall. The froth, which may b⸢e c⸣alled the flower of the decoction, is an ingredie⸢nt⸣ of remedies for the eyes. The rest of the juice is used for clearing spots from the face and for the cure of itch, chronic fluxes of the eyes and corroding sores in their corners, pus in the ears, sore tonsils and gums, cough and spitting of blood. For these a piece the size of a bean is swallowed, or if there is discharge from wounds it is applied locally, as it is to chaps, ulcers of the genitals, excoriations, fresh, spreading and also festering ulcers, excrescences in the nostrils and suppurations. It is also taken in milk by women for excessive men-

ancient monuments, were the real truth of architecture. They represented cultural order; not the order of Beauty in its Vitruvian, eurhythmic sense, but the harmony of natural systems and cycles, indeed, a whole *language* of nature, venerated by the rituals of agrarian life. By envisioning architectural origins this way, architecture could maintain its ability to express the accrued knowledge of the world *and* the mystery of nature. By so doing, it proposes a ground for meaning.

A cursory flip through the *Lettres* reveals that Viel de St-Maux was familiar with the ancient agricultural treatises of Cato, Varro, Columella, and Virgil, among others. He makes reference to Ovid and Lucretius and he seems to have completely absorbed Pausanius's *Guide to Greece*. Most of these ancient writers of pastorals, georgics, and bucolics gush with an Epicurean (or, in the words of the Enlightenment, a materialist) ontology; Virgil, Lucretius, and Ovid were all Epicureans. They chose to see the soul as the vital spark of life that was a *property of matter*, not a product of divine breath, occult force, or metaphysical constructs. These texts helped St-Maux piece together a *rustic* history of architecture that went beyond the scope of his contemporaries and ideological cousins, the Physiocrats.

Viel de St-Maux was also a student of Enlightenment archaeology, ethnology, and antiquities. As a result of the flood of new and undigested data pouring in, he was able to select images, reports, and hypotheses that suited his revised history of the beginnings of ancient civilization. In addition to the rustic history that is surmised from the Roman agricultural literature just mentioned, the *Lettres* also suggest that the physical environment struck so-called "primitive" man as a sacred sign to be deciphered, not as an object to be studied. Indeed, the sacred, encoded world was revealed for all to see *and worship* when the deciphered nature-signs were re-inscribed and placed on what we can call "geomantic" monuments. This provided a physical, embodied way of understanding the world and cosmos for the primitive agrarians. Viel de St-Maux's research resulted in his radical hypothesis of the original, absolute meaning of classical architecture: that it was wholly subsumed to the liturgies of semi-primitive agrarian societies which – and this is the most pervasive idea of the *Lettres* – worshipped *Fecundity*: "[W]e proclaim symbolic monuments and the *Poëme parlant* of Fecundity, in what [the Moderns] call the *Order of Architecture*."[9]

THE VEGETAL SOUL

The contemporary scientific discoveries of the celebrated Georges Louis Leclerc, Comte de Buffon, were used as proof of the ancients' precursory wisdom and helped to underpin the idea of the generative forces of nature, or fecundity, as the basis for the construction of the agrarian cosmos and its architecture. To be sure, Viel de St-Maux lived in the "prison house" of scientific language, but he strove to prove the ancients' possession of the same "scientific" knowledge, expressed by them, however, with symbol, metaphor, and allegory. The language, methods, and assumptions of contemporary science and its construing of Nature only reiterated the more eloquent symbols of the ancients: "I like to think that the heads of sphinxes or of lions which serve as rain gutters in ancient temples, that one is a symbol of the Divinity that gives the rains to the earth, and the other indicates to mortals that the sun gives up to it these very waters that it had acquired through its *force of attraction*."[10]

If, in the Enlightenment, Nature was a new-found book open to discovery, then for St-Maux its text had already been inscribed on the walls of antiquity: "How good it would be to desire that Botanists studied the plants retraced upon the temples of antiquity; a study which according to some instructed Hippocrates himself."[11] For Enlightenment natural philosophers such as the Comte de Buffon, to know Nature meant to distill from muddy, conventional language a more transparent language that represented exactly the observed world. For St-Maux, it meant to resurrect that symbolic language from the agrarian past.

Viel de St-Maux fashions a natural history of architecture in the same way that Buffon fashions a history of Nature: both go beyond an abstract taxonomy and work through an empirical collection of hard facts – facts that are sifted into a story of the world and a new language of science. For Buffon, this scientific language speaks of the qualities of the world, not just its quantifiable facts. He states: "As in civil history, one consults titles, one studies medallions, one deciphers antique inscriptions to determine the epochs of human revolutions, and proclaim the dates of moral events, also in natural history, one must scrounge about in the archives of the world, pull from the entrails of the earth the aged monuments, pick off the debris and re-assemble in a body of proof all the indices of the physical changes that allow us to gather together the different ages of nature."[12]

Buffon and Viel de St-Maux can in this sense be doubled in methodological terms. Buffon's project is to posit the natural world into the real time of history, and then to expose relationships among the things of the world. The *Lettres* insist that the ancient tendency of "retracing the causes of nature" on monuments is the prescient mirror to this. Indeed, as far as the *Lettres* are concerned, ancient architecture and ancient natural philosophy were the same discipline: architecture was nothing less than the explication of the living world through the relationships among its parts, its symbols, and its hieroglyphs. The signs and "text" of nature were placed on agrarian monuments for all to read.

With the rise of the physiological and "pneumatic" study of the human body in St-Maux's time, representations of forces acting upon the body were discussed in terms of liquidity, spirits, or the Epicurean flux of the chaotic world imprinting itself upon the human soul. The body – whether plant or animal – was no longer a solid, fleshy enigma but now an organism: composed of organs that communicated with each other

11.4 Tableau; from Buffon's *Histoire Naturelle*; author and date unknown.

and were acted upon by spirits or nerves or the soul (depending on whom one believed) coursing through the increasingly voided body. The priority of ocular authority gave way as "hearing, smell, taste and touch promised to expose the camouflage confounding conventional sight."[13] Here we see the rise of the organic, sensual body, its voids becoming the media within which the material soul could operate. The soul, as the receptacle and reservoir of bodily sensory experience, becomes newly invested with the power of organic vitality. The soul becomes *vegetal*.

The ancient Atomists – from Democritus to Lucretius – and certain radical French physicians of St-Maux's time, such as LaMettrie, saw the universe as composed of matter and motion. Man was an integral part of that material universe, eliminating any need for occult explanations of the soul. Living matter for them was *vegetal*. Derived from Aristotle's "Vegetal" or "Nutritive" soul, the term "vegetal" was used to explain matter that was extended, motile, and "irritable" or capable of sensing. According to Aristotle, souls were a part of *physis*; therefore, plants had souls too: "It seems that the principle found in plants is also a kind of soul; for this is the only principle common to both animals and plants."[14] LaMettrie defined the soul as incontrovertibly *of* nature and not simply in it. Man's natural organic processes explain the soul; the soul, LaMettrie

11.5 View of the Buffon and Baudet greenhouses in the Jardin des Plantes, Paris, after a drawing by F. Huet. Vegetal discoveries excited the imaginations of Viel de St-Maux's contemporaries. Bibliothèque du Musée d'Histoire Naturelle, Paris, c. 1800.

insists, is *material*. LaMettrie's materialism is, however, organic – living matter truly derived from *mater*, the mother of life. This coincides with the radical meaning of *physis* as the essence or primary composition of objects, and of *natura*, rendered by Lucretius as the invisible power of *Venus Genetrix*.

A telling and relevant example of the redefinition of soul is the popularity of hypnotism and trance-cures as promoted by Mesmer, the Austrian hypnotist, and his proselytizers. L.M. de Puységur was one such staunch disciple of Mesmer. He published a testimonial cure book[15] at the same time as the *Lettres*, wherein he insists that all objects in the universe are saturated and charged with a superfine, vivifying fluid – a kind of cosmic energy. Man is "une machine électrique animale," both receptacle and reservoir of this energy. Of interest here is his study of magneto-vegetal (*magnéto-végètal*) treatments involving the powers of plant life. How could the discoverers of plant respiration and combustion, he asks, not have concluded that the process of vegetation was due to the "universal fluid"? He performed curative sessions on the peasants of his estate around a "magnetized" tree. This power of healing by animal and vegetable magnetism is, like sexual reproduction, a mystery

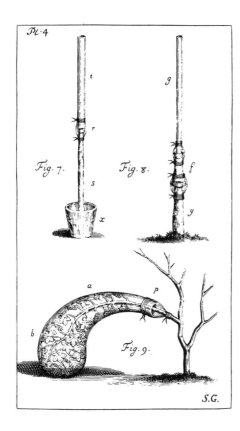

11.6 From Stephen Hales, *Vegetable Staticks*, Plate 4 (reprinted in London: MacDonald 1969 [originally published in 1727]).

of nature that cannot be understood. "For, as when speaking of a plant, we say that the juices of the earth spur the growth of seeds … so the touching of the sick [with the magnetized tree] communicates a kind of fecund spirit, analogous to his seed or vital principle which serves to reinforce him."[16] The earth is now seen as a conduit of this energy of fecundity and plants are seen as the outlet.

The *Lettres* present the idea of the vegetal soul and cosmic energy: "[O]ne sees on another [frieze] that active principle, regarded by the Poets as the bond and the soul of the universe, the creator of form, of movement and of life."[17] Some of the components of classical architecture represented the vegetal soul for him: "The arrows or darts that are mixed in among these eggs, could they express anything but the rays of this star of the day, soul of all vegetation?"[18] This vegetal soul, this fecundity that Viel de St-Maux reiterates and insists on, is for him the absolute meaning of classical architecture.

Materialists and vitalists (those who believed that matter was alive or contained a vital spark) could not see nature and its matter as rational and lifeless and subject to abstract scientific laws. The point of view of the *Lettres*, coupled with the materialists' position, casts a grotesque shadow over the human inhabitation of nature; because the body was animated by the vegetal soul, it became a medium for invisible communication with *every living thing* of the world. This new imprinting of the soul of the world onto the soul of the body brought about a sensitivity to the Sublime, the horrific, and the weird in Nature. The final *Lettres* describe a fascination with subterranean temples, awesome mountain aeries, and grotesque sculptures, while Buffon casts his tale of the violent, terrible beginnings of the world: the very cataclysms that produced the natural monuments of the Sublime.

With Buffon's *Epoques de la Nature*,[19] the history and age of the planet were radically revised and lengthened into the darkest recesses of time. Buffon defined seven stages or *époques* in the earth's prehistory, belying a structural relation to the Genesis creation. First was a molten stage; next, a too-hot-to-touch stage; thirdly, a Neptunist stage when a universal sea covered the planet (hence, the sea shells found in the Alps); fourthly, a stage of volcanic upheaval; a fifth stage characterized by the emergence of land animals; a sixth stage when the ancient continents sank, thereby defining the present ones and explaining the disappearance of Atlantis; and finally the age of man.[20] The first men witnessed the frightening convulsions of the earth, and it is through their fear and respect that religious rituals developed. More appropriately, it is from the belief in an angry underworld that gods and goddesses were invented. The first religious impulse (therefore the first architectural impulse) comes from the violence of the earth's crust.

Viel de Saint-Maux takes this history and suggests that many ancient monuments were allegories of those vast and horrific changes: a primordial memory of cataclysm: "Here they say, a part of the earth was consumed by a volcano; there such and such a monument was rebuilt with the same symbols and dimensions which had existed several thousand years before."[21] He wants to know the age of the earth and the story of its various strata so he can read the palimpsest of a very deep antiquity: "without telling us, neither when nor how the Volcanos of Auvergne became extinguished, as layers of lava are noticed at different depths. Can one not presume that the ravages of the most ancient monuments commenced only in our dark ages[?]"[22]

The verity of Saint-Maux's claims relied on his belief that the ancient agrarians' speaking monuments had been destroyed by warlike societies

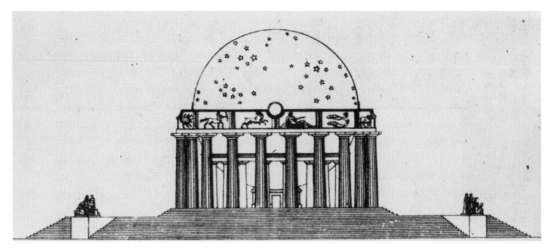

11.7 Antoine Laurent Thomas Vaudoyer, *House of a Cosmopolite*, 1785; from Van Cléemputte ed., *Collection des prix*, II, 127, Plate 64.

unsympathetic to the old religion. Only by careful study could the existence of these monuments be proved. The *Lettres* are the collation of Saint-Maux's proofs.

FECUNDITY

As discussed earlier, for these hypothetical agrarian societies, the worship of the natural force of *fecundity* and the agricultural bounty that results from it supplied the radical base for the iconographic and symbolic types that they applied to architecture, social structures, and even language itself: "The Earth, the honoured recipient of the sublime language of these monuments, presented to the World Master the Poem or *Ex-Voto* to *Fecundance*."[23] As employed in the *Lettres*, the term fecundity defines not only the unknowable force of Nature, manifest as an agricultural rhythm, but also as a natural language of the universal soul. Pre-Hellenic and "Oriental" societies, themselves couched in a mythological time, revered this universal soul and, in return for their faith, were privy to its wisdom. The force of fecundity ultimately gave birth to and instructed their cultures, institutions, and religions. Fecundity and agriculture, in their eighteenth-century embodiments, become metaphors for cultural

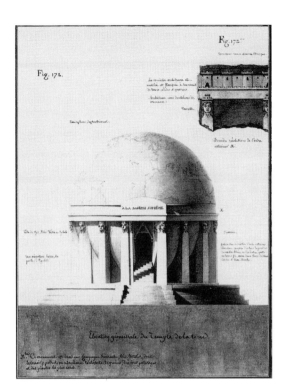

11.8 Jean-Jacques Lequeu, *Temple of the Earth*, 1790. Figures 4 and 5 show the influence of Viel de St-Maux's theory of zodiacal and geographical symbol in ancient architecture on contemporary *projects*.

harmony, enlightenment, and a re-fusion of the mystery and vitality of *physis* into everyday life: "Its Sublime origin, much to the astonishment of those who profess to be the most able in this field, is Agriculture itself, and the cult which issues forth from it; it is the *Poëme parlant* [of Architecture]: it is in its assemblage that the ancients instructed themselves as if from a book, not only of primitive theogony, but also of the way in which their cosmogony was put together; in a word, it is in its totality that all knowledge came to be gathered and depicted by ingenious allegories, with emblems that could not be misunderstood."[24]

The claim of the *Lettres* is that agrarian life was *symbolically* mediated to appease "divinity" or, more appropriately, the *sacredness* of nature. The land was laboured upon in accordance with the lessons given by nature herself. The resulting architecture portrayed and re-presented this agrarian universe:

In the ancient Temples, out there ready to be analyzed, everything exhibits symbols and mysterious types; throughout them one discovers the great attributes of Divinity. Indeed, one sang only the marvels of Creation in these temples, the perpetual miracles of fecundance, the wonders of statics, the laws of movement &c., one even saw upon the walls of these Temples the geographic maps of the known world ... lessons on the cultivation of soils were also portrayed; the annual divisions of the course of the Sun were represented upon them ... under the form of the bounty of the land; these very divisions, the Sun itself, were always considered as attributes of the Divinity: thus the people became enlightened, laborious and grateful.[25]

Votive columns and standing stones of deep antiquity and the distant Orient are constantly invoked as the first moments of the architectural impulse discussed earlier. Viel de St-Maux offers this interpretation: "Lone rocks, raised some distance from one another, the number of which equals the planets, the months of the year or else the days of the month, composed this sacred place that was the point of reunion of neighbouring families and societies."[26] These sacralized stones eventually took on a denser set of religious figurations as society developed:

One can consider these same rocks as the source of the Arts & Sciences, it is they that carried the first hieroglyphs or representative signs, signs to which we owe the origin of Painting and language; it is these same rocks or votive altars that were seen adorning and representing, by some characteristic marks, the months, the seasons and the elements; it is they that through these symbols express the course of the Sun; they are, finally, these very stones chiselled into mysterious columns, so vaunted in antiquity which, afterwards, served as supports and suggested the idea of a new structure for Temples.[27]

The eventual decorative programme of architecture was born from the incorporation of symbolic icons into these sacred markers: "The columns were engraved, says Manéthon, quoted by Eusebius, with the principles of the Sciences, the decrees of the stars and public instructions. The columns were not only the interpreters of agriculture and the laws but they also retraced useful plants, since in those times one only had stone and marble to instruct with."[28]

In his fifth letter, Viel de St-Maux explores the mysteriousness of the dark Plutonic underground, a perspectiveless site for communion with the fecund forces of the earth: "Sacred archives, Temples to Serapis and Proserpina, protectresses of seeds, the temples consecrated to Agrarian mysteries, as well as the places set aside for the study of the 'causes of nature' were always burrowed in such souterrains and served as shelter from the excessive heat of burning climes. These souterrains, which

11.9 "Tuning in to Nature": the author's uncle as field telegraph operator c. World War II.

should not be confused with the immense grottoes bored from rock throughout the greater part of the earth ... often formed queer sinuosities and proffered mysterious types and symbols."[29]

Here, finally, Viel de St-Maux connects the earth and *Venus Genetrix* – the feminine power of fecundity, the power of *physis* – with the underworld, and therefore, death. Perhaps he realized, like Lucretius in *de rerum natura,* that any poem on the creative powers of nature, of life, must also be a poem about the mystery of death and destruction, facts incomprehensible to science. St-Maux construed the *souterrains,* the underground temples, as sacred sites where death and fecundity collapsed in the ritual veneration of Demeter, Venus, Proserpine, and Cybele, the goddesses of fecundity. As Puységur the mesmerist indicates through his experiments, the earth is now an electrical conduit for the force of fructification. This charged crust is sacralized with the Physiocratic temples of antiquity, where *physis* is personified, allegorically, as *Venus Genetrix*: "Some so-called learned men, it seems, exist only to support Barbarity. What then, do the Temples signify for them, raised to Diana of Ephesus, to Diana of Dindymene, Venus Athera, Astarte or Astartagis, Minerva, Pallas or Athena, finally to Isis, Ceres, Proserpine, Vesta, Juno and Anna – always the same divinity designating the Earth and the force which

11.10 Robert Fones, *Moraine*, 1987. The artist explores the alphabetical inscription of our "gaze" on the landscape. Black and white photograph with plastic laminate on plywood construction. Courtesy of S.L. Simpson Gallery, Toronto. Photo by Robert Fones.

fructifies it. Named *Ertha & Adama* by the ancient peoples, did it not exhibit the same Monuments and the same symbols?"[30]

CONCLUSION

Viel de St-Maux believed that his primitives knew the truths of nature, truths that were based not on scientific observation but on subjective experience, on a primordial and somehow direct dialogue with the world. He was convinced that these agrarians were sutured to nature and he thirsted for the basis of that seam between human and non-human. The primitives that he invented could coerce nature, not through science, but through something akin to mimesis, through the expression of felt experience and through the medium of architecture. This suggested to him an empathetic means of perceiving *and* revealing the world, based on the body's erotic knowledge of the world. Behind his sardonic rhetoric he asked: can we be reconciled with nature by expressing the flesh of the world through architecture?

Viel de Saint-Maux's world had been exposed as conventional, as *unoriginal*. "National" customs and religion were revealed as only relative to one another, and at some point in history they had been sundered from the newly discovered "natural order." By re-wedding society to a re-animated nature, the elevation of progress, technocracy, and the rationality of positivist science as paradigms of modernity would be forestalled. A phenomenal, speaking nature would be bound to the material human subject in a seamless flow of communication.

We are now, I think, more or less aware of our complicity in the invention of this nature system, and this anthropocentric attitude that utters, "Us human, you beast." Sooner or later we will have to admit our role in the constitution of reality.[31] The presumptions of science and its instrumentalized technology have caused nature to disappear as a *real presence*. The subject-generated sense of place has been relinquished in favour of the abstraction of universal space. The landscape has lost its presence to us through the abstract veil of mathematics and the scientific tendency of observing the world from an enframed distance. This is the predominant construing of the world in the West and particularly on the North American continent.

Science has a solution to this problem: ecological science reveals an interconnected planet, and that is a start. But it is still the homogenous time-space planet of science that cannot allow the uniqueness of place as an embodied limit and disdains the primacy of perception in the way we live the world. Unfortunately, the science of ecology is not radical enough, because it maintains the mental apparatus of science that keeps us in its objectifying constraints, which got us into this mess in the first place.

The bonds of language also do their part to keep us constrained. Alphabetization is one method of objectifying reality that we have perfected. If the written characters of language were once drawn after the recognizable but mysterious things of the world – the plants, animals, stars, and so on, as St-Maux believed – then it could be argued that, with the development of the abstraction of these characters into the alphabet, the "participatory proclivity of the senses was simply transferred from the depths of the surrounding life world to the visible letters of the alphabet." With the spread of phonetic writing, the rest of nature began to lose its voice.[32] As a result, nature was no longer language as such, nor was architecture its medium. The memory of this sacred text

11.11 David Bierk, *Grainstacks Toward Glen Sutton #2*, 1991–92. Oil on photo on 19″ × 44″ board. The artist completes the aura of the landscape photograph with painted gesture. Courtesy of the artist and Wynick/Tuck Gallery, Toronto.

became a mere decorative code applied to buildings. Conventional scientific language that we speak daily detaches us from the "surrounding life-worlds" or "wild otherness" that the ancient monuments "spoke."[33] It seems clear that we must break through that way of "speaking the world" and expose Nature as a conventional, social creation.

Fecundity, the word we could give to a mimetic understanding of nature, can only be intuited, felt, not easily quantified. To attempt to grasp other life-worlds entails a new way of being open to them, away from the objectifying stance of nature-as-resource. One way is best described as *camouflage*: the mode that feels out local systems of fecundity and reveals their presence through architecture.[34] This is not the camouflage that hides things, but one that communicates with more primordial elements, requiring some sort of carnal reciprocity. This act blurs the division between human artifice and natural intention and accepts "wildness" as strange, unknowable, and therefore unconquerable.[35] It conceives of an architecture written with this wild language of the strange, one that can become, in the words of Viel de St-Maux, a *"speaking poem of fecundity."*

NOTES

1 For excellent scholarship on this subject, see William Leiss's *The Domination of Nature* (Montreal and Kingston: McGill-Queen's University Press 1994).

2 David Abram, *The Spell of the Sensuous: Perception and Language in a More-Than-Human World* (New York: Pantheon Books 1996). See especially the chapter entitled "Animism and the Alphabet."

3 This term was coined by Neil Evernden in his *The Natural Alien: Human-kind and Environment* (Toronto: University of Toronto Press 1993).

4 J.M. Perouse de Montclos, "Charles-François Viel, Architecte de L'Hopital Général et Jean-Louis Viel de St- Maux, Architecte, Peintre et Avocat au Parlement de Paris," in *Bulletin de la Societé de L'Histoire de l'Art Française* (Paris 1966), 267.

5 The first two letters – one to the Comte de Wannestin and the other to the Comte de Luxembourg – appeared separately in published form in 1779 and 1780 respectively. These two were then collated with five new letters and published in Paris in 1787. The latter five were addressed to, in order: the Comte de Buffon; the Imperial Academies of Sciences, Belles-Lettres and Arts of Saint-Petersburg; the Royal Academy of Sciences and Belles-Lettres of Berlin; the Baron of Marivetz; and the Comte de Vaudreuil.

6 A.N. Whitehead, *Adventures of Ideas* (Cambridge: Cambridge University Press 1947 [first ed. 1933]), 150. Emphasis mine.

7 For a discussion of these concepts, see Paul Virilio and Sylvère Lotringer, *Pure War* (New York: Semiotext(e) 1983).

8 In one of its oldest meanings, *Physis* was fraught with the idea of birth and so could be cast as "the birth of things." In everyday language and popular medical texts of antiquity as well, *physis* signified genitals. So one of the radical articulations of *physis* is the *essence* or primary composition of objects – the beginning of life – and this critical term emerges in Lucretius's great poem (*de Rerum Natura*) as *natura*, restored to *its* original and infrequently used articulation of birth and genesis – the invisible power of *Venus Genetrix*. The connotation of *physis* with *natura* has more to do with genesis, origins, and birthplace, its root sense in Greek *and* Latin, and contains a fluid subtext of sexual reproduction. *Physis,* then, is the *prima materia* from which Venus manipulates the world, both bringing things to their birth and driving them towards death *as a part of life.* See John Winkler, *The Constraints of Desire: The Anthropology of Sex and Gender in Ancient Greece* (New York: Routledge 1990), 112.

9 Jean-Louis Viel de St-Maux, *Lettres sur l'Architecture* (Paris 1787), Letter Two, 10: "[Q]ue nous annoncions des monuments symboliques, & le Poëme parlant de la Fécondance, dans ce qu'ils appellent *Ordre d'Architecture*." This translation and all subsequent translations of Viel de St-Maux are by the author.

10 Ibid., Letter Four, 30: "J'aime à penser que dans les têtes de sphynx ou de lions, qui servent de gouttières aux anciens temples, l'une est le symbole de la Divinité qui donne les pluies à la terre, & que l'autre indique aux mortels que le soleil lui rend les mêmes eaux qu'il avoit acquises par sa force attractive." Emphasis added.

11 Ibid., 44, n28: "Combien seroit-il à désirer que les Botanistes étudiassent les plantes qui sont retracées sur les temples de l'antiquité; étude qui , selon quelques uns, forma Hippocrate lui-même."

12 Georges Louis Leclerc, Comte de Buffon, *Œvres Complètes de Buffon: Tome Neuvième; Introduction aux Minéraux – Époques de la Nature.* (Paris: Garnier Frères 1855 [1749]), 455. The *Histoire Naturelle* was published between 1749 and 1804. Buffon died in 1788, one year after the publication of the *Lettres*.

13 B.M. Stafford, *Body Criticism: Imaging the Unseen in Enlightenment Art and Medicine* (Cambridge, Mass.: MIT Press 1991), 403.

14 Aristotle, *De Anima*, in *The Works of Aristotle*, volume 3, trans. J.A. Smith (London: Oxford University Press 1931), Book I.5 (411[6] 26.)

15 Armand-Marie-Jacques Chastenet, Marquis de Puységur, *Mémoires pour servir à l'histoire et à l'établissement du Magnétisme Animal,* (Paris 1784).

16 Puységur, *Mémoires pour servir à l'histoire*, 219.

17 Viel de St-Maux, *Lettres*, Letter Four, 24: "[O]n voit sur une autre ce principe d'activité, regardé par les Poëtes comme le lien & l'âme de l'univers, le createur de la forme, du mouvement & de la vie."

18 Ibid., 24: "Les triats ou dards qui sont mêlés parmi ces ovaires, peuvent-ils exprimer autre chose que les rayons de cet astre du monde, âme de toute végétation?"

19 Buffon, *Époques de la Nature*.

20 Otis E. Fellows and Stephen F. Milliken, *Buffon* (New York: Twayne Publishers 1972), 69.

21 Viel de St-Maux, *Lettres*, Letter Three, 5: "Ici, disent-ils, une portion de terre fut consumée par un volcan; là, tel monument fut rebâti avec les mêmes symbols & sur les mêmes dimensions qu'il avoit existé quelque mille ans auparavant."

22 Ibid., Letter Seven, 51, n17: "sans nous dire ni quand, ni comment les Volcans de l'Auvergne se sont éteints, puisqu'on remarque des couches de

lave à des profondeurs différentes. Ne pourroit-on pas présumer que le ravage des plus anciens Monumens n'a commencé que dans nos siécles de ténébres."

23 Ibid., 7: "La Terre, honorée du langage sublime de ces Monumens, présentoit au Maître du monde le Poème ou l'*Ex Voto* à la *Fécondance*."

24 Ibid., Letter One, 16: "Sa sublime origine, au grand étonnement de ceux qui se prétendent les plus habiles en ce genre, est l'Agriculture elle-même, & le culte qui en fut la suite; il en est le *Poëme parlant*: c'est dans son ensemble que les anciens s'instruisoient comme dans un livre, non-seulement de la théogonie primitive, mais encore des combinaisons de leur cosmogonie; en un mot, c'est dans son complément que venoient se réunir toutes les connoissances, & qu'elles se peignoient par des allégories ingénieuses, & des emblêmes auxquels on ne pouvoit se méprendre."

25 Ibid., 17–18: "Dans les Temples anciens, tout prête à l'analyse, tout y présent des symboles & des types mystérieux; par-tout on découvre les grands attributs de la Divinité. En effet, on ne chantoit dans ces Temples, que les merveilles de la Création, les miracles perpétuels de la fécondance, les prodiges de la statique, les loix du mouvement, &c. on voyoit même sur les murs de ces Temples, jusqu'à des cartes géographiques du Monde connu, avec les époques des révolutions diverses qu'il avoit essuyées; on y appercevoit également des leçons sur la culture des terres; les divisions annuelles de la marche du Soleil y étoient représentées, ou sous la figure d'autant de personnage, ou sous la forme des productions de la contrée; ces mêmes divisions, le Soleil lui-même, y étoient toujours considérés comme des attributs de la Divinité: anisi, les peuples devenoient éclairés, laborieux & reconnoissans."

26 Ibid., Letter Two, 8–9: "Des pierres seules, élevées à quelque distance les unes des autres, & dont le nombre égaloit celui des planetes, des mois de l'année, ou enfin des jours du mois, composoient ce lieu sacré, qui étoit le point de réunion des familles & des sociétés voisines."

27 Ibid., 9: "On peut considérer ces mêmes pierres comme les meres des Sciences & des Arts; ce sont elles qui porterent les premiers Hiéroglyphes, ou signes représentatifs, signes à qui nous devons l'origine de la Peinture & du langage; ce sont ces mêmes pierres ou Autels votifs, que l'on vit s'embellir & représenter par quelques marques caractéristiques, les mois, les saisons & les éléments; ce sont elles qui, par des symboles, exprimoient la marche du Soleil; ce sont enfin ces mêmes pierres, taillées en colomnes mystérieuses, si vantées dans l'antiquité, qui, par la suite, servirent comme de supports & suggérent l'idée des Temples d'une nouvelle structure."

28 Ibid., Letter Four, 36, n9: "On gravoit sur les colonnes, dit Manéthon, cité par Eusebe, le principe des sciences, les décrets des astres, & les instructions publiques. Les colonnes furent non seulement les interprètes de l'agriculture & celles des loix, mais elles retraçoient les plantes utile, puisque dans ces temps on n'avoit d'autres secours que la pierre & le marbre pour instruire."

29 Ibid., 10: "Les archives sacrées, les temples à Serapis & à Proserpine, protectrices des semences, les temples consacrés aux mystères Agricoles, ainsi que les lieux destinés à l'étude des causes de la nature, étoient toujours pratiqués dans des souterrains semblables, & servoient d'abri contre les chaleurs excessives dans les climats brûlans. Ces souterrains, qu'il ne faut pas confondre avec ces grottes immenses pratiquées dans les rochers sur la plus grande partie de la terre, & dont nous parlerons en son lieu, formoient souvent des sinuosités singulières, & offroient des types & des symboles mystérieux; leur entrée étoit pratiquée le plus souvent dans une colonne."

30 Ibid., Letter Seven, 9: "Quelques prétendus Savans ont paru n'éxister que pour être le soutien de la Barbarie. Que signifioient donc pour eux les Temples élevés à Diane d'Ephèse, à Diane Dyndimène, Vénus Athir, Astarté ou Astargatis, Minerve, Pallas ou Athénée, enfin Isis, Cérès, Proserpine, Vesta, Junon, & Anna, toujours même Divinité, désignant la Terre & la puissance qui la fructifie? Nommée *Ertha & Adama* par les anciens Peuples, ne présentoit-elle pas les mêmes Monumens & les mêmes symboles?"

31 Neil Evernden, *The Social Creation of Nature* (Baltimore: Johns Hopkins University Press 1992), 94.

32 David Abram, *The Spell of the Sensuous: Perception and Language in a More-Than-Human World* (New York: Pantheon Books 1996), 138.

33 Evernden, *Social Creation of Nature*, 132.

34 This is an idea that Roger Caillois calls "Legendary Psychasthenia." His essay "Mimetism and Psychasthenia" can be found in *Impulse* vol. 15, no. 3, (Toronto 1989): 6–9. This version was adapted from *Le Mythe et L'Homme* (1938) and translated by Ronald de Sousa.

35 Evernden, *Social Creation of Nature*. See epilogue, 129–33.

Domesticity and Diremption: Poetics of Space in the Work of Jana Sterbak

Irena Žantovská Murray[1]

> One need not be a Chamber – to be Haunted –
> One need not be a House –
> The Brain has Corridors-surpassing
> Material Place –
>
> Emily Dickinson[2]

JANA STERBAK IS A VISUAL ARTIST, but she would make a good writer. She might find verbal expression "limiting and not always subtle," as she says, yet her notebooks are fraught with literary excerpts from Mallarmé to Marx, and her attachment to language is palpable. Her own texts, such as the one accompanying her installation *I want you to feel the way I do*, are equally revealing.[3] They establish an extra dimension, simultaneously space-defining and space-defying, a dialectic between the visual and the verbal, an inward-directed view.

The body as a focus of Sterbak's work has been frequently discussed, most thoroughly perhaps by Diana Nemiroff in her catalogue for Jana Sterbak's exhibition at the National Gallery of Canada, but in many other commentaries as well.[4] Less frequently considered are her methods of grappling with the issues of space – the cladding of the body, not just in a succession of membranes and surface layers, but ultimately framing it in an array of exteriors and interiors. This process of framing is umbilically connected to a close examination of shelter, the testing ground par excellence for both sexuality and space.

A core example of Jana Sterbak's approach is a 1987–88 conceptual project entitled *House of Pain: A Relationship*. The axonometric drawing of a roofless house allows for multiple interior readings of the space, in which all action happens on the periphery. The house has no windows to give visitors at least a glimpse of the experience that awaits them upon entering, or rather stumbling, through a doorway with a two-foot drop on the interior. Note that one is to report in the reception room, which serves simultaneously as an exit room.

What are the traces of life in this room? A table with a large knife placed upon it, an empty swivel chair, and, against the wall opposite, a metal bar clutched by a man seated uncomfortably upon it – a guest perhaps or already a host? The act of "reporting" in this reception/ rejection room abruptly confuses the visitor; the idea of pain and discomfort is adumbrated here in the cyclical beginning/end. Proceeding back down the blind corridor, the visitor has a chance to escape through

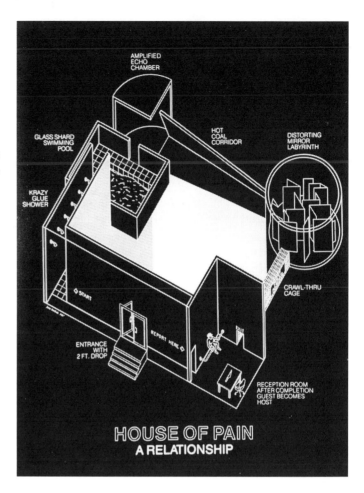

12.1 *House of Pain.
A Relationship,*
1987–88. Axonometric
drawing 137 × 102 cm.

the door but is instead drawn irrevocably to walk about. It is a highly tactile walk, as Jennifer Fisher pointed out in her own haptic journey through the project.[5]

The long and narrow Krazy Glue Shower corridor culminating in the boxy Glass Shard Swimming Pool feels like a postmodern improvement on the tar-and-feather procedure. The Amplified Echo Chamber then seizes the tormented visitor, whose skin has been raked with sharp pieces of glass, and assaults him/her with infinite reverberations of sound. The visitor's flesh is further seared in the Hot Coal Corridor to emerge grotesque, unrecognizable perhaps, in the circular space of the Distorting Mirror Labyrinth. Finally, this crazed creature – for what visitor could escape such a radical immersion in physical and emotional pain unscathed? – crawls through a narrow rat cage (even the Guest Parking Sign is a referent of sorts) and into the Exit room, in a seemingly "final" loop of the cycle. A man. A knife. A relationship.

One can find numerous parallels in other fields, such as in Marilyn Chandler's essay on Charlotte Perkins Gilman's short story "The Yellow Wallpaper," which offers a literary precedent for the idea that "the house assumes the position of the shadowy Other against which an internal conflict can be played out; ordinary facts or events assume extraordinary interpretative possibilities." In Sterbak's *House of Pain*, too, "as an outer shell, the house duplicates the body as enclosure or limiting wall."[6] In her essay "Topophobic Touch: The Spectatorial Wake-up Call in Jana Sterbak's House of Pain," Fisher rightly sought to explore Sterbak's work in the context of "the relationship of touch which is essential to sensing space." In the country of Jana's birth, Czechoslovakia, a young architect named Pavel Janák (1882–1956) contemplated this very relationship in the second decade of the century, exploring cubism in relation to building typology. For him, optic intuitions were related to the architecture of the longitudinal façade, while haptic intuitions were connected to the architecture of the round plan.[7] Janák emphasized the duality of sight and touch, "indivisibly present between the creating subject and his work." He further postulated that their coexistence and co-activity "truly represent the way through which the work is realized: each elicits, according to its possibilities, perceptions in which a common idea of things is apprehended."[8]

Jana Sterbak freely mixes the geometry of her spaces, but she uses a circular geometry (echo chamber, distorting mirror labyrinth) for some of her most painful tactile experiences. The aerial form of her drawing maximizes the voyeuristic, spectatorial voyage for the observer, but the true visitor's sense of touch is engaged and his tormented senses draw together the composite, tentacular "knowledge of things" which Janák considered fundamental to the experience of a work of art.

What is particularly striking in Sterbak's architectural concept, however, is the absence of the middle, the traditional essence, the sacred centre of a shelter. Inside the *House of Pain* we are looking at the very antithesis of the well of heaven, the courtyard house, the centripetal force of domesticity. This hollow, blank centre, this empty pit of hell, of nothingness, embodies the radical reversal of how we think about the domestic space: not as a safe place of retreat, but rather as a menacing hole of incarceration.

One cannot but be reminded of Poe's "The Pit and the Pendulum," in which the narrator first apprehends the evolving space of his prison through touch, and even when it is finally revealed to him through sight, the duality of the haptic and the optic is maintained. In the advancing heat of the burning iron, a change in form takes place: "The room has been square. I saw that two of its iron angles were now acute – two, consequently obtuse ... In an instant the apartment had shifted its form into that of a lozenge ... into the pit was the object of the burning iron to urge me."[9] In this final stage of Poe's story, the circular pit, "typical of hell and regarded by rumor as the Ultima Thule of all punishments," becomes irresistible by its coolness, the coolness of impending death.

An additional insight into Sterbak's literary sources is evident in a quotation copied alongside the negative of the *House of Pain* project in one of her notebooks: "Since I came in here and have stacks of leisure time my fancy runs away with me and I liken love to a great house, a mansion, that once you go in, the big door shuts behind you and you have no idea, no premonition where it will lead to. Chambers, vaults, confounded mazes, ladders, scaffolding, into darkness, out of darkness – anything. Sometimes you get left there all alone, stranded, while the loved one has got out, has bolted and gone away, and what do you do then; you sit or you cry, or you scream or become insensible. What do you do then."[10] Thus speaks the narrator of Edna O'Brien's novel *I Hardly Knew You*, a prisoner, a woman who has killed her lover in the midst of his monstrous metamorphosis during an epileptic seizure.

This charged passage powerfully evokes the close relationship between sexuality and space, one of the themes probed by participants in a 1990 Princeton University symposium and its attendant book, edited by Beatriz Colomina.[11] In her own essay, "The Split Wall: Domestic Voyeurism," Colomina speaks of "the look folded inward upon itself," a look that posits architecture "not simply as a platform that accommodates the viewing subject," but rather as "a viewing mechanism that *produces* the subject."[12] From this basic premise, Colomina develops a striking representational dichotomy in the work of two pioneers of modern architecture: Adolf Loos and Le Corbusier.

It was Loos, in Colomina's view, who valued "the bodily experience of space over its mental construction," thus reversing "the Cartesian schism between the perceptual and conceptual."[13] This, too, seems to apply to Jana Sterbak's approach to her architectural project. She would probably agree with Loos's statement in his famous essay, "The Principle of Cladding": "The artist, the architect, first senses the *effect* that he intends to realize and sees the rooms he wants to create in his mind's eye. He senses the effect that he wishes to exert upon the *spectator.*"[14]

It is not surprising that Jana Sterbak often contemplates different, companion pieces in her spatial deliberations. The *House of Pleasure* is still on the boards, and her notebooks are replete with verbal fragments of the exteriors and interiors which may or may not happen: "house of frustration," "house for a person of a particular sensibility," "a palace of intricate feelings," "room of bad humours," and "room for a person with low defenses." The house metaphor has its olfactory and gustatory variants in her project proposals such as the *House of Lavender* and the *House of Parsley*, variants that draw on her observation of cultural space – the sod houses of the vast Canadian prairies and the green garden patches of her Bohemian childhood.

The radical juxtaposition of the vast spaces of her country of adoption and the miniscule, by turns intimate and suffocating, spaces of the country of her birth regularly intervenes in Jana Sterbak's work. Whether just in her mind or more overtly, she is intrigued by the distortions of personal-space perceptions in, for instance, schizophrenics (many schizophrenics fear closeness with others and are unable to find a secure space), and she often draws on the literary experience of space, as embodied for example in one of her favourite poems, by the Czech artist and author, Frantiek Gellner (1881–1914):

> I love the skies of the North,
> white and impenetrable,
> where the sun disentangles its path,
> chilled and insensible.
>
> I love the plains of the North
> from snowdrift-saddened roads,
> I love the fogs of dusk
> in great cities to the North.
>
> I love the men of the North,
> with their lumbering, weary bodies
> and their mute, impossible longings
> in sorrowing hearts.

> I love the women of the North,
> fearfully folded in the nights,
> whose experience of love
> is only in dream and in memory.[15]

Sterbak's spatial probing and shifting are in themselves the result of a certain aloofness she feels towards both her birth country and her adopted country, a deliberate act of distancing and of suspension of preconceived ideas, which she repeatedly plumbs in her work. She herself likes to point out the often contradictory "readings" of both natural and cultural space as expressed by the continental European and American literary traditions – much in the way described by W.H. Auden in his essay on Robert Frost and discussed more recently by Joseph Brodsky.[16] Both the artist herself and critics of her work have pointed out how Sterbak's own cultural "dislocation" has repeatedly provided her with "a sense of freedom from cultural constraints," a liberating break to see anew.[17]

Let us try to see anew as well and imagine some of Jana Sterbak's other works situated in that hollow middle of the *House of Pain*, works straining the thin blank walls with a subversive force of our feelings, simultaneously pushing and pulling apart in an act of diremption, or forcible separation, from the conventional symbolism of domestic comfort.

A literal, etymological meaning of domestic spaces gave birth to some of Jana Sterbak's projects of the 1980s, such as the sensuous felt hanging of her *Sulking Room* (1988) or the bench-inscribed *Drawing Room* (1988). Only an artist-reader, someone for whom words represent a procession of enigmatic, unfolding personae, would think of the relationship between the French word *boudoir* and its originating verb *bouder* – to sulk, or to follow the traces of "withdrawing" to a drawing room. These rooms, as Diana Nemiroff pointed out in her text for Sterbak's exhibition catalogue, embody the dichotomy between the public and the private realm.[18]

These conceptual spaces also seem to corroborate Beatriz Colomina's observation that "comfort is paradoxically produced by two seemingly opposing conditions – *intimacy* and *control*." Colomina posits as the subject of Loos's houses "a stranger, an intruder in his own space," and the overall impression on the spectator as "that of someone about to enter," while, in her view, Le Corbusier tends to throw the subject

12.2 *Sulking Room*, 1988. White embroidery on black felt 137.2 × 182.9 cm. Collection: National Gallery of Canada, Ottawa.

"continuously towards the periphery of the house," with the overall impression of "someone who has just been there."[19] In her "architectural" projects, Sterbak seems to weave in and out of the maze of both the deep and the shallow spaces of our psyche, alternating between the "inward gaze, the gaze turned upon itself, of Loos's interiors" and "Le Corbusier's gaze of domination over the exterior world."[20]

Imagine further, for a moment, how Sterbak's rooms might be furnished, which activities are taking place in them, what domestic tranquillity exists inside the walls of these rooms. The *Sulking Room* might be the perfect setting for the artist's *Seduction Couch* (1986–87), a skilfully crafted modern variation of Mme Récamier's own, a sleek elongated wedge of perforated steel armed with a Van de Graaff generator – an enticing prospect of love, rest, and electroshock. Intimacy and control are potently present here in the lines of the object, in the sheen of the metal, in each warning spark staking out the danger zone.

The Drawing Room perhaps is where the sewing basket stands with its collection of the artist's tape measures, *The Measuring Tape Cones*

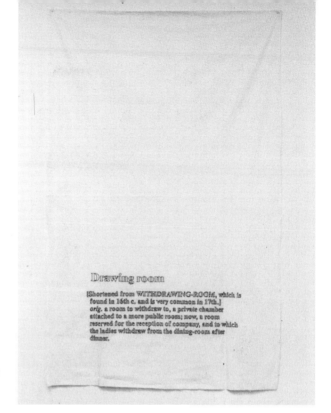

12.3 *Drawing Room*, 1988. Black embroidery on white cotton 166 × 108.5 cm.

(1979) and also *Vies sur mesures* (1988). The former group uses the actual tape measure in a series of tautly coiled extensions prodding the space, simultaneously playful and protective, measuring and measured. The latter project takes the idea of the tape measure and combines it with the celluloid tape of film – a cinema of our lives. The drawing room is transformed into a screening room and we watch unfold, along the length of the vinyl strip, the scenes of family life made up of mail order catalogue images of childhood, courtship, marriage, aging, the works. In its finite form, the tape even suggests an army-honoured custom of snipping away the last metre – the hundred days separating soldiers from the freedom of civilian life. Snipping away towards another form of banality.

Next let us walk through these spaces of suppressed feelings, of muffled sounds, of Calvino's "The King Listens," and proceed to the imaginary Living Room, the very locus of domesticity. Here you reign supreme, this is your own private "throne room," your ear to the rest of the house, as Calvino describes it: "[E]very footstep, every click of a lock, every sneeze echoes, rebounds, is propagated ... Into the great lake

12.4 *Declaration (the Jacobsen version)*, 1993. Collection: National Gallery of Canada, Ottawa.

of silence where you are floating rivers of air empty, stirred by intermittent vibrations. Alert, intent, you intercept them and decipher them."²¹
It is here that we become engaged with another seemingly cozy domestic scene, one of the artist's most recent works – "a declaration."

Déclaration (1993), Jana Sterbak's first foray into the domain of video art, is consistent with the body of her earlier work in the economy of its means, on the one hand, and the complex semantic reading, on the other. Its deceptively simple setting – two brightly coloured chairs and a television monitor – embodies the archetypal domestic situation of contemporary life, with its attendant reduction of our nesting instincts to the vacuous space of the "idiot box." Activated, however, this space generates a complex dynamic of exchange – between the viewers and the "program," between those occupying the chairs and others coming or going.

Most important, what one sees on the monitor is not some escapist pap, nor the instantaneous "théâtre de guerre" somewhere on the far side of the globe. It is a reading of one of the most portentous pieces in the collective repertoire of Western civilization, the text of the 1789 *Déclaration des droits de l'homme et du citoyen*. In the rich iconography of the French Revolution, an undated engraving by Jacques-Louis Perée,

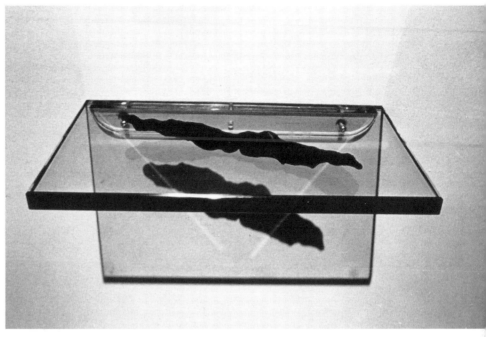

12.5 *Tongue*, 1990. Bronze. Private collection, Montreal.

L'homme enfin satisfait d'avoir retrouvé ses droits, seems to offer a striking antecedent: a young man reborn, yet struck speechless by a lightning bolt which bisects the night of history.[22]

In Sterbak's piece, a stuttering young man struggles through the seventeen articles of the declaration with the quiet determination of those who know that each sentence is potentially a death sentence, a spectre of muteness that must be vanquished through speech. This is the polar opposite of the ideas embedded in the earlier *Sulking Room* (a room in which one seeks refuge by a refusal to speak), a direct enactment of the declaration, a forward-looking sequel to another earlier project, *Tongue* (1990). The latter stands out as a bronze metaphor inspired by another kind of diremption, the excision, in 1621, of the tongue of a tragic figure from Czech history, the rector of Charles University, Dr Jessenius, a humanist and fearless and courageous speaker on behalf of the Czech Estates.

In *Déclaration*, the artist pitches the organic comfort of the 1950s furniture by the Danish designer Arne Jacobsen against the organic discomfort of the voice on the screen. In this highly charged space, the ringing clarity of Sièyes's text collides with the ineptness of its delivery. The chairs embrace, the screen strips naked. The medium implodes the

12.6 *Attitudes*, 1987. Private collection, New York.

message and in the process reveals its larger meaning. The journey to the affirmation of that which is morally just and equitable is fraught with the struggle of rising above the impediments of the self.

Let us further imagine a bedroom situated somewhere in the hollow of Sterbak's *House of Pain*. Here we find a bed – *Attitudes* (1987) – as roomy and perfectly conventional as any of the "letto matrimoniale" variety, strewn with an assortment of pillows in fine cotton cases embroidered in the old-fashioned script of our grandmothers. A comforting sight from afar, this pastoral domestic metaphor is textually subverted in a series of disquieting, ambiguous traces: Disease, Greed, Reputation, Sexual Fantasies ... Words again, like the tracks of someone who has just been here, who has slept in the bed perhaps, are a message recalling Walter Benjamin's descriptions of "an abundance of covers and protectors, liners and cases ... on which the traces of objects of everyday use are imprinted."[23] In Sterbak's case, these are the traces not just of objects but of buried thoughts, shameful feelings, secret, pervasive, omniscient.

Further developing this complex web of traces is a notebook-inserted Polaroid for a proposed project inspired by Mallarmé's "Brise Marine" – a vast bed smothered in books and pillows, with the body's faded imprint lingering under the eiderdown: "La chair est triste, hélas! et j'ai lu tous les livres!"[24] Unspoken, the line resonates in the muffled maze of the bed linens, another example of the forcible separation from the matrix of intimacy and domestic comfort. The artist-reader is only too painfully aware of the limitations of words, but her installation idea takes this awareness and makes it eloquent.

Jana Sterbak's most recent projects, still in progress, such as *The Hair Whip on a Medical Bed*, also employ the structure of the bed as a framing for an intrinsically ambiguous situation. The traditional supporting, sustaining function of bed is dislocated, compromised, questioned. Its status as the place of ultimate comfort is infused with tension. As Colomina points out in her essay, "the tension between sensation of comfort and comfort as control disrupts the role of the house as a traditional form of representation."[25]

The spatial dimensions of Sterbak's work are extended into other types of enclosures – cages, caskets, even catacombs. Her 1992 work entitled *Sisyphus I* is a sleek open shell of chrome and aluminum ribs enframing a small platform. The project simultaneously evokes feelings of instability and solidity, confinement and struggle for freedom. Its very constraints beckon the viewer inside. This duality is accentuated by a film clip projected in the background, in which the dim figure of an athlete gyrates effortlessly within the mirror image of the shell on the ground. Balancing awkwardly inside the real frame, however, we are torn between the fragile equilibrium of our bodies and the compelling desire to test ourselves against the intractable, vulcanian limits of the cage. Just for a moment, through movement, we precariously regain our balance, only to lose it again – through movement. The circumfluent, slickly packaged screen image offers an ironic juxtaposition to our own clumsiness. And yet, with each renitent gesture, with each wobbly step, we affirm our defiance of what is given, of the circumscribed outside edge. We confront the built-in disequilibrium, and the unyielding quality of the material, with the lunatic expectancy of desire unencumbered by experience. Trapped inside the law of gravity, we are engaged in an effort to escape the confines of the inevitable, thus perpetuating the dualism of self-punishment and self-creation.

If, in its intentions, *Sisyphus I* resembles the more recent *Déclaration*, its form advances an idea introduced in Sterbak's earlier project, *Remote Control II* (1989), a cage-like giant hoop dress mounted on a set of motorized wheels inside which a woman is suspended in a canvas

12.7 Above: *Sisyphus I*, 1990. Private collection, Chicago.

12.8 Right: *Remote Control II*, 1989. 150 cm × 405 cm (circumference). Collection: MAC, Barcelona.

harness. Here again, control shifts as the remote-control device changes hands between the woman suspended and an outside operator, thus expressing the private and public struggle for control. At one moment, the woman is in full charge of her destiny, liberated from the confines of the earth, manipulating space, shrinking it and expanding it with the touch of her finger. At the next minute, she is helpless, aloft in the air, with someone else manipulating space, her space. Her mobile shelter is no longer protective and liberating, it is confining and paralysing.

Here again, one is reminded of Calvino's "The King Listens": "Your every attempt to get out of the cage is destined to fail: it is futile to see

yourself in the world that does not belong to you, that perhaps does not exist. For you there is only the palace, the great reechoing vaults ... the hurried footsteps on the staircase which each time could be announcing your end. These are the only signs through which the world speaks to you; do not let your attention stray from them even for an instant; the moment you are distracted, this space you have constructed around yourself to contain and watch over your fears will be rent, torn to pieces."[26]

Sterbak's spatial explorations informed her 1992 project *Catacombs*, a chocolate confection whose very perishability subverts the notion of

catacombs as the most secure and resistant form of subterranean burial place, a sequence of crypts and recesses hidden both from view and from interference. Yet the gustatory nature of the material even suggests a connection to cannibalism. Alternating between a close relationship between material and form and a pronounced dichotomy between them is another strong "architectural" element in Sterbak's work. Furthermore, she is particularly attracted to the use of active, transient, mutating materials – be it the decaying strips of flank steak of her *Vanitas* project or the radioactive fermium of her *Malevolent Heart*, among others. Emanation holds a special place in Sterbak's work and underscores her transmutative, frequently subversive approach to both literary and visual encoding.

12.9 Left: *Catacombs*, 1992. Collection: Musée d'art moderne de Saint-Étienne, France.

12.10 Right: *Vanitas: Flesh Dress for an Albino Anorectic*, 1987. Collection: MNAM, Centre Georges Pompidou, Paris.

If, as Loos argued, the meaning of the house (or another enclosing space) in "all its richness must be made manifest by its interior," Sterbak both corroborates and challenges that idea, most particularly in her 1990 work entitled, appropriately enough, *Inside*. Consisting of two caskets, one inside the other, the larger casket is made of glass, and the smaller, interior one of mirror glass. Here the mirror acts both as a boundary and as a reflection, much in the way that, as Colomina describes it, "the placement of Freud's mirror between interior and exterior undermines the boundary as a fixed limit."[27]

Our curiosity, our voyeurism, is sorely tested: within each inside, another inside is perhaps hidden, an inside invisible to our senses, a conjectured core, convoluting the relation with the outside. This notion

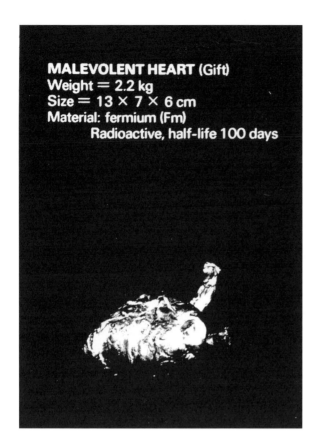

MALEVOLENT HEART (Gift)
Weight = 2.2 kg
Size = 13 × 7 × 6 cm
Material: fermium (Fm)
        Radioactive, half-life 100 days

12.11 Left: *Malevolent Heart*, detail from *Golem: Objects as Sensations*, 1979–82. Collection: Musée des beaux-arts, Nantes.

12.12 Right: *Inside*, 1990. Private collection, Chicago.

is in direct contradiction to the more benign interpretation of Gaston Bachelard: "Chests, especially small caskets, over which we have complete mastery, are objects *that may be opened*. When a casket is closed, it is returned to the general community of objects; it takes place in exterior space. But it opens! … The outside has no more meaning. And quite paradoxically, even cubic dimensions have no more meaning, for the reason that a new dimension – the dimension of intimacy – has just opened up."[28]

But Sterbak's caskets do not open; inside there is always another inside, and to reach it, the caskets would have to be broken – an act of intimacy to be replaced by an act of aggression. Freud's mirror symbolizing the psyche garbs an impenetrable secret – a secret of the ultimate inside. Perhaps the smooth layering of transparency and impenetrability bespeaks the opacity of memory, the Bergsonian "pure recollection," as Bachelard describes it: "The pure recollection, the image that belongs to us alone, we do not *want* to communicate. Its very core is our own, and

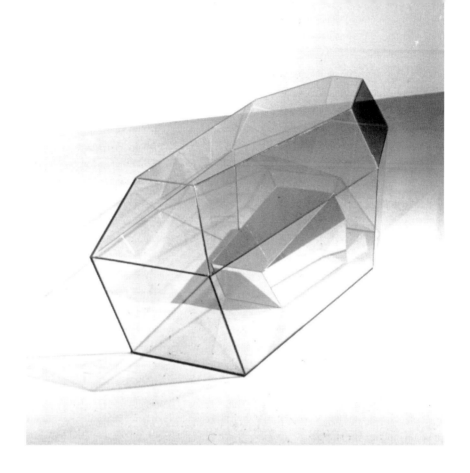

we should never want to tell all there is to tell about it ... Every secret has its little casket, and this absolute, well-guarded secret is independent of all dynamism ... Surrounding certain recollections of our inner self, we have the security of an *absolute casket.*"[29]

In the dubious "security of an absolute casket," our inner self roams the mirror labyrinths of the house of doubts, the house of pain, but also the house of possibility to which Jana Sterbak, unwittingly perhaps, has led the spectator. If, as Colomina writes, "to address the interior is to address the splitting of the wall," Sterbak continues her determined enquiry of both the centre and the periphery. The house, the rooms, the cage, the catacombs, the caskets – all but a form of cladding, an envelope for the body – can be read as controlling or confining, dominating or intimate, but ultimately as a telling sensorial narrative. If to "dwell in possibility" appealed to Emily Dickinson, it is more the idea of a haunted house that Sterbak espouses – a place where not just the corridors of the brain but the swinging doors of the senses open onto the watchful void.

NOTES

1 This text was first published in the catalogue *Jana Sterbak. Velleitas* (Barcelona: Fundació Antoní Tàpies 1995), on the occasion of the exhibition of the same title, held at the Fundació Tàpies 6 October – 10 December 1995. The author would like to thank Dr Manuel Borja, Director of the Fundació Tàpies, for permission to reprint the original text. All reproductions courtesy Galerie René Blouin, Montreal.

2 *American Poetry: The Nineteenth Century*, 2 vols. (New York: Library of America 1993), 2:284.

3 Diana Nemiroff, *Jana Sterbak: States of Being/Corps à corps*, Catalogue no. 5 (Ottawa: National Gallery of Canada 1991). "I want you to feel the way I do: There's barbed wire wrapped around my head and my skin grates on my flesh from the inside. How can you be so comfortable only 5" to the left of me? I don't want to hear myself think, feel myself move. It's not that I want to be numb, I want to slip under your skin: I will listen for the sound you hear, feed on your thought, wear your clothes. Now I have your attitude and you're not comfortable anymore. Making them yours you relieved me of my opinions, habits, impulses. I should be grateful, but instead ... you are beginning to irritate me: I am not going to live with myself inside your body, and I would rather practice being new on someone else."

4 Nemiroff, *Jana Sterbak*, 14–39; Nancy Spector, "Flesh and Bones," *Artforum* 30 (March 1992): 95–9; Cornelia Lauf and Olaf Hanel, special issue of *Výtvarné Umění* (Prague) (April 1992): 2–7, 8–13; Richard Noble, "Jana Sterbak: Chaos and Self-creation," *Parkett* 35 (March 1993): 8–12.

5 Jennifer Fisher, "Topophobic Touch: The Spectatorial Wake-up Call of Jana Sterbak's House of Pain," unpublished paper, Montreal, August 1992. Fisher writes of the bodily awareness of space in the artist's project: the "structure of feeling" which "transposes directly a particular "structure," a "house," and a particular "feeling," in this case "pain" (2).

6 Marilyn R. Chandler, "*The Awakening* and 'The Yellow Wallpaper,'" in *Dwelling in the Text: Houses in American Fiction* (Berkeley, Calif.: University of California Press 1991), 143.

7 See Irena Žantovská Murray, *Sources of Cubist Architecture in Bohemia: the Theories of Pavel Janák*, M.Arch. thesis, McGill University, 1991.

8 Ibid., 55–7.

9 Edgar Allan Poe, "The Pit and the Pendulum," in *The Works of Edgar Allan Poe* (New York: Random House 1938), 257.

10 Edna O'Brien, *I Hardly Knew You* (Garden City, N.Y.: Doubleday, 1978), 18.

11 Beatriz Colomina, ed., *Sexuality and Space* (Princeton, N.J.: Princeton University School of Architecture 1990).

12 Beatriz Colomina, "The Split Wall: Domestic Voyeurism," in *Sexuality and Space*, 83.

13 Ibid., 91.

14 Adolf Loos, "The Principle of Cladding," in *Spoken into the Void* (Cambridge: MIT Press 1982), 66. Here quoted from Beatriz Colomina, "The Split Wall," 90.

15 Frantiek Gellner, *Spisy* (B. Hýsek 1926–28). For his help with the English translation of this poem I would like to thank Dr Eric Ormsby.

16 Joseph Brodsky, "On Grief and Reason," *The New Yorker* (26 September 1994): 70.

17 See, for example, Christopher Noble, "Jana Sterbak: Chaos and Self-Creation," an interview with Sterbak in *States of Being*, and Sterbak's "Artist's Statement" in the *Impossible Self* (Winnipeg: Winnipeg Art Gallery 1988), among other writings.

18 Nemiroff, *States of Being*, 37–8.

19 Colomina, "The Split Wall," 98.

20 Ibid., 112.

21 Italo Calvino, "The King Listens," in *Under the Jaguar Sun* (New York: Harcourt Brace Jovanovich 1990), 38.

22 [*L'homme enfin satisfait avoir retrouvé ses droits rend graces à l'Etre suprême*]. Bibliothèque Nationale de France, Département des Estampes et de la Photographie. I would like to thank Professor Kurt Forster of Zürich for his kindness in bringing this image to my attention.

23 Walter Benjamin, "Paris, Capital of the 19th Century," in *Reflections* (New York: Schocken Books 1986). Here quoted from Colomina, "The Split Wall," 74.

24 Stéphane Mallarmé, "Brise Marine," *Œuvres complètes* (Paris: Gallimard 1945), 38. "The flesh is sad, alas! and I have read all books."

25 Colomina, "The Split Wall," 92–3.

26 Calvino, "The King Listens," 59.

27 Colomina, "The Split Wall," 86.

28 Gaston Bachelard, *The Poetics of Space* (Boston: Beacon Press 1994), 85.

29 Ibid.

Absent Bodies
Writing Rooms

Ellen Zweig[1]

Chora

13.1 From the Lumière brothers' *L'Arrivée du train en gare*, 1895. Courtesy Museum of Modern Art Film Stills Archive.

OUTSIDE/INSIDE

1   The camera waits outside the building, examining a façade. Inside, someone is dying.

1.1   The camera stops at a wall, covers the distance, surveys the flat, opaque surface, caresses the protuberances and the holes.

1.2   When the camera encounters a window, a gate, or a door, it takes the opportunity to look in or to enter. Inside, it looks around the room, looks out again through the window, goes out again through the door.

1.3   The camera is writing rooms, moving like a hand with a pen. The camera draws curved or straight lines from its fixed centre. Inside is a room (camera obscura) for an image, more often than not the image of a body, the discovery of a corpse.

1.4   In 1888 Louis-Aimé Augustin Le Prince created a one-lens camera with which he photographed moving images. The camera was also a projector and Le Prince might have shown films to large audiences if he had not mysteriously disappeared in 1890. After visiting his brother in Dijon, he boarded the train to return to Paris and was never seen again. Neither his body nor his baggage were ever found.

1.5   The camera projector implies three rooms. First is a little dark room, camera obscura. Inside, the image is upside down, right left reversed; tiny bits of light writing an image on film, a small moving wall. When the camera is transformed into a projector, it sends this image outward in a visible stream of light to a large dark room where we sit entranced. We're looking at an image that fills a screen, a large wall that becomes another room. On this screen is the room without a body. This room anticipates death, waits for the murder as the camera pans, tilts, and zooms, looking for the corpse. We sit in the large dark room, relaxed, almost asleep. Our bodies are linked with the movement of the camera; we see through our haptic sense.

Benjamin asks us to consider architecture as an example of habituated physiognomic knowing. How do we get to know the rooms and hallways of a building? What sort of knowing is this? Is it primarily visual? What sort of vision? Surely not an abstract blueprint of the sort the architect drew ... [An] indefinable tactility of vision operates here.[2]

1.6 Architecture is that which creates inside and out-side – boundaries, borders, walls, windows, and doors. It hems us in. Outside it is a barrier, some-thing we have to move around. Inside, it is a shell, hollow, something we move through in order to fill a void.

1.7 The movement of the camera gives the illusion of filling in space. The image on the screen seems full. An empty room on film has a paradoxical volume: simultaneously spatially deep and flattened out to the depth of the material of the screen itself.

1.8 The tension between these two depths is erotic. The body leaks out all over the place.

DEAD BODIES

2 A building is static, fixed, a position, or a place. It does not move. The camera, the little room, is also fixed.

2.1 Zooms, pans, and tilts move from the centre. The zoom penetrates depth with a continuous adjustment of focal length from a central and static point; the pan traverses the horizontal, the tilt moves through the vertical or diagonal; one rotates on the vertical axis, the other on the horizontal or diagonal from a fixed position. The apparatus moves but the little room stays in place.

2.2 Even when the camera is put on a dolly or a crane, even when it rides around the room as though it were on a train, the camera is only a passenger. It doesn't drive the car.

2.3 Architecture makes boundaries; eroticism rubs up against them, pushes at them, tries to dissolve them.

Eroticism requires an "overall view," a view of the whole, and only movement can be overall, specifically only the movement that leads to the destruction of the object.[3]

If we posit the movement of film as this overall view, what does it destroy? It sets its scope on architecture, narrative, and bodies. It wants them dead.

2.4 But film is an object itself, an image, a partial view. It has to go hunting for the body, surveying the local architecture for a clue. It gets caught up in a room. The suspense is killing …

2.5 Death is an anchor, a fixed position from which the narrative unfolds backwards. We can't tell the story of a life until it's over. The end is our camera, our little room.

2.6 We can't get our minds off death. We read mystery novels, thrillers, ghost stories. These same plots show up in the movies. But the odd thing about these stories is that we don't care much about the corpse. It's the fixed point, the anchor, the place to begin. Without it, we would have no motivation, no reason to go looking for clues. Death is the mother of structure, of time, of narrative.

2.7 Death is the thing we don't want to see. We'd like it kept hidden, swept under the rug. We'd like to pass over it without comment. We'd like the body to vanish, without a trace. We'd like to stop time, so that stories can be structures, like buildings that never fall into ruin, impediments to the mess of life itself.

2.8 But death gives meaning to life. It fascinates us. Literally, we are forced to stare. Going to the movies to see death, our eyes don't get enough lubrication; we aren't even allowed to blink at the usual rate. We keep on looking because it isn't there; death eludes us, always in another room, another building, across the street, on the other side of town. This is the pleasure of suspense: to be slapped in the face with the image of a corpse.

WINDOW/SCREEN

3 Alfred Hitchcock's *Rear Window* begins with a large picture window, the boundary between inside and outside. The camera frames this window with its three blinds. As the credits appear over the window, the blinds go up, one at a time from left to right in an elegant choreography revealing the window as an instrument of revelation and surveillance. As the blinds go up, the light intensifies outside, as though we were looking at a theatre set and watching the lights fade up. Also, during this sequence we see people

13.2 The window from Alfred Hitchcock's *Rear Window*, 1954.

moving and birds flying across the frame. Across the way, we see an apartment building with many windows.

3.1 Then, the camera moves towards the window in a shot that at first appears to be a simple forward-moving dolly shot. However, this camera movement is more complex; as the camera moves forward, it adjusts slightly in a wavelike movement so that it finally winds up with the middle frame of the casement window filling the frame of the film screen and becoming one with that screen. For this moment, looking out of the window is almost the same as looking at the movie.

3.2 The camera is not simply moving towards the window. If we examine this shot more closely, we see that the window is actually moving towards the camera. This is the basis for the real discomfort that this sequence engenders in the viewer. Although the camera does move forward, the window – the architectural element we trust will be stable – is mobile. Suddenly, architecture is brought into doubt. This is the world of the film set, of illusion, and possibility. Here architecture is mutable to serve the shot.

3.3 The camera will go outside, penetrating the depth of the image – outside to survey the courtyard. However, the initial image of the window establishes it as a membrane, a sort of barrier that protects the viewer from the life outside. As a screen, it is both transparent and opaque. Throughout the film, references to this window will use metaphors that remind us of its similarity to a movie screen. "Show's over for tonight," says Lisa, as she closes the blinds, "Time for coming attractions." She leaves the room and enters again in a filmy white nightgown. This seduction scene is interrupted by a scream.

3.4 The curving, adjusting movement of the camera as it approaches the moving window will occur again in the first complex shot that makes up the beginning of the film. The feeling is slightly uncanny, not mechanical. It signals a body that holds the camera (although this is a dolly shot, some of the movement is awkward because it is simply technically difficult). A hesitant body, but curious. Note, I refer to a body and not eyes – for this curve of movement has something of the hand in it. Typical of Hitchcock, that small detail – the way the camera seems to curl slightly as it gets to the window sill – foreshadows the climax of the film when Jeff (played by James Stewart) is thrown out the window. We feel here a bit of vertigo – because of the curve and because the window itself is moving. Windows here become unmoored, separated from architecture. The window is both symbol and character, a creepy figure, unstable and unpredictable.

CONE OF VISION

4 Cut to a cat, walking up a concrete stairway. We don't know where we are at first. The camera seems to follow the cat, tracking it, but really the camera is tilting – first up the stairs – the cat goes off to the right, out of the frame, meowing, a false lead, but preleptic in that it foreshadows another use of these stairs. Then the camera continues up the wall – up a metal ladder attached to the wall – pans left, tilts down when it gets to the window directly across from the window where we started, and pans left again. We don't see the stairs again until Lisa (Grace Kelly) and Stella (Thelma Ritter)

13.3 The fourth side; from Alfred Hitchcock's *Rear Window*, 1959.

use them to sneak into the back courtyard of the building across the way in order to dig in Thorwald's (Raymond Burr's) flower bed to see why he's killed the dog. Again, Hitchcock signals the climax of the film, by disorienting us, filming the architecture so that we don't know exactly how it's structured. In fact, the physical layout of the buildings becomes clear to us only slowly as we are given more and more hints throughout the film. Michel Chion has pointed out that there are parts of these buildings we never see (some of these parts probably don't exist at all) because for the most part we see everything from Jeff's point of view. We don't see Jeff's window from the outside, nor do we see other windows on Jeff's side of the courtyard. We also see only one room of Jeff's apartment. Although Lisa enters both the kitchen and the bedroom, we never follow her there, confined to our chairs just as Jeff is confined to his wheelchair. Chion describes this configuration as though it could be diagrammed with a cone from Jeff's eyes (and binoculars and telephoto lens) out to the rest of the courtyard.[4]

4.1   As a peeping Tom, Jeff is curiously immobile, fixed, static, as though he himself is a camera. Descartes's description of the workings of vision compares the human eye to a camera obscura. This cone of vision is one eyed, one lensed. When Jeff begins to spy on his neighbors, he first uses his eyes, then binoculars, but finally settles for a telephoto lens on his camera. It is in this *single* lens that we see a reflection of the building.

4.2   The camera comes back along a brick wall and does a rack focus in the window to Jeff's head as he lies sleeping inside. He's sweating. Curiously, this first pan has not been through his eyes, since the

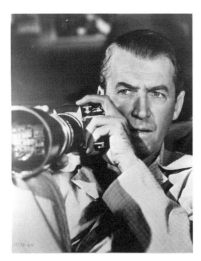

13.4 A reflection of the building; from Alfred Hitchcock's *Rear Window*, 1954. Courtesy Museum of Modern Art Film Stills Archive.

back of his head is to the window and he's asleep.
The window appears like a dream or fantasy space,
like the balloon in a cartoon, hovering behind his
head.

4.3 The next sequence of shots, starting with a cut to a
thermometer that reads 90 degrees, is a series of
clues to the time, place, and characters of the movie.
All of the following shots tell us that it's hot and
it's morning. From the thermometer, the camera
rack focuses out and pans left until it gets to a
window that fills the frame. Here we see one of the
neighbors shaving. Cut to a couple asleep on the
balcony of their fire escape. Tilt down and pan left
to the sexy girl who dances as she gets dressed; pan
left and zoom out at the alley that leads to the
street. Here we get a series of adjustments, the
camera hesitating and moving as though it doesn't
quite want to leave the view of that alley. This is
partly because the camera is doing something difficult and we're seeing the awkwardness, a technical
error really, but then the camera moves faster back
to Jeff. This alley is the way out, the way Thorwald leaves the building with the body, the way Jeff
might leave if only he could walk. This is the
avenue of escape from the enclosed world of the
backs of these buildings. This alley is also another
cone of vision, a narrow space through which Jeff
can see outside. The camera gets back to Jeff, fast –
which gives the illusion that it's lingered at the alley
– and we see that we still have not been looking at
any of this through Jeff's eyes – he's still sleeping,
his back to the window.

One never is inside the labyrinth, because, unable to
leave it, unable to grasp it with a single glance, one never
knows if one is inside. We must describe as a labyrinth
that unsurmountably ambiguous, spatial structure where

13.5 Above: Window as Jeff's dream;
Alfred Hitchcock's *Rear Window*, 1954.

13.6 Below: Courtyard showing alley;
Alfred Hitchcock's *Rear Window*, 1954.

one never knows whether one is being expelled or enclosed, a space composed uniquely of openings, where one never knows whether they open to the inside or the outside, whether they are for leaving or for entering.[5]

4.4 From Jeff's face, the camera pans down to his leg in a cast and then moves around his room, moving almost parallel to the survey of the windows outside. This time the clues are contained in objects. From the cast, zoom out and a fast pan left to a broken camera, then tilt up to a photograph of a car accident, a tire wildly spinning too close to the camera. More photos and equipment, the negative of a photo and then its positive on the cover of a magazine. This is how we first meet Lisa, Jeff's girlfriend and a fashion model – the image on the other side of his camera. This is, also, how we learn that the injured Jeff has almost died, his death whirling towards him in the form of a tire. The parallel survey of Jeff's room helps to establish it as a camera obscura, a mirror image of some place outside, perhaps Thorwald's room. Jeff is immobile, Lisa mobile; Thorwald mobile, his wife an immobile invalid.

4.5 Many critics have pointed out the psychological significance of the camera obscura as an image referred to in *Rear Window*. First, according to Mladen Dolar,[6] the kind of surveillance here is not like Foucault's Panopticon, where frightened prisoners are watched from a central tower. Here, those who are watched are unaware of Jeff's spying, unafraid. It is Jeff who watches in order to find that which he fears. He's looking for an absent body. Lisa, his beautiful girlfriend, is pressing for marriage. Miran Bozovic[7] points out that Jeff imagines himself in all the other windows, fearing his options, his desire to murder. Looking in the windows, we see vignettes, mini-narratives that Hitchcock will exploit throughout the film, coming back again to revisit each window, developing these small plots. Each of these plots presents fantasy options to Jeff, who is struggling against getting involved with Lisa. There's the lonely old maid, the just-married couple in love, the sexy dancer with lots of suitors, the misunderstood composer, the comfy boring married couple, and most of all there's Thorwald, the man who murders his invalid wife.

PENETRATION OF THE PHYSICAL SPACE

5 Jeff sleeps through the murder. The body is missing. Jeff, who cannot move, depends on sight, the same sight we depend on, to solve the crime. He also depends on his girlfriend, his masseuse, and a friend who happens to be a police detective. These characters penetrate the physical space of the courtyard, crossing it finally to enter Thorwald's space and confront him with his crime. This violation of the space, which is meant only for the eye, causes Thorwald to enter Jeff's space, throwing him out of the window. Only in this way can Jeff become part of the picture.

5.1 Although psychological interpretations of *Rear Window* are valid, a look at the physical plan of the film and the camera's involvement with architecture brings us to other conclusions. Lisa is asking Jeff if he likes her nightgown; this seduction scene is interrupted by a scream. The little dog, lovingly lowered in its basket from an upper floor each night, has been murdered, brutally strangled. The distraught woman shouts out to her neighbors who have rushed to their windows at her scream: "You don't know the meaning of the word neigh-

13.7 Penetrating the space of the courtyard; from Alfred Hitchcock's *Rear Window*, 1954.

bors. Neighbors like each other, speak to each other, care if anybody lives or dies, but none of you do."

5.2 We are shown the buildings, windows, vignettes throughout the film so that we understand the architectural structure that will control the plot and the vision of the film. *Rear Window* depends on architecture. It is a movie about negative space: a courtyard and an empty bed, a missing body and an urban world of social isolation.

5.3 The film ends as it begins with a complex shot surveying the courtyard, showing us happy endings to all the little stories, coming back to Jeff, who now has two broken legs but has resolved his own romantic problems. (Perhaps commitment has made him immobile.) In *Rear Window* the body was not in the building – it had been taken out in a trunk and left checked at the train station. But bodies, confined to their small worlds, began to penetrate the space between the buildings. The courtyard, which serves as a space for surveillance, is transformed into a space for social intercourse. Only by entering the space between the buildings can all the problems of the film be solved.

5.4 The empty space of the courtyard is filled with human interaction. This is why we can't know the space until we're in it – when the dog dies and when Jeff falls. The camera, moving around the architectural space, creates a false space, an invented space, full of absences, voids, disappearances, even windows that can move towards us, unattached to any restraining wall. In *Rear Window*, instead of asking what the camera is looking at, we might ask what it is looking for. It seems to be searching the space, gliding along the walls, stopping at the windows. Looking, yes, out of Jeff's fear and our own – a fear of involvement, of being outside in the space that creates connection – looking for answers – which, because it's 1954 and a comedy, it finds in a flurry of happy endings. As Stella says early in the film: "We've become a race of peeping Toms. What people oughta do is get outside their own house and look in for a change." The architecture of *Rear Window*, described through complex camera movements, mutable architecture, and disorienting cuts, enables us to do just that.

THE WALLS HAVE EARS

6   Harry Caul (played by Gene Hackman), the audio-surveillance specialist in Francis Ford Coppola's *The Conversation*, is betrayed at every step: by his friends, a lover, his boss, even by his own need to expiate a mistake made long ago in which he caused the death of some innocent people. The people Harry tries to save are, in this case, the murderers; those who appear innocent are indeed guilty. Throughout the film, Harry imagines a body. As an audio-surveillance expert, he has evidence of the ears but not the eyes. He invents what he cannot see. The camera shows us the body of a beautiful young woman – shows us blood in a shower – shows the scene obsessively over and over.

6.1   At one point in the film, Harry checks into a hotel room next door to Room 773, the room where he believes the murder will take place. Under the bathroom sink of his room, he installs a listening device, but he cannot interpret what he hears. He cannot see. This adjoining room is not a camera obscura – the image cannot appear – but it is in this room that Harry's fantasy images of murder are most intense. Through hearing, he invents seeing.

13.8 Under the bathroom sink; from Francis Ford Coppola's *The Conversation*, 1974.

13.9 First and second images, above: Harry tears apart his apartment; from Francis Ford Coppola's *The Conversation*, 1974.

13.10 Third and fourth images, above: alone in the devastated apartment; from Francis Ford Coppola's *The Conversation*, 1974.

6.2 When Harry picks the lock of Room 773, he finds nothing: no evidence of a crime, no body. Just a room identical to his own. Harry is listening, but he can't hear murder. When he tries to see, he sees only his own fantasies. In the bathroom, he opens the sealed toilet and blood gushes out, overflowing and covering the floor with imaginary red.

6.3 Near the end of the film, when Harry is playing his saxophone along with a record, he receives a phone call on a private phone in his apartment, a phone no one knows is there. "We know that you know, Mr. Caul," says the voice. "For your own sake, don't get involved any further. We'll be listening to you." Harry, renowned for his expertise in audio surveillance, searches his own apartment for audio bugs. Finding nothing, he begins to tear the place apart: stripping the walls of plaster, prying up floorboards, breaking even the little statue of the Virgin Mary. Harry Caul, with his symbolic name, tears at the caul of his apartment, stripping the rooms so that he may be born. Like Jeff in his cast, Caul is a chrysalis, a corpse himself, waiting to be resurrected.[8]

6.4 At the end, the camera, situated in an upper corner of the room, pans left; we look down on the bare devastated apartment – even the walls have ears – Harry playing his sax, alone in the empty destroyed space, stripped to its framework; camera pans right, then left as the credits roll. Here the pan, swaying back and forth through the apartment, shows us Harry alone with architecture. Although the camera finds Harry twice, he doesn't seem to be all that the camera is looking for. When the camera first pans left, it stops only when Harry is at the far right of the frame, going beyond him but not so much that he is out of the frame. It shows us Harry as part of the architecture, the structure of this apartment, isolated and mournful and impotent. Waiting for death, hoping for birth, as the camera moves back and forth over the devastation of the rooms that could be a preparation for a new order, Harry is not safe in his own isolation. Where once he played at the illusion of connection, playing his sax with others on a record, now he plays completely alone. The camera, fixed in one position like Harry, moves back and forth on its vertical axis. Someone watches, from above, more powerful than he imagined, invading his privacy, as he has invaded the privacy of others. Everything is double, ambiguous, torn open, and kept uneasily closed. This is the image of the rooms exposed to their structure, holding Harry loosely in their unsafe arms.

STILL DEAD

7   In *India Song*, the dead are rumors, figured by the smoke of incense and a photograph, an altar on a piano that remains central, as if the whole of the action revolves around it – the music, the smoke, the mirror, the camera circling it or framing it, finding it. Still dead.

13.11 Altar from Marguerite Duras's *India Song*, 1974.

7.1 Shots often alternate between inside and outside. The camera looks at the surface of the building and pans around the room. This building, this shell, is created as a space where time overlaps. The main character, Anne Marie Stretter, is dead, a picture on an altar, yet in this room, we see her – or someone re-enacting her story.

7.2 Outside, a shadow moves on the stairs – like smoke, like the shadow left at Hiroshima, the

13.12 Building from Marguerite Duras's *India Song*, 1974.

13.13 Empty clothing; from Marguerite Duras's *India Song*, 1974.

13.14 "We see them but in the mirror"; from Marguerite Duras's *India Song*, 1974.

shadow of the absent body. Earlier, inside, we've seen the camera play lovingly over a red dress, a wig, a necklace; it sensually caresses the empty clothing. Again, when Anne Marie Stretter lies on the floor, the camera cuts to her empty clothes. Just as the performers seem to absent themselves from their bodies, to move as tools for Duras's exploration of depth, movement, and stillness, so also these clothes, emptied of bodies, and the shadow and the smoke are alive and dead, staggered and stuttering like the entrances and exits of the performers, like the camera's alternating exploration of inside and outside, present and past, looking, always looking, for the dead.

7.3 "We see them but in the mirror," writes Marguerite Duras in the shooting script for *India Song*.[9] Throughout the film, this shot of the private drawing room recurs. The mirror is a kind of inside outside, a device used to distance the bodies of the performers from their images. "I see them, yes, as absent, therefore, restored to themselves in this film," writes Duras, "cleansed of a self-esteem that usually conceals the star's performance and deprives the viewer of seeing beyond the performer to his function. I see their absence as parallel to our own when we watch them in the film, and when, having gone astray, we meet up with one another."[10]

7.4 The visual displacement of the mirror parallels the audio displacement that is a unique aspect of the film. The characters don't speak on camera; what we hear are voices: party talk, gossip, rumor, speculation … haunted by the death of a beautiful woman, by sorrow and desire, by madness, by India.

The image of what body rushes by and flees into the mirror? Going where? Beyond the frame? Who returns in this mirror-hole with its virtual, false, true and oblique images that shut off representation as one stops a hemorrhage?[11]

7.5   In *India Song*, the camera is a mirror, an absent body. Here what is not seen, what is outside the frame, has the power to define the frame. We're too late and too early, uneasy in a world we cannot understand. The sensuality of the room, the incense smoke from a small altar on the piano, the absence of the body, the void of history, someone just left the room, all these haunt us and leave us unsatisfied. This, for Duras, is India, from the point of view of the colonials. "He looks so troubled ... She doesn't like people who get used to it," the voices say. But the camera stays still while people walk in and out of its gaze or the camera studies the room carefully, describing it, inscribing it, getting us used to it, not showing us events, or death, still with an evocative eroticism, waiting for something that will never happen. She will never get used to it nor will he. Desire is intense and unrequited, a scream in the darkness. The camera cannot help us; it stares at architecture. The camera is a room attached to another room by a lens, but this other room is only a series of reflections in a mirror. This is how Duras makes our desire visible: a camera obscura of longing, the impossibility, "the refusal,"[12] the suicide that haunts the reception, reflections of our own position, sitting in a certain isolated stillness.

DESTROYING ARCHITECTURE

8   A Soho loft, four tall windows at the end of a large open room. Two women carry a bookcase into the space, then leave. The camera zooms in. The women re-enter and turn on a radio that plays all

13.15 First image, above: "He looks so troubled ...": the vice-consul in Marguerite Duras's *India Song*, 1974.

13.16 Second and third images, above: Another view of the altar; from Marguerite Duras's *India Song*, 1974.

13.17 First and second images, above: Opening shot from Michael Snow's *Wavelength*, 1967.

13.18 Third image, above: Falling man; from Michael Snow's *Wavelength*, 1967.

of *Strawberry Fields Forever* and the women leave. Alternation of action and zoom. Here the actors, usually the initiators of narrative, are secondary. We are soon embroiled in the visual lurching, undeniable forty-five-minute zooming-in of the camera in Michael Snow's film *Wavelength*.

There is … no way to describe a system without resorting to the vocabulary of architecture. When structure defines the general form of legibility, nothing becomes legible unless it is submitted to the architectural grid.[13]

8.1 The space of the room we enter is made physical by this camera action. The camera is not the eye of the viewer; no one looks in the same way that a camera zooms. For ten minutes there is nothing but this zoom and an occasional flicker of color. There is the inevitable movement forward, but the movement and color changes occur in unexpected segments, making us aware of the body of the camera, the physicality of the film … shaping our identification with the camera and film as body. We hear the sound of breaking glass, a man stumbles into the room and falls …

8.2 The zoom continues to describe the geometry of the room, marked now by the refusal of the camera to follow the action. In fact, the camera never moves and as the zoom continues we are frustrated in our attempts to see the fallen man. His body is inexorably passed over, finally completely out of the frame. We see only what the camera allows us to see from its fixed position. Just as the camera is fixed, so is the body. We are trapped in an architecture of grids and focal lengths; light comes from the windows, which at first seem to be the goal of the zoom. In vain, we try to follow the narrative of the action, while the body is embedded in the building.

8.3 Near the end of the film, one of the women re-enters, finds the body, and calls someone named Richard. She asks him to come over because she thinks the man is dead. Then, she leaves the loft, perhaps to meet Richard or perhaps because she doesn't want to stay inside with the body. The zoom continues. The room, which began as a deep space, has now become a wall with one photograph. The goal of the zoom is a photograph of the ocean: a pun of, course, on wavelength, but also a flattening of the space. The camera rests finally when the image of ocean fills the screen. The zoom, which has allowed us to penetrate the space of the room, betrays us to an image we cannot enter. Paradoxically, as the image of ocean fills the screen, we hear sirens – through sound, the world outside the window intrudes.

13.19 The final image from Michael Snow's *Wavelength*, 1967.

8.4 In *Wavelength*, the architecture of a room provides a grid through which the camera lens moves, zooming in from wide to close, changing our view of the room. Through the manipulation of film stock, filters, lighting, and so on, everything is constantly changing in the room, or perhaps it is better to say that the room itself is constantly changing, because this room is subject to the physicality of film itself. This is why the final image of the film is not the room at all, but rather a photograph.

8.5 Similarly, Snow gives us an outline of a narrative, the elements of detective fiction, but doesn't flesh them out. The body is passed over without comment, relegated to a place outside the frame of the zoom, because only the possibilities of the camera are important here. This is a joke on our expectations of narrative, transferring our interest from the mystery, the search for clues, the examination of the body that is both our desire and our fear. We want to see that body, but we're relieved when it's neatly excised from the picture. We want to see the picture, a visual image that has no room for the desires of a linear narrative. Instead, we traverse a space in a frame, our view limited by that little room through which we see the world.

13.20 First image, above: La Pedrera; from Michelangelo Antonioni's *The Passenger*, 1975.

13.21 Second and third images, below: Locke and Maria meet on the roof of La Pedrera; from Michelangelo Antonioni's *The Passenger*, 1975.

8.6 In *Wavelength*, Snow dissolves both architecture and narrative through the use of a simple but strict constraint. He leaves us with something more chaotic, a calm ocean or a drowning. The room is a camera obscura of the limits of our own vision; the photograph of the ocean will liberate us from the room, but trap us in another vision – the kind that is only an image, flat and unresponsive.

THE DEATH OF NARRATIVE

9 In Michelangelo Antonioni's *The Passenger*, David Locke (Jack Nicholson) meets a young woman (Maria Schneider) in Barcelona; she is a student of architecture. They meet in Gaudí's Palacio Güell; later he finds her in La Pedrera (Casa Milá). These buildings by Gaudí introduce a kind of architecture quite different from the buildings and spaces we see throughout the rest of the film. When Locke first meets Maria he asks her about the building they're in. "What is it? Do you know? I came in by accident." "The man who built it was hit by a bus," she replies. She shows him around. "Do you think he was crazy?" Locke asks. This conversation is illogical, surrealistic, perhaps a reflection of the architecture in which it takes place. Other spaces in the film are flat, white, empty, barren, abandoned. In them, we feel exposed. Of Gaudí's buildings, Maria says, "they're all good for hiding in. It depends on how much time you've got." On the roof of La Pedrera, Locke spots Maria but they

can't figure out how to reach each other. The camera wanders through the labyrinthine space until the two finally connect.

9.1 Locke, a well-known journalist, has taken the identity of a casual acquaintance, David Robertson, whom he meets in Africa and later finds dead of a heart attack in an adjoining hotel room. Although Robertson told him that he's a businessman, he turns out to be a gunrunner with access to the very rebel groups Locke has been trying to contact. The Gaudí scenes are set between the earlier scenes of bleak Central African desert – the blank walls of villages and hotels – and similar scenes in small towns near Barcelona where Locke attempts to keep Robertson's appointments – in empty plazas, sitting in front of a blank white wall, waiting. Both Gaudí and the girl represent the kind of identity that eludes Locke, first in his quest for information on the rebels in Central Africa and later when he's switched identities with Robertson. In Barcelona, we are mostly inside the buildings, close up, or walking on the roofs amid the fantastic towers. The space is disorienting, but the girl knows her way around and Locke is safe – both from detection by his wife and friend, who are seeking information about his death, and from Robertson's enemies, who want to kill him. In Central Africa and the towns in Spain, Locke waits outside in vain – the man whom Robertson was to meet has been assassinated. These scenes of waiting have a kind of suspense or suspended time. Locke waits and the camera wanders on to look at nothing.

13.22 Locke in Africa; from Michelangelo Antonioni's *The Passenger,* 1975.

9.2 Antonioni's signature technique, in which the camera wanders from its subject or stays after the subject has left the frame is commonly referred to as *temps mort*. Sam Rhodie describes it as "this place at which the narrative dies."[14]

OUTSIDE/INSIDE II

10 David Locke is a journalist who can't get inside his subject. In one telling scene, an African witch doctor whom Locke is interviewing turns the camera on Locke himself. "Now we can have an interview," he says. So Locke takes the identity of Robertson, a man who looks uncannily like himself, a man who seems to exist inside. When Locke becomes Robertson, he goes "outside the window"[15] of media to be inside "reality" and he looks back at himself.

10.1 This passage from outside to inside, from one identity to another, depends on Robertson's death, but from the beginning, it is Locke who is dying. In some ways, the whole film is his long slow dying. Losing all interest in work and life, he takes Robertson's death as an opportunity to inhabit another life. From the moment he puts on this false skin, he realizes that he can't inhabit it either. He watches himself as Robertson in order to find himself as Locke or not Locke. This film is not about the dead body we see in the beginning, but about the process of dying. It is, as film might appropriately be, about duration and its inevitable end.

13.23 Setting up the penultimate shot; from Michelangelo Antonioni's *The Passenger*, 1975.

10.2 At the Hotel de la Gloria, Locke meets his fate. In a penultimate seven-minute shot that describes a courtyard, Antonioni creates a fluid architecture of passage. He needed a special apparatus to accomplish this tour de force. First, the camera runs on a track along the ceiling of the hotel room. It is picked up outside by a hook suspended from a

giant crane, nearly thirty metres high. A system of
gyroscopes was mounted on the camera, a kind
of jury-rigged Steadicam before Steadicam was
invented.

10.3 The shot begins inside Locke's hotel room. He's
lying on the bed, resting, looking out the window,
smoking a cigarette. He closes his eyes, then slowly
turns over. What we see next will not be through
his eyes. As in the first scene of *Rear Window*, the
camera seems to give us an "objective" view.

10.4 The camera frames the bars on a French window;
outside we see an old man and a dog. As Locke
turns over, the camera begins to move forward,
also zooming slightly so that the space outside
begins to get flatter as we go forward. Throughout
this forward-moving shot, a series of actions occur:
ordinary, chaotic, indecipherable. As we watch, we
search for clues, but the detective fiction has
become derailed. The actions are carefully choreographed, each person or vehicle crossing the space,
sometimes oblivious of each other, sometimes inter-
acting. None of these is especially dramatic. For
example, a driver-training car enters from the far
right, goes toward the bars, then veers to the left
and goes out of the frame. Maria enters from the
near right, turns to look in through the bars, and
continues to the far left. Then the driver-training
car crosses the space from left to right. Has there
been any interaction off screen? Who is learning to
drive? Should we see this as symbolic or acciden-
tal? Is Locke learning to die? All of the actions are
insignificant but potentially crucial. We wait in suspense, suspended as the camera is suspended. This
is *temps mort*, pregnant: "[T]he undulating, just
perceptible movements of the camera ... I was
trying unconsciously to find the same movement

13.24 The penultimate shot begins inside
Locke's room; from Michelangelo
Antonioni's *The Passenger*, 1975.

our imagination makes when it tries to give birth to an image."[16]

FLUID ARCHITECTURE

11   The camera approaches the bars of the window and appears to go outside. In fact, the illusion was accomplished by taking the bars apart, swinging both sides out just as the camera moved forward and zoomed in. The removal of the bars is invisible; the whole thing looks like it's only the motion of the camera. At the same time, the hook is attached to the camera to suspend it from the crane. Throughout the 180-degree pan of the outside space, we cannot be sure that any of the architectural elements are stable or static. We see a wall, a gate, a ramp, a landscape; we return to the doorway of the Hotel de la Gloria, to the hall outside Locke's room, and finally back inside his room. We cannot be certain that this is the same room from which we started – in fact, if we look closely at the scene a number of times, we can't quite work out the physical space. It is as though all of the rooms have been moving around.

11.1 The old man who sits outside, opposite the camera, is an anchor, a measuring tool – *la vie quotidienne*. He witnesses everything and sees nothing. Throughout the scene in which the camera moves forward, he remains seated; the camera seems to approach him. As the camera begins to move outside, first to follow the police car to the left, this man is forgotten, although when the camera begins to follow Maria and the policeman as they walk to the right, we see him still seated in his place. We don't see him again until the very last shot of the film, after Locke has been found dead. There is a cut to the driver-training car, then a pan to the front of the hotel. The man and his dog walk down the road as the sun sets and the credits roll. Although the camera misses the murder, it is possible that the old man witnesses it. He never leaves his spot, the one stable element in a fluid scene. This anchor, this ordinariness, betrays us because it gives us no clue. It's a false lead and falsely static – life goes on.

11.2 The 180-degree pan that takes us back to Locke's room is a complex shot in which pan and zoom combine to widen and condense space outside the hotel. At first casual and indifferent, the camera movement speeds up halfway through the pan and begins to suggest that it is following significant action. Locke's wife arrives, rushing, because she now knows that she has led Robertson's enemies to him; Maria, the police, a government official, all running. The camera zooms in on a conversation with the manager at the hotel door. As he points toward Locke's room, the camera outside continues to move in that direction while the people move inside the hotel. Looking in a window, we see Maria frantically knocking at Locke's door on the right. Here the crane has actually been repositioned to get a wider view as everyone enters another door on the left. Finally, with mounting suspense, the camera moves past a blank wall to rest, framing the window that it left at the beginning of its journey around the courtyard. This time the camera looks in. The body lies on the bed. The camera lingers.

13.25 The body lies on the bed; from Michelangelo Antonioni's *The Passenger*, 1975.

11.3 In this brilliant penultimate sequence of *The Passenger*, the camera defines space as a passage. The empty courtyard is filled with events; viewed by the camera, these events move in a choreographed trajectory towards death. The camera replaces architecture as a framing device; it defines space and the place of the body in space, as architecture once did. In *The Passenger*, buildings are either blank, empty of content, or filled with death; buildings such as Gaudí's, illogical, chaotic, offer only a temporary respite from that blankness. The camera moves as though it is seeing itself moving. It is not following anyone's point of view. This kind of movement gives the impression that neither the space nor the narrative is fixed. But we have come too late to prevent a death.

11.4 It is true that Locke seeks death, and the penultimate scene of *The Passenger* is his slow acquiescence to his own end. His death is an image, and all images, especially photographic images as Barthes describes them, are images of absence, of a trace of something no longer there. But film as a fluid medium must first destroy both narrative and architecture in order to become the static picture that is a picture of the dead.

TEMPS MORT: THE STARE, STILL

12 We can stare. According to Vanessa R. Schwartz, the word *morgue* comes from an archaic verb that means "to stare."[17]

12.1 A travelling incarceration. Immobile inside the train, seeing immobile things slip by. What is happening? Nothing is moving inside or outside the train ... Inside there is the immobility of an order. Here rest and dreams reign supreme ... Outside there is another immobility, that of things, towering mountains, stretches of green fields and forests, arrested villages, colonnades of buildings, black urban silhouettes against the pink evening sky, the twinkling of nocturnal lights on a sea that precedes or succeeds our histories ... being outside these things that stay there, detached and absolute, that leave us without having anything to do with this departure themselves ... However, these things do not move. They have only the movement that is brought about from moment to moment by changes in perspective among their bulky figures ... [V]ision alone continually undoes and remakes the relationships between these fixed elements.[18]

12.2 The Paris Morgue, opened from 1864–1907, was situated behind the cathedral of Notre-Dame. The Morgue was open to the public from dawn to dusk, seven days a week, with free admission. Presumably created for the identification of corpses, the Morgue was arranged like a Salle d'Exposition. There were two rows of corpses laid out on marble slabs. Viewers stood at a large glass window that had green curtains hanging at either side.[19]

12.3 On 29 July 1886, a four-year-old girl was found dead in a stairwell. The corpse was taken to the Morgue, where it was clothed in a dress and exhibited in a chair covered with a red velvet cloth. By 3 August, about 50,000 people had come to view this corpse. Each night the corpse was strapped to the chair and put into a refrigerated room to preserve it. An autopsy was performed on 6 August. Subsequent visitors to the Morgue complained because they could not see the child.[20] It was as though death should be stopped for the spectacle of death.

THE PASSENGER

13 The camera is at the station, waiting for the train. *L'Arrivée d'un train en gare. L'Histoire d'un Crime.* On the earliest European trains, first-class passen-

gers travelled in compartments that were completely cut off from each other. They entered the compartment from the platform and when the door closed they were captive. In 1861 Chief Justice Poinsot was found murdered in his compartment when the train arrived at the Paris station. The isolated train compartment had become the scene of the crime.

13.1 The motion of the train through the landscape appeared to the nineteenth-century traveller as the motion of the landscape itself. Using two related metaphors, Wolfgang Schivelbusch describes the new perceptions created by the speed and motion of the train. First, it was a kind of panoramic vision: "[T]he traveller saw the objects, landscapes, etc. *through* the apparatus which moved him through the world."[21] Secondly, the train inscribed itself in the landscape. "The hurtling railroad train appears as the very motion of writing and the telegraph poles and wires are calligraphic instruments with which the new perception inscribes the panoramic landscape upon the real one."[22] Through the windows of the train, the traveller saw a film. The train and telegraph wires were the apparatus, the flickering poles creating the illusion of persistence of vision.

13.2 Why have historians focused on the iron and glass architecture of Paxton's 1851 Crystal Palace, ignoring the architecture of light of the darkrooms of the same period? On the one hand, the development of transparence was established as a result of the materiality of large surfaces of glass, held up by an impressing array of metal scaffolding. On the other hand, transparence entered secretly in the unnoticed architectonic mutation of a wall-screen. The images on this wall increasingly assumed the value of space, taking over all the dimensions in the projection room, and finally fusing and confusing architecture with projection technique.²³

13.3 The myth that spectators ran from the first showing of *L'Arrivée d'un train en gare* is nicely dispelled by Tom Gunning in his article "An Aesthetic of Astonishment: Early Film and the (In)Credulous Spectator."²⁴ Apparently, at early showings of this and other films of trains, a speaker would present the film by showing its first image as a still. Then, he would explain that by the miracle of this new invention, film, the picture will begin to move. Not only was the audience prepared in this way for what was to come, but also, the audience was astonished by the apparatus's ability to create illusion, rather than being fooled by the illusion itself. "The spectator does not get lost in a fictional world and its drama, but remains aware of the act of looking …"²⁵

13.4 In other early films, especially those of filmed landscape panoramas, spectators were aware of the camera pivoting on its tripod. They were amused and amazed at the wonders of motion. Many of these landscapes were shot from the front or back of trains.

13.5 At showings of Lumière's *Destruction of a Wall*, the film was often projected twice: first forward and then backward, so that the wall would miraculously reassemble.

13.6 For his 1965 film *Playtime*, Jacques Tati built a modern city on the outskirts of Paris. The office blocks were on wheels and tracks so that they could be moved for particular shots. The hilarious and joyful traffic circle scene near the end

13.26 From the Lumière brothers' *Démolition d'un mur (Destruction of a Wall)*, 1895.

depends on the fact that the cars aren't moving, but the whole traffic-circle is rotating like a carousel.

13.7 In 1971, Tony Cridlin used tracking dollies, cranes, and even wheelchairs for Stanley Kubrick's *A Clockwork Orange*. We sit to watch while the camera sits to move. The camera dissolves our stasis while it glues us to our seats.

WRITING ROOMS

14 Film destroys nothing, not narrative, not architecture. It's all an illusion. Narrative and architecture renew themselves, only to be destroyed again.

14.1 Film is the uncertainty of this special space, where zoom and pan, tilt and track inscribe the room. And we, only passengers, out for a ride or forced into the car, find pleasure in going.

14.2 What the dead tell us is this: we are alone. Of all the films we've looked at here, it is only in *Rear Window* that architecture serves to suture the pain of each lonely passage. In the others, rooms isolate us, buildings create boundaries and impossible obstacles. This is because we look alone; no one else can see through our eyes. The camera represents this solitary looking; it cannot bring us together, except in astonishment at its own devices.

14.3 Nevertheless, we get on the train. We are already on the train. Narrative helps us along, carries us. We ride through the tunnels of architecture, go in and out the door. Every space, empty space, is filled by our passage.

ABSENT BODIES: EXITS AND ENTRANCES

15 Maria: "People disappear everyday."
Locke: "Every time they leave the room."

15.1 Film is erotic because it moves; because we move
through it, it takes us along. The world of film is
only in front of our eyes, but sometimes comes in
through our ears. All this is deceiving. The body is
missing, absent, turned to light.

Matter, for example, like architecture, is no longer even
what it pretends to be, since this matter is "light." It is
the light of an emission, of an instantaneous projection that results in a reception rather than in a
perception.[26]

15.2 Perhaps architecture has always had this quality of
reception, an aspect of empty space that opens
itself to the possibilities of social interaction or of
solitary dying. Perhaps architecture has always been
made entirely of light.

NOTES

1 Special thanks to Patrick Clancy and Tom Zummer for brainstorming in the
early stages of this writing, to Toni Dove for reading and commenting on
the first draft, and to the extraordinary filmmaker Leslie Thornton who
helped me, most of all, to *see* the camera's illusionary moves.
2 Michael Taussig, *Mimesis and Alterity* (New York: Routledge 1993), 25–6.
3 Denis Hollier, *Against Architecture* (Cambridge, Mass.: MIT Press 1993), 75.
4 Michel Chion, "The Fourth Side," in *Everything You Always Wanted to
Know About Lacan But Were Afraid to Ask Hitchcock*, ed. Slavoj Zizek
(London: Verso 1992).
5 Hollier, *Against Architecture*, 61.
6 Mladen Dolar, "A Father Who Is Not Quite Dead," in *Everything You
Always Wanted*, 144.

7 Miran Bozovic, "The Man Behind His Own Retina," in *Everything You Always Wanted*, 169.

8 Bozovic, writing on *Rear Window*. Ibid., 172–5.

9 Marguerite Duras, *Duras by Duras* (San Francisco: City Lights 1987), 20.

10 Ibid., 11.

11 Joël Farges and François Barat, "Introduction: India Song," *Duras by Duras*, 3.

12 Duras, "Notes on India Song," *Duras by Duras*, 12.

13 Hollier, *Against Architecture*, 33.

14 Sam Rohdie, *Antonioni* (London: British Film Institute 1990), 51.

15 Ibid., 150.

16 Ibid. Rohdie is quoting Antonioni.

17 Vanessa R. Schwartz, "Cinematic Spectatorship Before the Apparatus: The Public Taste for Reality in Fin-de-Siècle Paris," in *Viewing Positions*, ed. Linda Williams (New Brunswick, N.J.: Rutgers University Press 1994), 89.

18 Michel de Certeau, *The Practice of Everyday Life* (Berkeley, Calif.: University of California Press 1984), 111–12.

19 Schwartz, "Cinematic Spectatorship Before the Apparatus," 89.

20 Ibid., 91–3.

21 Wolfgang Schivelbusch, *The Railway Journey* (Berkeley, Calif.: University of California Press 1986), 64.

22 Ibid., 31.

23 Paul Virilio, *Lost Dimension* (New York: Semiotext(e) 1991), 88–9.

24 Tom Gunning, "An Aesthetic of Astonishment: Early Film and the (In)Credelous Spectator," in *Viewing Positions*, 114–33.

25 Ibid., 121.

26 Virilio, *Lost Dimension*, 69.

About the Authors

Myriam Blais

Myriam Blais was born in Canada in 1960. A registered architect, she received a bachelor of architecture degree from Université Laval in 1983, a master of architecture degree from the same institution in 1987, and a doctoral degree from the University of Pennsylvania in 1994. She is associate professor of architecture at Université Laval in Quebec City, where she teaches undergraduate studio and a technology course which includes the theoretical and iconographic aspects of techniques. Her main interests focus on the poetical and ethical role of technology in architecture and on the figurative potential of materials. She is currently pursuing research along those lines of inquiry.

Ricardo L. Castro

Ricardo L. Castro received the title of "Arquitecto" from the Universidad de Los Andes in Bogotá, Colombia, and later received a master's degree in art history and a master's degree in architecture at the University of Oregon. He has taught design, history, and visual communication at the Universidad de Los Andes, University of Oregon, Kansas State University, Université Laval, and, since 1982, McGill University. Currently, his activities take place on several fronts: he teaches architectural design, history, and criticism at the McGill School of Architecture, he is a regular contributor to several publications in Canada, the United States, and Colombia, and he uses architectural photography as an expressive medium. In 1990 he received the prize Paul-Henri Lapointe from the Order of Quebec Architects in the category History, Criticism, and Theory. This year he was awarded a Graham Foundation Grant to complete a monograph on the work of the Colombian architect Rogelio Salmona.

Janine Debanné

Janine Debanné is currently assistant professor of architecture at the University of Detroit Mercy. Born in Ottawa, she received a bachelor of architecture with high distinction from Carleton University in 1988, and a master's degree with honours in architectural history and theory from McGill University in 1995. She has taught in schools of architecture in Canada and was recently a visiting professor at the Faculty of Architecture of the Warsaw University of Technology. She has worked in private practice in Ottawa, Hull, and Toronto. Her current work focuses on the city of Detroit.

Katja Grillner
Katja Grillner was born in Gothenburg, Sweden. She holds a professional degree in architecture from the Royal Institute of Technology in Stockholm and a master's degree in history and theory of architecture from McGill University, Montreal. Her academic studies include art history and philosophy at the University of Stockholm. She is currently employed as a doctoral student and part-time teacher in the Department of Architecture and Urban Planning at the Royal Institute of Technology in Stockholm. She has published articles on contemporary criticism, architecture, and art for the *Nordic Journal of Architectural Research*, *Arkitektur*, and *The Fifth Column*. Her current research investigates the role of literature in the development of the English landscape garden during the eighteenth century and its relation to Enlightenment art theory.

Maria Karvouni
Maria Karvouni was born in Athens, Greece. She holds a degree in mathematics from the National and Kapodistrian University of Athens, Greece, a master of architecture degree from Syracuse University, and a master of science degree from the University of Pennsylvania. She is currently completing a doctoral dissertation at the University of Pennsylvania. The thesis, entitled "Treading on the *Rhythmos* of a Greek Temple," is an exploration of the connections between music-dance and building in ancient Greece. Maria Karvouni is an assistant professor of architecture at the Virginia Polytechnic Institute and State University, teaching at its Washington Alexandria Centre.

Alberto Pérez-Gómez
Alberto Pérez-Gómez has taught at the universities of Mexico, Houston, Syracuse, Toronto, and Carleton, and is now the Saidye Rosner Bronfman Professor of the History of Architecture at McGill University, where he has directed the graduate program in history and theory of architecture since 1987. He was also the director of the Institut de recherche en histoire de l'architecture from 1990 to 1993. He is a prolific writer, author of *Architecture and the Crisis of Modern Science* (MIT Press 1983) and *Polyphilo or The Dark Forest Revisited* (MIT Press 1992). His numerous articles have been published in North American and European journals. His most recent book (co-authored with Louise Pelletier) on the history and theory of modern European architectural representation, with special reference to the role of projection in architectural design, was published in 1997 by MIT Press.

Henrik Reeh

Henrik Reeh was born in Copenhagen, Denmark, in 1958. Since 1995 he has been senior research fellow at the Centre for Urbanism and Aesthetics at the University of Copenhagen. Previously, Henrik Reeh was research fellow at the Humanities Research Centre–Man & Nature (1993–95) and at the Department of Comparative Literature (1989–92), both at Odense University, where he obtained his doctoral degree in comparative literature. Initially, Reeh studied the social sciences in Denmark and received his Magister-degree in history and social sciences from the University of Roskilde. During the 1980s Henrik Reeh lived in Paris where he was awarded a master's degree and a diplôme d'études approfondies in comparative literature by the University of Paris VII-Jussieu. In 1986–87 he was a DAAD–scholar in the Department of Philosophy of the Johann-Wolfgang Goethe University in Frankfurt am Main, Germany. From 1983 to 1986 he was a member of the Groupe de Travail Interdisciplinaire at the École Normal Supérieure de Saint-Cloud, France.

Apart from essays in French, English, Danish, and German on urban theory and analysis, Reeh is the author of two books: *Storbyens Ornamenter – Siegfried Kracauer og den moderne bykultur* (The Ornaments of the City: *Siegfried Kracauer and Modern Urban Culture*) was published in 1991 by Odense University Press; *Den urbane dimension – tretten varationer over den moderne bykultur* (*The Urban Dimension: Thirteen Variations on Modern Urban Culture*) will be published shortly by the same press.

Mark Rozahegy

Mark Rozahegy is pursuing a doctoral degree in the interdisciplinary humanities doctoral program at Concordia University in Montreal. Born in Hamilton, Ontario, he received a bachelor of science degree in physics with honours and a bachelor of arts degree in English with honours from McMaster University, and a master's degree from the Centre for the Study of Theory and Criticism at the University of Western Ontario. While completing his master's degree, Rozahegy became interested in the issue of space in the context of modern French philosophy. For his doctoral thesis, he is planning to investigate the ontological dimensions of space as expressed in the body-centred philosophy of Maurice Merleau-Ponty.

Sören Thurell

Sören Thurell was born in Örnsköldsvik, Sweden, in 1933. He received a master of architecture degree from the Royal Institute of Technology (KTH) in Stockholm in 1959, did post-graduate studies from 1986 to 1989, and received a doctoral degree also from the KTH in 1989. He owned a design partnership, ARKITEKTVERDSTAN, from 1970 to 1985 and was assistant professor at the Royal Institute of Technology from 1990 to 1994. Since 1995 he has been doing freelance research and writing. He is currently launching STAR, the Institute for the Study of Architectural Relations, with different projects in the area of design and ecology.

Franca Trubiano

Franca Trubiano is an architect in the pursuit of happiness. To this end she is currently dwelling in the text at the University of Pennsylvania, paradoxically tracing a path back to the praxis of architecture. She is a recent graduate of McGill University's master's program in the history and theory of architecture and received her professional degree from the same institution in 1988. At present her research includes carnivals, masks, and games of entertainment – sites that gave voice to architecture during the seventeenth century – and the role played by architectural drawings in the edification of the architect since the sixteenth century. An artist's grant from the Canada Council will allow her to explore, more concretely, ways in which architectural representations define the urban artefact that is the city of Montreal, her birthplace.

David Edward Winterton

David Winterton graduated with a bachelor of architecture degree in 1991, the centennial year of the University of Toronto's School of Architecture. There, he developed an interest in representations of the landscape, especially that of his birthplace in rural southwestern Ontario. In 1995 he earned his master's degree in history and theory of architecture from McGill University, where he further cultivated ideas on the presence of concepts of nature in architecture. In Montreal he also translated the *Lettres sur l'architecture* [1787] of Viel de Saint-Maux. He currently resides in Toronto and continues to research how culture inflects ideas about nature.

Irena Žantovská Murray

Irena Žantovská Murray was educated at Charles University in Prague, now the Czech Republic, and moved to Canada in 1968. She holds a master's degree in library and information science from the University of Western Ontario and a master's degree in history and theory of architecture from McGill University. Currently she is a doctoral candidate in architectural history and theory at McGill.

Prior to her employment at McGill, Murray held positions with the National Library of Canada and the National Archives of Canada. From 1981 to 1996 she served as head librarian and curator of the Blackader-Lauterman Library of Architecture and Art at McGill University. She is currently head of the Department of Rare Books and Special Collections, McGill University Libraries, and curator of the University's Canadian Architecture Collection. As well, she is a faculty member of the Institut de recherche en histoire de l'architecture (IRHA).

Murray's research interests focus on the history of European Modernism between the two World Wars, on issues of architectural representation, and on Prague. Among her current projects is a translation of selected texts for *Karel Teige: Architecture and The European Avant-Garde*, to be published by the Getty Center for the History of Art and the Humanities. At McGill, she recently edited *Moshe Safdie: Buildings and Projects, 1967–1992* (McGill-Queen's University Press 1996).

In recent years, Murray served as guest curator for several architectural exhibitions, notably *Soviet Avant-Garde Publications* and *Czech Cubism: Architecture and Design, 1910–1925*, both of which took place at the Canadian Centre for Architecture. In 1994 she was guest curator of *The City Off-Centre: the Architecture of New Prague*, shown at the World Financial Center in New York City.

Ellen Zweig

Ellen Zweig is an artist who works with text, video, performance, and installation. In her installations, she uses optics to create camera obscuras, camera lucidas, and video-projection devices. She has presented work in Europe, Australia, and the United States and has received two NEA grants. Her most recent work includes *Hubert's Lure*, an installation in a storefront on 42nd Street in New York City, and *Critical Mass*, a collaborative project that is currently on tour. Among other projects are a permanent installation of a camera obscura for the Exploratorium in San Francisco and the novel *Surveillance* (written with Lou Robinson), soon to be available on the World Wide Web.